Technical Theater
——— for ———
Nontechnical People

Drew Campbell

Illustrations by Kis Knekt

ALLWORTH PRESS
NEW YORK

05   04   03   02   5   4

Illustrations © 1998 Kis Knekt

Published by Allworth Press
An imprint of Allworth Communications
10 East 23rd Street, New York, NY 10010

Cover design by Douglas Design Associates, New York, NY

Page composition/typography by Sharp Des!gns, Inc., Lansing, MI

ISBN: 1-58115-020-2

Library of Congress Catalog Card Number: 98-74538

Printed in Canada

For Schrader

Table of Contents

Acknowledgments

As I say several times in this book, theater is a collaborative process and there is no such thing as a one-man show. My deepest thanks to all who helped me through the years of birthing this book.

Thanks to all the people who read my work and gave generously of their ideas and reactions: Denise Martel, Sheila McNerney, Jolene Obertin, Wendy Austin, Reid Edelman, Diane Frohman, Harry Magalong, Robin Morris, and Kathleen Cunneen.

Thanks to my teachers: John Lucas, David Schrader, Richard Isackes, Craig Anderton, James Berton Harris, Dean Markosian, Dave Loftin, Bernie Works, Ron Beebe, and many others.

Thanks to all of my students for teaching the teacher and keeping the excitement alive, especially: Kita Grinberg, Anita Pederson-Arbona, Chris Wong, and all the members of the Lick-Wilmerding High School stage crew.

Thanks to my family: my mother, Phyllis Campbell, a theater expert herself, my father, David Campbell, who gave countless writing tips, my brothers Jim and Charles, who are the finest I could ever hope for, and Heather Radley, for learning to cope with Campbell men.

And finally, to my ever-patient and supportive wife, Ann Marie, who makes every day a holiday of love and laughter, my deepest appreciation.

Why This Book

When I left graduate school in the eighties, I headed to the Pacific Northwest, to Seattle, which, at the time, was considered a hotbed of theatrical innovation. I had received my degree in "theatrical technology" and I was a hotshot—as those who suffered through me can tell you. I was ready to practice my craft with the best theater artists I could find, indulging in a feast of high-tech theater. After a brief stint at the Seattle Repertory Theater, however, I found myself working for a theatrical lighting and sound company that supplied rental equipment for anybody who was doing anything, well, "theatrical"—not only plays, but also weddings, bar mitzvahs, conventions, press conferences, whatever. We even lit a night-time bike race and a thoroughbred horse show.

One of my jobs was to organize rental equipment for pickup, a task that put me in the vicinity of the front counter. As I was setting up a package to go out one day, a thirty-something, office-dressed woman came in the door. Glancing around the shop, she edged over to the counter and smiled at me, clearly uncomfortable. She was in a wilderness, surrounded by racks of unfamiliar equipment, and she had evidently decided to "go for it."

"Hi," she said nervously, "I'd like to rent some sound."

I looked down at the two-inch-thick catalog of sound equipment sitting on the counter and considered my options. Educate—or embarrass? I was not in a particularly good mood, as I recall, so I went for the latter—a genuine cheap shot.

"Excuse me, could you be less specific?" I said, and immediately regretted it.

"I'm sorry," she said, smiling with relief as she realized what she had forgotten to say at first. "It's for a big party." She settled back, now satisfied that I had all the information I needed.

That's when I decided that both of us needed this book.

As human beings, we are constantly showing ourselves to each other. Much of the time, it is just a private, personal act between individuals, but now and then, we decide to go public and make some sort of hoopla about it. We present plays, throw parties, hold conventions, play concerts, introduce new products, meet the press, get married, sing opera, and dance the story of the tadpole. We create "shows" of infinite variety. Some of us do it professionally. Some of us do it at Sunday services or the company kegger. Some of us would rather not do it at all; but whether we are showing off, showing skin, showing gratitude, or just showing up, it's all the same thing. It's a "show." And it does not take long before that show grows beyond our own technical knowledge, especially for that substantial portion of the population whose VCRs are still flashing "12:00." I cannot count the number of times that someone has said to me, "Oh, don't worry, it's a simple show, we just need a few lights," or "No, no, we don't need anything special, just a microphone."

That's fine, I thought. So, why do you need *me?*

Why do you need a technician? Because there are a lot of people in the world who have no desire to be technicians, no desire to go through the years of training, mistakes, and experience that are necessary to bond with things mechanical, electric, or electronic. These same people, however, still need the technology in everyday living, particularly when it comes time to do the "show." They don't want to master the technology; they want to use it. They want to stand in the right place on stage. They want to communicate with a designer or a technician. They want to walk into a rental company and know what to ask for. They just want to survive backstage.

So here was this well-meaning and otherwise competent woman, standing next to my counter, biting her lip and casting her eyes around the shop, looking for something familiar so she could point to it and say, "There! I'll take one of those!" unaware that a few magic words like "mixer" and "microphone" would go a long way toward getting what she needed. She was not stupid. She was not prejudiced. She just didn't have the vocabulary to communicate in a foreign language. Actually, after talking for a while and sounding out more information, I discovered that she was short on facts because she wasn't even in charge of the event. She had been sent by her boss, who did not have any idea what was required either. Hey, people get busy sometimes.

But I digress.

If you want to be a technician for a career, and learn all the ins and outs of everything that was ever plugged into a wall, more power to you and the pun is intended. Enjoy your life! The world will depend on you more and more. But put this book back on the shelf. There are some really thick, detailed ones that will serve you better.

If, however, you have something else to pursue in your life—whether you are a dancer, drama teacher, playwright, actor, fashion show coordinator, meeting planner, minister, publicity person, or anyone else who needs to go public—read on. This book is for you. We are going into a jungle, but have courage. By the time we are through, the trees will be the right size, the animals will howl on cue, the sunlight will filter mysteriously through the leaves, and all those scary technical tigers will be rugs in front of your fireplace.

General Notes

A Note about Gender

One of the as-yet-unsolved problems in the English language is the absence of a gender-neutral, third-person singular pronoun. Unlike the French, who have the glorious use of the pronoun "on," we must struggle along with only "he" and "she" and all their related forms (his, hers, himself, herself, etc.). The closest approximation—"one"—has a cold, businesslike quality to it, and, personally, I find using "his or her" a bit awkward. Therefore, I have decided to simply alternate between the masculine and feminine forms. While you are reading, you may encounter generic technicians or designers who have assumed one sex or the other. Please do not interpret this to mean that any job is limited to only half of our population. I am often heartened that jobs in the theater business tend to be less gender-specific than those in other industries. The word "actor" seems to have become a neutral word for both sexes, however, so I will stick to that rather than alternating with "actress."

Highlighted Words

As you are reading, you will notice that many terms appear in **boldface type**. This is to indicate a term that you should know. All terms in boldface appear in the glossary at the end of the book.

CHAPTER 1

Breaking It Down: Who Does What

Theater is collaborative. We never do it alone. There's no such thing as a one-man show. Being backstage means being surrounded by people—people who assume a wide variety of titles and responsibilities. As a show person, you do not need to know how to do all their jobs. You do not have time to do all their jobs. You need to know who to talk to when the carpet is coming up behind the podium, or the work light backstage is burned out, or the Frosty the Snowman costume is ripping open. Scenic designers, prop coordinators, stage managers, tech directors, first hands, flymen—they surround you at every turn, and, if they are any good, they are there to help you. So who are all these people? And who can help you staple down that carpet?

Not an easy question. There are constant overlaps between areas of responsibility, and many things must be worked out on a case-by-case basis. Sometimes a simple task requires input from several departments. Consider this example: The script calls for a lamp to be sitting on a table. The **scenic designer** talks to the **director** and decides what the lamp should look like. Then the designer shows the design to the **propmaster**, who either buys the item, pulls it from stock, or builds it. The finished lamp is brought to the stage, where the **electrician** wires it up. The **lighting designer** decides how big of a bulb to put in it and when it should be on (with more input from the director). The lighting designer then communicates that information to the **dimmerboard operator** who, under the direction of the **stage manager**, operates the light during the show. If the light has to move during a scene change, that task is the responsibility of the **stage crew** chief. One object—eight people. Hard to believe we get anything done at all.

If we are to work together, then, it must be with a set of predetermined areas of responsibility. Most things fit pretty neatly into one of the following six categories: costumes, props, lighting, sound, stage management, and scenery.

Costumes

Any kind of clothing, or anything at all worn by a performer, including masks and jewelry, is considered a costume. Makeup and wigs are sometimes handled by separate departments, but they are usually treated as a subset of the costume shop. This area is designed by the **costume designer**, and is managed by the **costume shop manager**, who is assisted by a **first hand**, as well as **cutters**, **stitchers**, and **drapers**. During the run of the show, costumes are handled by the **dressers**.

Props

Anything that is carried by an actor, or *could* be carried by an actor within the context of the play, is a prop. Pictures on the wall, for example, are props, because an actor, while portraying a character, could move them. A kitchen countertop, however, is scenery because the character he is playing would not rip up and move a real countertop, even though the actor himself might be able to do so. It is a tenuous definition. The distinction between props and scenery gets muddy at times, and clear assignments should always be made at the start of the building process. Props are designed by the **prop designer** (or the set designer if there is no prop designer), and managed by the **propmaster**. Props are built by **prop carpenters** and **craftspeople**, and handled during the run by the **props crew**, a subset of the **stage crew**.

Lighting

Anything electrical that is not sound equipment is the responsibility of the lighting department. There are two exceptions to this: the "running" lights, which are the small (generally blue) lights that allow people to see in the darkened backstage areas, and the "ghost" light, the naked bulb on the tall stand that gets set out on the stage when the theater is empty. Both these lights are usually set up by stage managers. In a theater with union stage crews, the ghost light is the only light on the stage that does not have to be turned on by a union electrician. The arrival of the ghost light center stage means that the work call is over, and the union workers must clock out. Whether you are union or not, the ghost light keeps people from killing themselves in a dark theater. Lighting is designed by the **lighting designer** and managed by the **master electrician**, with the assistance of the **electrics crew**. The lights are operated during the run by the **dimmerboard operator** and, if spots are used, the **follow spot operators**.

The **lighting cues** (the instructions that tell the lighting operators what to do and when to do it) are handled by three different people. The lighting designer creates the *content* of a cue (what lights are on and how bright) as well as its *time* (how fast the lights change from one "look" to another). During the performance, however, it is the **stage manager** who tells the operator when to perform the cue and the **dimmerboard operator** who actually pushes the buttons and pulls the levers. In technical terms, we say that the stage manager "calls" the cue and the operator "runs" it. So, if you would like a cue to occur in a different place in the script, tell the stage manager. If you want it to look different, talk to the designer. Talking directly to the dimmerboard operator is rarely a good idea. For one thing, the operator may not have the big picture and he may screw something else up by making changes on his own. For another thing, the designer's name is going on the show, so it is only decent that he supervise the changes himself. Finally, if you go straight to the operator, you will screw with everybody's recordkeeping and the possibilities for mistakes will multiply. Nothing is worse than sudden confusion on the headset during the show when the stage manager calls a cue and the following conversation takes place:

Stage Manager: Light Cue 49 go.
Dimmerboard Operator: No, not yet.
SM: What?
DBO: Not yet, he said he wants it later.
SM: Who?
DBO: Steve.
SM: What? When?
DBO: Before the show.
SM: No, I mean when does he want it? He didn't tell me. Are you sure?
DBO: Are you saying I don't know my job? Hey, I'm just doing what I'm told here.
SM: Well, I want to be sure. Where is he?
Assistant SM (from backstage): I think he's in the bathroom.
SM: Well, um . . .
DBO: All I want is for somebody to tell me what to do.
Lighting Designer (suddenly coming onto the headset): Hey, what planet are

you people on? Cue 49 is late and you've missed two more. Let's go!

SM: Well, Don says Steve said to wait on 49 and make it later.

LD: What? When?

SM: Before the show.

LD: No, I mean, when does he want it? And why the heck haven't you called Cue 50?

SM: I should call it now?

LD: YES!! Go now! GO, GO, GO!!

Follow Spot Operator: Is that Go for us?

SM: Yes, I mean No! Who said that?

DBO: Well, I think we should Go.

SM: Fine, Go! Everybody Go!

Stage Crew Chief: OK, main curtain coming in!

Meanwhile, Steve, the well-meaning director, returns from his trip to the bathroom to find follow spots crisscrossing the auditorium, the main curtain bouncing up and down, and a gaggle of actors standing bewildered on the stage, trying to improvise themselves into the wings to find out why the blackout at the end of the scene never happened. The bottom line is, talk to the right people when you want a change.

Sound

Microphones, sound effects, and the playback of recorded sound are all part of the sound department. Sound people also should handle headsets for backstage communication. The **sound designer** is in charge of this area. Sound is often a one-person operation, but if the sound designer doesn't run the show, there will be a separate **sound engineer**. If you have a large live band on stage, there also might be a second engineer running a separate mixer, called a **monitor mixer** that feeds the **monitor speakers** that the band uses to listen to themselves. When the sound system is first installed, there may be additional sound crew people in the theater.

Stage Management

The **stage manager** handles rehearsal schedules, runs the rehearsal itself, provides assistance to the director, and, during the run, is in charge backstage. The SM is also responsible for being a clearinghouse of information about the entire production process. *When in doubt, ask the stage manager,* particularly if the question has to do with schedule.

Almost all stage managers have at least one assistant, the ever-useful **ASM**. The ASM is the gofer position, the essential yet thankless job of getting done whatever needs to get done. It is impossible to predict when you will need an errand run, when you will need a prop handed to an actor, why you will need a curtain pulled back, a phone answered, or an animal fed, but one thing is for sure: It will be the job of the ASM. Besides being an everything-to-everybody position, it is also a primary training position, the entry-level job in the backstage world.

The **company manager** makes all travel, lodging, and food arrangements for the cast and crew.

Finally, many companies have a **production stage manager** (PSM) who oversees the entire production process. The PSM is responsible for coordinating the entire process. In the Broadway theater world, the PSM works for the producer and moves from show to show, releasing day-to-day control of each show to the stage manager when it opens. In regional or repertory theater, the PSM is in charge of the entire season while each show has its own stage manager. In one-shot productions, the PSM is often the stage manager as well.

You should not forget the position of PSM just because your theater is nonprofessional. It is mighty useful to have someone overseeing the entire process; especially if she does not have to worry about the moment-to-moment rehearsal process, as the stage manager does. A good PSM makes everybody's process smoother and more creative.

Scenery

Anything that I have not already mentioned is scenery. Not surprisingly, scenery is designed by the **scenery designer**, and is managed by the **technical director** (TD). "Technical director" is a very loose job description, one of the loosest in the business, but usually he is in charge of deciding how the set will be built. Sometimes, he also oversees the properties and lighting crews, particularly in small theaters. His oversight, however, is always limited to practical matters, such as money, equipment, and staff. He is *not* a designer, and should never be put into the position of making design decisions.

The TD is the voice of reason in the technical process, which, unfortunately, often makes him the bearer of bad news. The TD is the one who must tell you that the effect you want is too expensive, too time-consuming, or simply not possible. His opinion may bring you down occasionally, but it's better to know that your idea won't work ahead of time, instead of on opening night.

The scenery is built in the **scene shop**. This shop usually has a **scene shop manager** (unless the technical director does it) who is in charge of carpenters and welders. In the **paint shop**, **scenic artists** do the painting and decorating under the supervision of the **charge artist**. During the run, the scenery is handled by the **stage crew** and their chief. Flying scenery is operated by the **flyman**.

The point that I made about lighting (that is, if you have a problem, it is best to talk to the area head instead of to the crew) holds true for scenery as well. If the problem involves a change in how things look from the front, tell the designer. If it only involves a change in how things operate mechanically, out of sight of the audience, tell the head of the crew. If you are not sure, tell the designer.

_____

*Remember, if you have any doubt about who to ask, go to the **stage manager**. The stage manager is always the best port in a storm.*

_____

You might be saying to yourself at this point, "But we don't have all those people!" Don't worry. Lots of theaters combine some or all of these jobs. Your technical director might also be designing the lighting, your stage manager might also be running sound, and your master electrician might also be operating the dimmerboard. All of the above jobs are still done. People just do more than one.

Of course, every theater is unique, and exceptions exist for every rule that I have given here. Talk to the people you work with. Take some time to learn who does what. What you are really "breaking down" are the walls of miscommunication.

CHAPTER 2

Touring a New Space:
What to Look For

So you're going to do a show. Well, assuming that your uncle doesn't have a barn (and take it from me, barns aren't the greatest theaters in the world), you've searched around and found somewhere to put on the performance. Or, you are still searching and you need to evaluate several different spaces to determine their usefulness.

Theater can be done anywhere, as generations of street performers have shown us. Besides "real" theaters, I have done shows in and on basements, boats, rooftops, breweries, swimming pools, cafes, back yards, more hotel ballrooms than I'd like to remember, and, yes, barns. Every space has its peculiarities and its unique problems. Strange architecture, no easy access, low ceilings, moody lighting, and never, ever enough room. But don't despair. Enjoy! It's these peculiarities that make a theater what it is. You think you've got problems? The Trinity Square Theater in Providence, Rhode Island (a first-class repertory house), has a brick pillar right in the middle of the stage. There's no taking it out. It holds up the roof. Every designer who does a show in that theater must find a way to incorporate a brick pillar into the set. And these people win Tony awards.

So the first thing to do when entering a new space is relax. You can do your show here—the question is, do you want to? And if you do want to, how will your show have to adapt to fit this space?

When visiting a new space, these are the things you should bring with you:

- *A notebook and a pen* to take notes and write down measurements.
- *A fifty-foot tape measure.* Twenty-five feet is often not enough.

- *A flashlight* for lighting up those creepy spaces above and beneath the stage.
- *A camera* for documenting the details of the space. Having a Polaroid makes it easy, but in these days of one-hour photo developing, a regular one is okay. Make sure you have a flash. And film.

Ready to go? Let's walk.

Is This the Right Space for You?

Before you get into any of the details, you should make a general determination if the space you are looking at is even in the ballpark for your show. A few quick questions can eliminate a lot of miss-fits.

• *Is it big enough?*

Do you have enough stage space? Look at the chart in "How to Do a Show in a Hotel" (page 205) to see how much space you need for various kinds of shows. Is there enough space to store scenery that is not on stage? Is the audience area big enough for the number of people you are expecting?

• *What does it sound like?*

Different kinds of shows need different kinds of acoustics. Spoken-word theater needs a space with no distracting noises (like traffic or air conditioning) ,where an actor speaking on stage can be clearly heard. There should be very little echo in the space, so that speech is not garbled. Look for carpets, low ceilings, draperies, and quiet neighborhoods. Acoustical music and singing call for a space with *lots* of echo—it fills out the music. Look for hard surfaces, like marble, tile, and paneled walls. Electrified music (dance bands, rock bands, etc.) should never, ever be put in a space that is mostly hard surfaces. No matter how softly the band plays, the noise will be deafening.

• *Can the space be scheduled appropriately?*

Remember to give your tech people the time they need to set up. If you want to do a large party with a big lighting rig and a dance band, don't choose a space where a wedding will be winding down two hours earlier.

Space for Stuff

Do you have enough room? Don't estimate. *Measure.* Measure the **playing space**, the amount of the stage that will be visible to the audience. Measure it both horizontally (how wide and how deep) and vertically (how high). The vertical measurement will determine how tall your scenery can be and how much room there is for lighting.

Now take a look at the **wing space**, the part of the stage that the audience cannot see. Remember, whatever scenery is not on stage will have to be stored here, and any part of the wing that is visible to the audience is not usable as storage. Is there room for **prop tables**, **changing booths**, and actors waiting to go onstage? Check out surrounding hallways as well. Are you allowed to use them for storage during the performance?

I did a production of *Good News* some years ago that contained a full-size automobile, a 1920s roadster (it didn't work, unfortunately, but it looked *great*). When it came offstage, it took up so much room in the wings that we finally had to attach cables and a motor to it and hoist it up in the air. In the end, that still didn't save us any space, because the sight of a car hanging overhead was too spooky and nobody would stand underneath it.

What about access? Think about how the scenery will be brought into the space. What is the smallest door that the scenery will have to pass through? Measure its height, width, and, for good measure, the distance diagonally across it. Will the scenery have to turn any sharp corners? With a friend, stretch out the tape measure and pretend that it is solid, like a board. Try to figure out the longest board that could still turn the corner.

Are there stairs? How many? Stairs mean that scenery cannot roll—a serious obstacle, in some cases. Is there an elevator? How big is it? How much weight can it handle? Is there a **loading dock** where a truck can back up and park?

Space for People

How many performers are in your show? Look at the **dressing rooms**. Will there be space enough for the actors to dress, put on makeup, and warm up? Is there space to store the costumes, and is there space for the costume crew to work? Do you need separate rooms for principal performers? The conductor? Do you have **fast changes** in your show that require a changing booth to be set up in the wings?

Are there bathrooms? Can the toilets be flushed during the show without being heard in the theater?

Is there a stage door? A **green room** where actors can wait for their cue to go onstage? It's a very bad idea to have actors milling around in the wings waiting to go on. They will invariably make noise and distract the performers onstage.

One extremely important actor space that is frequently overlooked is the **crossover**. The crossover is the path that actors use to get from one side of the stage to the other without being seen by the audience. It also refers to the movement itself, as in "Do you have time to make that crossover?" The easiest crossover space is right behind the set, on the stage, but there may not always be enough room between the set and the back wall to get a person comfortably through. In some theaters, there is a hallway outside the stage space that is used as a crossover. Others go beneath the stage. Watch out for the theater where you have to go outside the building to cross over. There's always a chance that it might be raining, and backstage doors have a funny way of being locked when you least expect it. (In this situation, I generally tape over the locks during the performance.) You may be required to re-stage a scene so that a performer exits and later enters on the same side of the stage. Know your show. Is there a time when you need a way for the performer to get quickly from one side to the other?

The crossover seems to be a particular problem with dance companies, since they often have little or no scenery to hide a crossover and the dance space sometimes extends all the way to the upstage wall. Dance also creates more problems because dancers often exit and re-enter several times during a piece with little time to spare. Again, in extreme cases, be prepared to re-choreograph.

A good crossover can allow for some tricks as well. In the show *Desert Song* (a delightfully sappy 1920s Sigmund Rombard operetta), the show opens with the rebel forces onstage, planning their next raid. Suddenly, the alarm is sounded offstage and the rebels have to flee stage *right*, running from the French Army. Two French officers run on from stage *left* and have a brief conversation, giving the actors playing the rebels enough time to make the crossover and a quick costume change. Moments later, the troupe enters stage *left*, now dressed as French soldiers, seemingly chasing the departing rebels but, in fact, chasing themselves. Good clean fun, and impossible without a fast crossover.

The Rigging System

Look up. Look at the rigging system over the stage. Is there one? If the space is not traditionally used for performances, you are probably looking at an ordinary ceiling. In this case, you will probably have to bring in **light trees** to put the lights on, and all your scenery will have to be freestanding. This usually means fewer lights can be used, unless you have a reasonable sum of money to invest in a **truss**. A truss is a long piece of gridwork supported by towers on each end. Trusses allow you to hang more lights (and hang them directly over the stage, instead of out to the sides), but they are considerably more expensive than trees, both in rental of equipment and in labor costs. For more about trees and trusses, see "How to do a Show in a Hotel."

If there is some kind of rigging system over the stage, then you are probably looking at rows of pipes that run parallel to the front of the stage.

These pipes are called **battens** and, if they are there, it's time to ask some questions. Are the battens rigged to fly, or are they **dead-hung**? In other words, is there some kind of system installed where the battens can be raised and lowered (rigged to fly), or are they just hung in one spot, unable to be moved (dead-hung). If the battens are dead-hung, forget about any piece of scenery bigger than a Draculean bat moving during the show. You can still install scenery or lighting on these pipes, but they cannot move during the show.

If the pipes are rigged to fly, then the tech people handling your show are going to want to know the answers to these questions:

• *How many line sets are there?*

Go to the wings. On one side of the stage or the other, there should be some ropes that come down from the grid, loop around a big pulley on the floor, and then go back up out of sight. These are the **purchase lines** that you use to operate the rigging system. Each one of them is attached to a metal cage, an **arbor**, full of metal weights, or **counterweights**, that offset the weight of whatever you are trying to fly. The arbor, in turn, is attached to a set of cables that pull a pipe (a batten), up and down. The batten is where you attach the thing you are flying. The whole enchilada—purchase line, arbor, cables, and batten—is called a **line set**. In general, each thing that you want to fly requires its own line set. The lighting people will also want some of the battens for lights.

• *Are any of the battens permanently wired for lights?*

Any pipe that is being used for lighting is called an **electric**, and a pipe that is *permanently* furnished with lighting circuits is called a **hard-wired electric**. You can still put lights on a pipe that isn't hard-wired, but using hard-wired electrics can save the lighting crew a lot of time. More than likely, your lighting designer will use the hard-wired electrics and then add a few temporarily wired electrics of her own. Often, the **first electric**, the one closest to the proscenium, is hard-wired, while the rest are not. This is because the first electric generally has more lighting instruments on it than any other electric. Furthermore, most lighting designers can agree on where the first electric should go. It's all the other ones that change from show to show and designer to designer.

• *What else is hanging?*

What hanging things are permanently assigned to battens, and cannot be moved? Many battens will be taken up with permanent lighting equipment (including work lights), draperies, and other equipment. **Acoustical shells**, those huge, curving walls that sit behind choirs and orchestras, are notorious for being stored in the air and eating up a lot of space. Look for them.

• *How high is the grid?*

This is a critical piece of information. If you have a twenty-foot high piece of scenery that flies, you will need another twenty feet above it in order to fly it up out of the audience's view. In practice, you will usually need a grid at least three times the height of your proscenium in order to pull scenery far enough out of sight.

Masking

Stand in the auditorium, or wherever the audience will be sitting. Walk from one side of the seating area to the other, looking at the backstage area. Pay attention to how much of the backstage area you can see. What kind of draperies does your space have? Are there **legs** on the sides to hide the wings? Are there **borders** overhead to hide the lights? Is there a grand drape to close at the beginning and the end of your show? If you are working in a very temporary space, like a hotel ballroom, you will have to rent draperies, in the form of **pipe-and-drape**.

The Lighting System

Your master electrician and lighting designer will want to ask some questions as well:

• *Where are the lighting positions?*

You've probably got part of the answer from the rigging section above. If the electrics aren't hard-wired, then the lighting and set designers have to sit down and decide who gets which battens. If, however, the electrics *are* hard-wired, then lighting will go on those and scenery on the rest, unless the lighting designer has special requests for more battens.

There are also lighting positions out over the audience. These are called **front-of-house** positions, often abbreviated "FOH." The horizontal ones are called **beams**, the vertical ones are called **booms**. Is there a follow spot booth?

• *What is the lighting inventory?*

The lighting people will want to know how many instruments are available and what type they are. The **lighting inventory** is a list of all the instruments and should include how many of each type there are, what wattage they are, and what accessories the theater owns for them. If not enough instruments are available, then you will have to either borrow them, rent them, or do without. If you are in a hotel, remember that track lights are rarely powerful enough to light a performance, so you should not count them in an inventory.

• *What kind of power is available?*

Is there a circuit plot? A **circuit plot** shows where you can plug in all the lighting instruments. You usually cannot plug lighting instruments into standard wall sockets. A dedicated stage lighting system needs far more power than those little electrical outlets can provide. The only time that those outlets are useful for stage lighting is when you only have a few small lights. Read "How to do a Show in a Hotel" to find out what kind of power you need for temporary setups.

• *What kind of a control board is it?*

How many **dimmers** are there? Is it a computer-controlled board, or a manual one? If it is a computer board, get the name of it. The designer will want to know which kind he is facing ahead of time. Ask how many dimmers are available. This may determine how many lighting instruments you can use.

• *What kind of plugs does the lighting system use?*

There are, at present, two kinds of plugs used for stage lighting: the **stage plug** and the **twist-lock**. These two plugs are incompatible. If you bring lighting equipment with stage plugs into a theater with twist-lock circuits, that equipment will be useless unless you change the plugs, a time-consuming process. Household plugs like the one on your reading lamp (known as **Edison plugs**) are rarely used on stage.

The Sound System

Make a list of everything that you need the sound system to do. Do you need to amplify a single person speaking? Multiple people speaking? Do you need to play a tape or a CD? Do you need to have wireless mics? Do you have a band that needs to be amplified?

Once you've determined the sound needs of your show, ask whoever takes care of sound equipment in the space if the system can handle it. If you are talking to the right person, you may be able to stop there. If you don't have a knowledgeable person who knows the space, at least try to get answers to the following questions:

• *What is the inventory of sound equipment?*

As in lighting, it's extremely useful to have some sort of list that shows everything that the theater is equipped with. This will help your sound person come up with a plan of attack.

• *If there is a mixer, how many channels does it have?*

Every piece of sound equipment has to be plugged in to the mixer, and each piece of equipment get its own **channel** in the mixer. Tape decks and CD players are generally in stereo, with a plug for left and right, so they each need *two* channels.

Monitors and Headsets

The people in your show will need to hear what's happening onstage when they are waiting for entrances. That is the purpose of a **monitor system**. A monitor system has a microphone hanging over the stage that feeds sound into speakers located backstage. When touring a new space, ask these questions about the monitor:

• *Which rooms can hear the monitor?*

You will want to warn the actors if, for example, they will not be able to hear their cues in the bathrooms.

• *Where is the microphone that's picking up the sound from the stage?*

This is useful not only because you should keep the lighting and scenery from hitting it, but also because you should know where to stand if you don't want your catty conversation being carried to the dressing rooms.

• *Is there a paging system?*

Can the stage manager make announcements over the monitor system?

• *Can the dressing rooms "talk back" to the paging system?*

Some snazzy systems allow the people in the dressing rooms to answer back when they are paged. This is a good thing, because the performers can let the stage manager know that they heard her.

A **headset system** is the system that the crew uses to talk to each other. It is just like a phone system where, if you plug your phone into the wall, you can join in on the party line. A headset system has four parts: a **base station**, **belt packs**, **headsets**, and a whole lot of **cable**. The base station provides power to the system and makes the whole thing work. You can't get by without one. It is often built into the wall somewhere. Each person has a belt pack that picks up the voices in the system and feeds them into a headset. The headset is the part that goes on your head and makes you look like an telephone operator. The cables plug everything together. Here are the questions you should ask about the headset system:

• *Is the system permanently built in, and, if so, where are the plugs?*

In a theater with a built-in headset system, there should be plugs all over the place where you can plug your belt packs in.

• *How many headsets and belt packs do they own?*

You will need one belt pack and one headset for everybody that you want to have on the system.

• *Do you have more than one channel?*

Some headset systems have more than one channel, so two different conversations can be going on at once without disturbing each other.

• *Are the headset and monitor systems connected?*

This allows the sounds from the stage to be broadcast into the headsets as well as allowing the stage manager to page the backstage area through her own headset. It can also allow the dressing rooms to hear the conversations on the headset, which prevents those conversations from straying into unprofessional territory.

Answering the above questions may help you to decide if you want to do your show in a given space. If your space passes the test, then you are ready to start planning your show there. Let's go on!

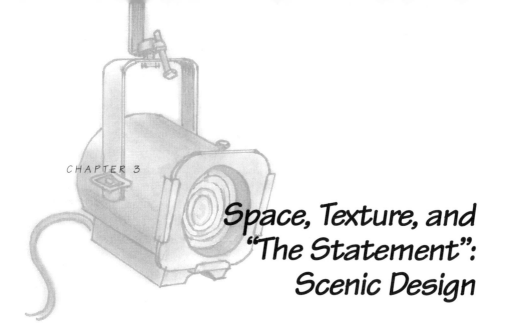

CHAPTER 3

Space, Texture, and "The Statement": Scenic Design

Why build scenery?

Good question.

Why take wonderful scripts; cast them with brilliant, lively actors; entrust them to spirited, creative directors; and then encase them in piles of expensive, distracting, noisy, heavy, monolithic scenery?

Like I said, good question.

When I was in graduate school, my brilliant scene design teacher, Richard Isackes, took all the tech theater students down to the stage and made us stand, one at a time, on a three-foot-high platform stuck out on the edge of the apron. From this uncomfortable position, we peered out through the blinding stage lights into the audience where he sat, hidden in the darkness. As we stood there, unaccustomed to being in the glare of the spotlights, he called out commands to us, sounding slightly annoyed if we did not respond to his liking.

"State your name, please!"

"Count to ten!"

"Do it backwards."

"Speak up!"

"Is there a problem?"

I have never forgotten that feeling of psychological nakedness, that sensation of being scrutinized and rebuked for the smallest mistake. When he was done harassing us from the darkness, Richard came down to the stage.

"That's what an actor does every day," he said, "Let's never forget that."

People come to the theater to see actors perform! So why do we persist in thinking that we have to have a truckload of scenery on stage? Just because a play takes place in Versailles does not mean that we have to have the Hall of Mirrors, complete with cascading cherubim, just to get the idea across. Somebody once told me that a set designer has five seconds to get his point across, "because that's how long the audience will look at the scenery." Granted, I have heard some gasps come out of the audience when the curtain went up, but if the performances did not carry the show, the audience was just as bored as if the scenery were made of cardboard. We all love to watch the chandelier crashing down on the stage in *Phantom of the Opera,* but we don't walk home humming the scenery—we remember the actors and their performances. We must have a gene kicking around in our collective pool that keeps telling us, "You're doing a show. You must build scenery." That has been the normal thought pattern for most of this century, after all, and even with the development of other design areas, we all have a tendency to fall back on scenery.

When modern theatrical design really began around the turn of the twentieth century, the entire playing field belonged to the scenic designers. Lighting was in its infancy, costumes were still being handled by the actors themselves, and sound had not been invented yet. This situation persisted until after World War II, when the costume designers began to gain prominence, showing their talents in the immense musicals of the period, such as *Camelot* and *My Fair Lady.* Later, in the sixties, lighting began to come into its own when the position of lighting designer was created as a separate entity from the stage electrician. In fact, with the advent of the rock-and-roll musicals (*Hair, Jesus Christ Superstar*), much of the design emphasis moved to lighting. In the eighties, with an audience that had become accustomed to movies, the sound designer became increasingly important. Audiences demanded a more complete sound environment and actors had to be clearly audible, even when speaking naturally. These days, actors use microphones more than ever before, and more shows make use of "ambient" sound—a constant stream of background sounds. Some people say that the growth of amplification has gone hand and hand with the decrease in good vocal training, but in my view, the growth of sound design—an abstract, emotionally evocative medium—is a positive trend, bringing us back to what is truly important in the theater: the imagination and the performer.

When dealing with scenery, the first and most important question you should ask yourself is: *What is the show about?* Then, ask yourself: What do we need, what do we really *need* to get that point across to the audience? Often, the answer might not even be scenic. A voice announcing departures can suggest "airport," the shadows from sunlight through a window can say "drawing room," a uniform can indicate "police station." Even if the answer is scenic, constant attention to that question—*What is the show about?*—can help you approach scenery in an intelligent way that won't end up stressing your technicians, your budget, or, most important, your show. After all, this is not *Field of Dreams*. Even if you build it, they may not come.

Having said all that:

The purpose of this chapter is not to turn you into a scenic designer. Rather, the purpose of this chapter is to help you see a script in a new, more visual way, as well as to help you understand why stage designers make the choices that they do. Scenic design can be thought of as the art of addressing three issues: space, texture, and the "statement." In terms of the director-designer relationship, the "statement" is the most important issue, and the most difficult to talk about, so we will do that first. Then, we will talk about space and texture (as well as texture's friend, color). Along the way, I will help you understand the most fundamental theatrical drawing— the **floorplan**.

The Big Picture: The Statement

A designer I worked with in college always began a new production by finding one defining object for that show in the real world. A few days after he started work on *A Streetcar Named Desire,* we were walking down a street in Providence, Rhode Island. It was winter, and the red brick colonials around us were frosted with snow. Most of the houses had little neoclassical facades over their front entrances and severe-looking paned windows with storm shutters. In short, it was about as far as you could get from the steamy New Orleans inner city of Stanley Kowalski and Blanche DuBois. Suddenly, he grabbed my arm and pointed. "Oh my god, *Streetcar!*" he gasped. Following his arm, I looked for what had gotten him so worked up, and sure enough, there was *Streetcar*. It was a tall, wrought-iron gate that closed in front of a set of brick stairs. The iron was ornately, even grotes-quely, wound around the gate, giving a sense of great wealth, with a hint of new money gone bad. Each vertical bar was capped with a little brass ball, and the handles were two languid curlicues. Best of all, the whole thing was completely rusted.

The next day we came back with the Polaroid and, for the entire design period, we covered the walls of the studio with photos of that gate. Time and time again, it pulled us back to what we really wanted to say about the play: the faded glory, the grotesque sensuality, the decay. We did not always use these "inspiration pieces" on the sets that they inspired, but this time, it was too good to pass up. We built a perfect replica of that gate on one side of the set, complete with the red-brick stairs, and it gave us immense pleasure to see Blanche pause in front of it every night to give her now-clichéd closing benediction: "I have always depended on the kindness of strangers." That gate said more about her condition than two tons of scenery could have.

The Statement is the ultimate answer to the question, "What is the play about?" It is the rallying point for all the designers. The Statement may be a visual (like the *Streetcar* gate), audible (like a piece of music, or Chekhov's "plucked bow string" at the end of *The Cherry Orchard*), written (a word, a speech), abstract or concrete, simple or complex, in the show or out of it. The Statement may be a painting, a piece of junk, a pop reference, or a newspaper article. Whatever it is, it gives the designers a place to start, and a place to return to when they need inspiration.

This is not to say that any production can be boiled down in its entirety to one sentence or object or thought.

The Statement is the talisman that the director gives to his flock. Discovering it, expressing it, and sharing it are all things that the director must do to get the ball rolling and keep it on the move.

How to Read a Script Like a Set Designer

The first time you read a script, forget about designers. Just read it! Enjoy. Visualize only if you want to. Follow the story and savor the characters. Read the script like an audience member.

Once you have finished being an audience member, however, take that hat off and put it away for a while. Now put on your designer hat and read the script again.

The most important thing that the set designer is looking for in the script is the number and kind of spaces that the show requires. The purpose of the scenic design is to service the actors and the script. Don't start out trying to make something that is visually impressive. Start by answering the question "What kind of space do I need?"

As you read through the script with your set designer hat on, start making lists. Make lists of locations. Is there more than one? Where are they? Are they interior spaces or exteriors? Do they require doors or windows? What kinds of specific physical objects do they require? Does the action require more than one of them to be visible at once? What is mentioned specifically? What is only suggested?

Sets break down into three rough groups and by the time you finish your read-through, you should have a pretty good idea which one fits your show best. It is worth noting that each of these groups has its own set of difficulties and none of them should be seen as "easier" to design or build than any other.

The One-Set Show

This is a show that takes place in one location, like a bedroom, an office, or a back yard. The set does not change, although furniture and props may be moved around within it. These shows are generally more realistic, and have a fair amount of detail on the set. One-set interiors—particularly those where the walls are built to surround all three sides of the set—are often referred to as box sets.

The Multi-Set Show

Shows that move from location to location sometimes require fully realized sets for each location. Large musicals such as *Guys and Dolls* are **multi-set shows**. Often, the designer creates a surrounding "frame" of scenery, while inserting different sets within the frame. For example, since *Anything Goes* takes place on a ship, a designer might create a shiplike atmosphere with decks, railings, and portholes, while changing walls around to create different rooms.

Multi-set shows aren't restricted to musicals, however. The nonmusical play *The Crucible* takes place in four different locations. Again, these locations have a common element: They are all rooms in wood-frame buildings in Salem, Massachusetts. The successful designer will tie them all together with common elements, reducing the number of pieces that have to be changed for each scene. The amount of detail on each set is usually less than for a one-set show.

Multi-set shows also require time during the play to change scenery. Hence, they are often written with the scene changes happening during intermissions. In the case of musicals, there are often short scenes between the long ones. These scenes, called **in-ones**, are made to be played in front of a downstage curtain in order to allow time for the scenery to be changed upstage. The name comes from the term used to describe the scenic drop that flies in behind them. This is called an "in-one drop" because it falls just behind the first set of drapery legs, the "in-one" legs. (The second set of legs is called "in-two," the third set is called "in-three," and so on.) Multi-set shows are usually the most complicated and expensive way to do scenery.

Sometimes, multi-set shows will have more than one of the locations onstage and visible to the audience throughout the show. This is necessary if the play changes quickly from location to location, as is sometimes the case when the playwright actually wrote a movie script but is trying to make it work on stage.

The Unit Set

Another solution to scripts with multiple locations—the **unit set** does not require full-blown sets for each scene. Rather, the designer creates a space that will accommodate lots of different scenes. Then, smaller pieces are added and subtracted to communicate specific locations. Major scenic elements, like the walls, do not change, while smaller elements—furniture, banners, window frames, coffins, ship's wheels, and so forth—are added and subtracted. The plays of Shakespeare are often done this way, particularly since Shakespearean stage directions are rarely specific about locations: "A ship." "A grove." "Rome."

Unit sets have different areas on them that are used for different scenes. If there are small, intimate scenes, then the designer must create some small, intimate places, and the lighting designer must turn off the lights on all the other areas. If there are crowd scenes, then there must be large, open spaces. The space should be designed to be subdivided in as many ways as necessary. Unit sets may tax the creativity of the design team, but they are often the most rewarding solution, offering simplicity and lowcost while maintaining the atmosphere of the show.

Whether a show really needs full sets, as in the true multi-set approach, or would be better served by a "unit" approach, is a stylistic decision as well as a budgetary one. The flow of the show is critical: If you cannot create a multi-set show without getting bogged down in lengthy scene changes, try a unit approach instead.

The Backstage Survival Guide to Reading a Floorplan

I would not even do Thanksgiving dinner for my family without a floorplan. It is the single most important drawing in the theater, and every single person on a theatrical team should know and understand the floorplan. A floorplan is how people talk to each other about space.

Find the Theater

No, don't get up. I don't mean find the actual space. Locate it on the drawing. Find the permanent part of the theater—the part that is always there, even when the set is gone. Look for thick, dark shapes, possibly with crosshatching inside them. In a proscenium theater, find the proscenium. In a thrust or arena space, find the audience or another landmark. In a hotel ballroom or other "nontheatrical" space, look for the walls and doorways. Get yourself oriented to the space as a whole before you try to understand where the scenery is.

A floorplan can be understood as a bird's eye view of the stage after someone came along with a gigantic chainsaw and sliced the roof off the

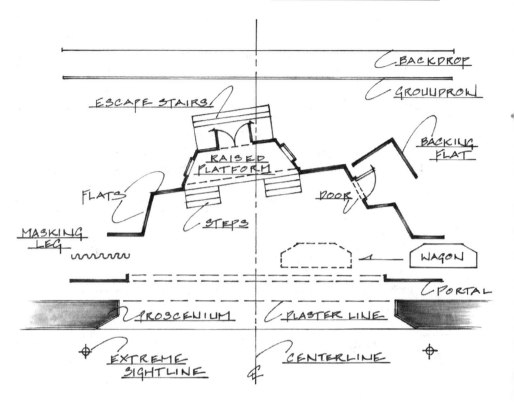

Figure 1. An example floorplan

theater. Actually, the slice is usually taken about head high, that is, about five to six feet off the stage floor. Any object that falls underneath the slice is shown as a solid line. Anything above it is shown as a dashed line. Anything that the chainsaw would actually cut through, like a wall, is shown as a heavier line with the interior of any shape filled in with crosshatching. (This is why the proscenium arch is drawn this way—the chainsaw would cut through it.)

Find the Center Line

The **center line** is the beginning of all measurements in a theater space. Look for a line that alternates between short and long dashes and ends at the bottom of the drawing with a symbol that looks like this: C/L. The center line, not surprisingly, runs down the center of the set, from upstage to downstage. The plaster line runs across the set, connecting the two proscenium arches. Technicians installing a set in a theater use the plaster line and the center line to get the set in the right place, and you should always find these first on any floorplan. Of course, there is no law that says these two lines have to be on a drawing, but they should be there if you are in a "real" theater and if the designer is theatrically trained. If these lines are not present, you will have to move on to the next step to get your bearings.

Find the Major Scenic Elements

Locate the principal walls and platforms. Remember, if they are "above the slice," that is, above the actor's head, they will be drawn as dashed lines. Anything "below the slice" is drawn as a solid object.

Find the Heights

Heights on a set are usually measured from the "real" stage floor, that is, the permanent floor, not whatever platforming is in the set itself. Heights are usually shown in circles, with a "+" or a "–" to show how much that platform is above or below the stage floor. A platform marked +8" is eight inches higher than the real stage floor, or one step up. A surface marked –1'6" is actually below the stage floor, so there must be an opening in the floor. Pay close attention to heights, since they will radically affect the performers' ability to move around the stage.

Look for Traffic Patterns

How will performers move around the stage? What alleyways exist for the performers to move through? Are there places for long crosses? Are there reasons to go to different parts of the stage? Is there a **crossover**?

Look for Doors and Windows

The floorplan should indicate which way they open, or if they open at all.

Pay Attention to Masking

Has the designer created enough walls or drapes so the audience won't be able to see backstage? A good floorplan will have a little "+" sign in each bottom corner showing the **extreme sightline**. This is the "worst" seat, the seat that, through the combination of being way out to the side and close to the stage, has the best view of the backstage area. There will be one on either side of the auditorium. If you design the masking so that these two people cannot see backstage, then you probably have prevented everybody else from seeing backstage as well.

Look for Moving Scenery

Any piece of rolling scenery should have more than one position marked, usually an onstage position and an offstage one. Flying scenery will only have one location marked (the onstage one), but it should be marked as a flying piece.

Look for "Weird Stuff"

This basically means anything that we have not covered so far. Every set is different, so there might be anything. *Make sure you understand what every single line on the drawing means, unless you are prepared for some tech week surprises.*

Note! Even with a good floorplan, it may be necessary to ask the designer to make a three-dimensional model. It is very difficult to imagine how a floorplan will translate into real objects. A model is the only way to really see how things will play together onstage. Even if you have a model, however, you must know and understand the floorplan. For one thing, in some situations, you may never *get* the model, no matter how much you want it. In addition, a floorplan is far more precise than a model, it contains real measurements, and it can be folded up and put in your pocket. Gotta love that.

Texture and Color: Giving the Show a "Look"

As you are reading the script, it is useful to try to imagine what kinds of materials would be appropriate. It is this choice of materials that gives the show its "look." Will you rely on painted muslin, or will you utilize three-dimensional sculptures carved out of foam? What about scaffolding and chain-link fencing? How about neon, vinyl, brick, or bales of hay? The list is endless. It helps to come up with a list of adjectives that describe the feeling you would like the set to convey to the audience. Make the adjectives as colorful and descriptive as you can. "Comfortable" might describe a room, but it may not tell the designer much. How about "academic," or "lived-in," or "like a rabbit burrow."

The texture of the set is derived from the mood and atmosphere of the script and characters. One thing to keep in mind about texture is how much it disappears over distance. Most of the audience will be a long way away from the scenery. If you put something textural on the stage and then step back ten feet to admire it, you are not seeing what the audience sees. Step back into the middle of the house and see how much of the texture actually shows. You will quickly see that what looked rough and coarse at ten feet looks like a Formica countertop from row M.

Color is another way of expressing texture, and all the same thoughts apply. Color brings out emotional responses and, as such, can be discussed with emotional adjectives. Again, stay away from "bright" and "dark." Try "belching" or "pasty" or "aggressive."

Coordinating Texture in Scenery and Lighting

Different textures call for different lighting treatments, so be sure to keep the lighting designer informed about how the scenery is going to look.

The direction of the lighting can reveal or destroy texture. Light coming from straight ahead will wipe it out. Light coming from the sides, above, or below will emphasize it.

Shiny textures and light colors may create problems for lighting, namely, **glare** and **bounce**. A textured surface will tend to "eat" light and not allow it to go anywhere else. Slick, smooth surfaces, especially floors, send the light on its way toward surfaces that should not be lit. Glare is produced when a light shining from upstage toward downstage—known as a **back light**—is reflected into the audience's eyes by a shiny floor. It can be extremely distracting to the audience. Bounce is the opposite: Light coming from downstage bounces off the floor and splashes onto the walls upstage. If you are doing *One Flew Over the Cuckoo's Nest,* for example, try not to give in to the temptation to build the hospital ward set completely out of shiny institutional white. If you do, the bouncing, glaring light beams will splash up onto the walls and into the audience and prevent you from getting the isolated pool of light that you will need when Chief strangles, oops, almost gave it away.

To control bounce, you must tone down the *color* of the floor. To control glare, you must tone down its *shine.*

The point is, shiny, light-colored sets make it difficult to isolate lighting. You may not think that isolating lighting is an issue for your show, but it almost certainly is. Isolation is how you steer the audience's eyes around the stage. With a bright, shiny set, you will constantly end up with light where you don't want it. Also, a shiny white stage will not go to blackout as easily as a dark-colored one. You would be amazed at how much light a set can pick up from an EXIT sign.

Be aware of the color wheel. Poor color combinations can be disastrous. As you will read later on, color filters change light in lighting instruments by *subtracting* colors, not by adding them. A light that has been colored red has had all the other colors removed. If that red light hits a green surface, that surface will turn black. There is no green in the light to reveal the green on the surface. I lit a punked-out production of *Titus Andronicus* once and the director asked for one battle scene to be lit entirely in red. Unfortunately, neither he nor I had talked to the costume designer. Turns out that all the actors in that scene had hair dyed green. Oops. Black hair everywhere.

Particularly offensive color combinations include red and green, blue and amber, and yellow and lavender. In these mismatched situations, it is usually the lighting that has to change—it is easier to change a color filter than to dye a costume. Remember, though, that the colors have to be strong and pure to be a problem. I solved the punk hair situation by just mixing in a little green light around the edges.

Coordinating Texture in Scenery and Costumes

Scenery and costumes are also closely related. It is even more important to coordinate them, since it is more difficult and time consuming to make changes.

Some things to think about:

It is important that the set and the costumes have similar palettes. This means that the set and costumes are using related sets of colors and textures. Notice that I did not say the *same* colors, just related ones. It can lead to visual confusion if the set designer uses neon colors while the costume designer is exploring earth tones. Of course, visual confusion may be just what your show is about, but at least make the choice consciously. It often helps if the set and costume designers can agree on a painting or two from which they can extract a palette.

It is equally important that the set and costumes not use the *same* colors. While the designers should agree on a palette, they should use different parts of it so that the actors will not appear to fade away into the set. *Most of the time, this means that the set should be darker than the costumes.* The set is not moving, the actor is. Therefore, the actors should get the brighter colors to allow the audience to track them more easily. Above all, avoid putting the exact same color on a wall and on a costume that stands in front of it.

CHAPTER 4

Surface, Texture, and Tricks: The Tools of Scenery

In the previous chapter, we discussed how scenery can establish mood, underscore themes, and reveal and support the characters on stage. This is the design perspective. From a more pragmatic standpoint, however, scenery basically does five things. First, it gives the actors a place to stand. Second, it gives the audience a physical surface to look at behind the actor. Third, it provides "real" physical elements, such as doors and windows. Fourth, it helps the play to move from one location to the next, through the use of multiple settings. Finally, it occasionally tricks the audience into believing something happened that did not really happen.

A Place to Stand: Platforms, Stairs, and Ramps

The most basic job of scenery is to provide a place for a performer to stand, feeling comfortable and clearly seen by the audience. Molière said that a platform and a chair was *all* you needed.

Platforms

Scenic platforms are made out of a variety of materials, but they all consist of a frame covered by some kind of top (or **skin**), all of which is held up by **legs**. Regular platforms tend to come in 4-by-8-foot sizes (usually abbreviated as 4 × 8), mostly because platforms use plywood for the top and 4 × 8 is the standard size for plywood sheets from the lumberyard. When you look at the stock platforming that most theaters have, you will see a lot of 4 × 8s. A platform can be built in any size and shape, of course, but, like

Fig. 2. Decks are made of platforms

mobile homes, it is easier and cheaper to build rectangles. If you are renting platforming, it will probably only be available in a few sizes, one of which will most certainly be 4 × 8. Other common rental sizes are 4 × 4 and 4 × 6.

Platforms are combined to build a **deck**. Stock platforms will sometimes have **coffin locks**—latches that lock the platforms together—built in. Otherwise, the platforms are bolted together.

Sometimes, for visual effect, a designer will decide to have the deck slant toward the audience. This is called a **raked stage**, or simply, a **rake**. There are lots of reasons to use a rake. It makes the performers easier to see, for one thing. A raked stage can also make the upstage area feel closer to the audience and it is a good device to improve the intimacy of the audience-actor relationship. It is best used in theaters where the audience seating area is raked very little, or not at all. A rake can also be used to increase the effect of **perspective**, the scenic trick used to increase the apparent size of the stage. If the tops of the walls slant downward as they go upstage, the combination of the top of the wall coming down and the raked floor coming up will make the stage appear larger, sort of like that railroad-tracks-coming-together-in-the-distance trick that you learned in fifth-grade art class. Using this effect to fool the audience is called **false perspective**.

The raked stage is firmly rooted in theatrical history. When scenic design was being invented in Renaissance Italy, false perspective was all the rage, and all the stages were raked. The trend continued into Shakespeare's day and actors had to get used to playing on a shallow hill. Since the actors were literally climbing up the hill as they walked away from the audience, the term **upstage** was created for this area. Conversely, **downstage** meant closer to the audience. As you know, these terms are used today on any stage, raked or not.

If you are considering a raked stage, you should know that actors adapt remarkably well to a slanted playing surface, as long as it is not too steep. Rakes are measured in "inches per foot." A one-inch-to-the-foot rake, for example, rises one inch in altitude for every foot you walk upstage. A one-inch rake is quite shallow, almost unnoticeable to the audience and easy to walk on, while a two-inch-to-the-foot rake feels quite steep, and requires some practice. Good rakes fall somewhere between one inch and two inches to the foot. For obvious reasons, dancers are not wild about working on rakes. Opera singers are less picky (they sing more and move around less). Surprisingly, runway fashion models seem to be able to work on anything short of a cliff.

Steps

The human body is remarkably rigid in its requirements for steps. If the steps rise too slowly, you constantly feel as though you are stumbling. Too quickly, and they exhaust you. Furthermore, the ratio of how high you have to lift your foot each time, the **rise**, to how far forward you move with each step, the **run**, is very important. Architects use a rather complicated

Fig. 3. Different staircases for different users

formula to determine these measurements, but for our purposes, we can use the "eighteen-inch rule." Simply stated, this rule says that *the rise plus the run should be about eighteen inches.* One of the most commonly used ratios is an eight-inch rise for a ten-inch run. This yields a staircase that is comfortable to climb, but rises fairly quickly. A six-inch rise and a twelve-inch run gives a more ceremonial look, suitable for a ballroom scene, an awards ceremony, or any scene where women will be wearing long dresses. Anything shallower than six-by-twelve, though, and the stairs start to get awkward. Performers may find themselves lurching up it, constantly trying to decide whether to put one foot or two on each step. Designers of large public plazas seem to get this one wrong fairly frequently, a good example of function being a slave to form. I live in San Francisco, and I always marvel at the awkwardness of the steps leading up to City Hall. Beautiful building. Lousy steps.

If you need a steeper, more utilitarian-looking stair (a scene in a basement, for example, or aboard a ship), or you just don't have as much space, you can use a nine-by-nine-inch stair, but any steeper and it begins to look and feel like a ladder. As it is, women in long period dresses or heels may need help getting up and down a nine-by-nine. One common use of this steeper stair is for getting actors off high platforms out of sight of the audience. Any staircase with this purpose is called an **escape stair**.

Another way in which the human body is very choosy is in each stair's height relative to the others. Put simply: *It is imperative that all the risers in a staircase are the same size.* As you climb a staircase, you tend to lift your foot only a fraction of an inch higher than necessary to clear each step. Whether this is because of human laziness or just a physiological obsession with efficiency is anybody's guess, but the result is that, if you make one or more of the steps higher than the rest, you will have created what technicians affectionately refer to as an **actor trap**, that is, a piece of scenery that lays in wait for preoccupied actors, causing them to trip, stumble, and forget their lines.

When I was in school at Brown University, we used to take our coffee breaks on the patio outside the theater, just above the post office. (It has since been moved.) We would watch the students come up the single flight of hundred-year-old steps from the basement and marvel at how often people would trip on the top step, spilling coffee and books all over the sidewalk. It literally happened every ten minutes. One day we took a tape measure to the step and, as we suspected, found that it was higher than the rest. How much higher? Less than half an inch. Ever since that experience, I have been impressed by how quickly and firmly the human body adapts to its surroundings. After climbing just a few steps, people's bodies were cutting the heights so close that a half-inch discrepancy was causing them to trip. I was no exception. Even after I knew the higher step was there, I still lost a cup of coffee to it now and then.

If you really need to have an uneven step in your staircase (if you are using a stock staircase, for example, and it falls a little short), put the odd step at the bottom. There are two reasons for this: First, people tend to pay more attention to the steps at the bottom of a staircase, and second, if they do trip, they don't have as far to fall. You laugh, you laugh. . . .

While we're on the subject of safety, any escape stair with more than two steps should have a hand rail (called an "Equity rail" after the actor's union that requires it) on at least one side. Any stair bigger than four steps should have it on both sides. Finally, make sure that you have a strip of white tape along the front of each step so people can see where they are stepping. Don't use phosphorescent "glow tape," though. It will never "charge up" in the backstage gloom and thus will not be visible.

Since the risers on your stairs are going to be six, eight, or (rarely) nine inches, it follows that the platforms that they lead to will also be multiples of six, eight, or nine inches in height. Because the eight-inch riser is such a common and comfortable step, stage platforms are often raised to multiples of eight: sixteen inches, twenty-four inches, thirty-two inches, and so on. The rental platform world is usually sized for six-inch-high steps (more platforms are rented for graduations than for Shakespeare), so their plat-forming tends to be in six-inch increments, that is, twelve inches, eighteen inches, twenty-four inches and so on.

A Surface to Look at: Walls, Drapes, Paint, and Fabric

In the theater, walls are called **flats**. Even if they're not flat. It's just one of those things.

Like platforms, flats can be built in any shape or size, but most theaters carry stock sizes in two-foot increments, such as 4 × 8, 2 × 10, and 2 × 8. When the size of a flat is listed, the width is first, followed by the height. A 4 × 8, for example, is four feet wide and eight feet high. People have been known to violate this rule, however, so if you're renting, be sure to check which is which.

Unfortunately, few rental houses carry flats of any size, although they might build them for you if you want to buy them. These companies make most of their money off corporate clients, and those clients generally prefer soft draperies.

Flats must be supported to stand upright. The best thing to use is other flats. Set the flats at angles to each other and then nail them together. If that doesn't do it, you can add braces on the back. Whatever you do, don't try to suspend the flats from the ceiling with wire or rope. This always

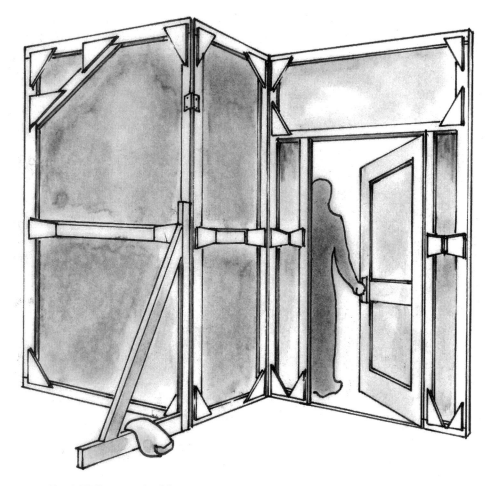

Fig. 4. Walls are made of flats

sounds like a good idea, but it won't keep the flats from swinging in the breeze. Attach the flats to the *floor*.

If you want some quick and easy texture to your walls, try covering them with a decorative fabric or with Styrofoam™.

Styrofoam comes in many different shapes and sizes, but the two most common are polyurethane foam, commonly known as **beadboard** (because it is made up of tiny white beads), and polystyrene foam, commonly known as **blueboard** (because it is blue). Beadboard is cheaper and less dense. It comes in big sheets, like plywood, weighs next to nothing, and makes marvelous-looking rocks if you gouge it out with whatever tools of destruction (screwdrivers, files, car keys) you have lying around. For best effect, dilute some ordinary white glue (one part water to two parts glue), get some cotton cheesecloth (*not* polyester cheesecloth), dip it in the glue, and lay it over the mutilated Styrofoam, pushing it into all the nooks and crannies with a paintbrush. The cheesecloth helps the Styrofoam take paint better, plus it will keep it from cracking and breaking when people rub up against it.

Blueboard is much more dense and can be cut with a fair amount of detail using standard woodworking tools. One good blueboard trick is to paint it with a little acetone. Acetone is a solvent that eats away at the Styrofoam, leaving behind a lovely, craggy surface that looks for all the world like stone. *Safety alert! The acetone trick produces dangerous fumes, so do it outside where there is a breeze blowing.* Like beadboard, blueboard also should be covered with cheesecloth before painting. The thing to remember about any kind of foam is that it will not take any weight at all, so do not use it anyplace where people are going to sit or walk. It has no structural strength; it is purely decorative. Incidentally, if you don't need a huge amount of foam, try prowling around lumber yards, contractor supply houses, or construction sites. They often have scrap pieces left over that are useful to you but not to them. Considering Styrofoam's well-deserved reputation as an environmental nightmare, why not put this scrap to use instead of buying new sheets?

Drapes

What says "show" more than draperies? From Fellini films to Las Vegas revues, the image of a grand drape slowly parting to reveal a spectacle behind it is a piece of cultural imagery that we can never escape. By the way, did you know that the Romans *dropped* the front curtain at the beginning of the show instead of raising it? It fell to the ground and was dragged away by slaves. The idea of raising the curtain up out of sight was invented during the Italian Renaissance, when many of the stage crew were former sailors and sailboat rigging was brought to the theater. To this day, many of the rigging terms we use backstage are actually sailing terms. It is also how the superstition about not whistling backstage got started. The sailors climbing around over the stage communicated by whistling. If you were standing around below them whistling *I Left my Heart in Verona,* people could get confused overhead and you were likely to end up with a sandbag on your noggin. I suspect that this whole don't-walk-under-a-ladder thing got started the same way. Today a safety rule, tomorrow a superstition.

Like the raked stage, draperies are an old tradition in the theater and, like anything else that is ancient, the terminology is extensive and rather particular. The fact that each variety of drape has its own name may seem excessive, but it is worth taking the time to learn them since this kind of terminology can make it easier to communicate with technicians, and isn't that why we're here?

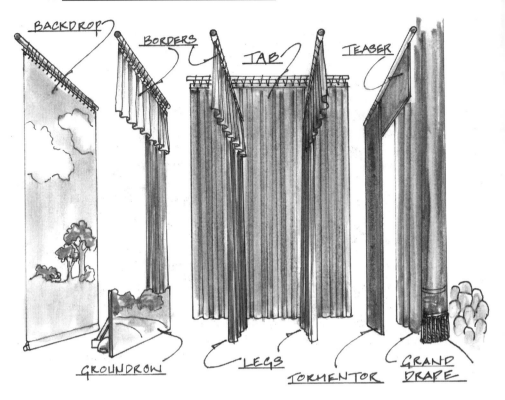

Fig. 5. Names of draperies

Okay, let's start downstage (closer to the audience, remember?). The first drape is the **grand drape**, also called the main drape, the grand curtain, or the main rag. It is the one that has to open for the show to start. It often has a decorative **valence**, a little short drape made of the same material, that runs all the way across the top and does not move. Sometimes a designer will design a main curtain with a logo for a particular show. This is called a **show drop**, and it is used in place of the normal grand drape. In Britain, the law states that the asbestos fire curtain must be down when the audience enters the theater (to calm their fears, I gather), so many theaters have beautifully painted ones.

When the grand drape goes up, you usually see a small drape running across the top of the stage behind the valence, hiding the first row of lights. Unlike the valence, this drape is dark (usually black) and is not meant to draw attention. This is called a **teaser** (I suppose because it "teases" the audience by barely covering the lighting equipment). The sadistic theme continues with the two vertical drapes hanging down from the ends of the teaser. These are called **tormentors**, or often, torms. Off in the wings, many theaters have another set of drapes that hang perpendicular to the proscenium, and help mask the wings. These are called **tabs**.

Moving upstage, we see several more sets of drapes hanging parallel to the arch—each set with one drape running across the top like a teaser and one hanging down from each end like tormentors. The one above is a **border**, the ends are **legs**. Hold it, you say. What's the difference between the teaser/torms and the border/legs? And the answer is, nothing really, except that the most downstage set of borders and legs is generally referred to as the teaser and the torms. Actually, sometimes the teaser and torms are framed draperies, like soft-cover flats, and they form a **portal**. What's more, the teaser and torms are sometimes painted in a design that matches the show and then they're put out in front of the grand drape. In this case, they are called a **false proscenium**. Confused? Check out the diagram.

Enough terms? *I know, it is difficult, but language is important when we seek clarity, and clarity can keep you alive backstage.*

For those of you who are working in the convention and meeting world, your drapes come as **pipe-and-drape**. This is a lightweight fabric panel that is pre-sewn with a pocket running along the top. The installers then slip a long pole into this pocket and suspend the whole thing between two vertical pipes on stands. These drapes usually come in ten-foot lengths, stand about eight feet tall, and are very high and sound-transparent. So you have to be quiet backstage. Sorry.

When hanging drapes, you should consider how thick the pleats in the fabric should be. This is called the **fullness**. A drape that is hanging in "zero fullness" is perfectly flat—no pleats whatsoever. A drape hanging in "100 percent fullness" is pleated, accordion-style, so that it takes up exactly half as much width as it would if it were not pleated at all. In other words, a drapery that is thirty feet wide when stretched out will be fifteen feet wide when hung with 100 percent fullness. Drapes may be hung with more or less fullness, as is appropriate. The more fullness, the grander and more regal they look. Drapes, especially grand drapes, are sometimes manufactured with **sewn-in fullness**, which means that the pleats are sewn in permanently. This makes them nice and crisp and all the same size, but does not allow you to ever spread the drape out flat. This is a nice feature for a front curtain, but you should consider carefully before committing yourself to this option for any other drape.

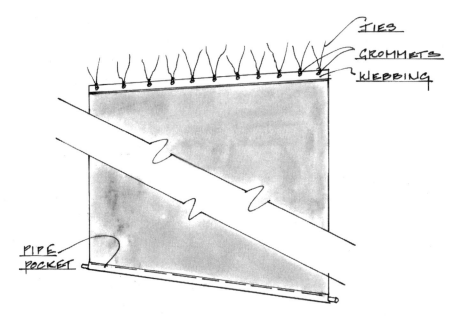

Fig. 6. Parts of a drop

Drops

What's the difference between a drape and a drop? Purpose, mostly. Drapes are considered part of the **masking**, that is, the things that you use to keep the audience from seeing what you don't want them to see. Drapes generally aren't meant to draw attention to themselves. Rather, they are the part of the stage that says: Don't look here. (Remember *The Wizard of Oz*? "Pay no attention to that man behind the masking!") Drops, on the other hand, are part of the scenery, and are meant to be looked at.

A standard stage drop is made from **muslin**. It has a strip of very heavy fabric, called **webbing**, across the top, which is studded with **grommets**—little brass rings embedded in the fabric. Small pieces of **tie line** are fed through grommets and then tied to the batten, the pipe above the stage that will hold the drop. The drop should also have a **chain pocket** running along the bottom, which holds a pipe or chain. The weight of the pipe or chain pulls the drop flat.

Sometimes, a designer will elect to cut out part of a drop (a "cut drop"), leaving an opening, if, for example, she wants the drop to look like leaves hanging down. Sometimes, when a drop comes up one side, across the top, and down the other side, it is called a **portal**.

There are also some special-use drops on stage that have names of their own:

A **scrim** is a commonly used piece of stage magic. When lit from the front, a scrim appears opaque. When the front light is turned off, however, and objects behind the scrim are lit, the fabric appears translucent. This effect, called bleeding through, is most effective when the lights on the front of the scrim are rather bright. When the effect happens, all the light should be taken off the scrim and those on the objects or people behind should be brought up as high as possible. You can use a scrim whenever you want this effect. The national tour of *Les Misérables* used a scrim as a show curtain, so they could start each act by bleeding through to reveal the actors going about their business upstage. Then the show drape was raised, the front lights came on, and the show started. Bleeding through is also a good effect for magic appearances (the talking mirror in *Snow White* is a classic), or for when an actor is onstage thinking (or, more often, singing) about somebody who is not present and that other person needs to be seen. If you're planning on doing *Brigadoon,* for example, you'd better start scrim-shopping for the moment when Tommy Albright sits drinking in a New York City barroom, singing about his mythical mistress in the Scottish Highlands.

For a truly clean effect, a scrim should have a black curtain, called a **blackout drop**, hanging right behind it until just before the effect happens. Then, at the last possible moment, the blackout curtain "flies out" (gets pulled up out of the way) and the lighting effect happens.

It's best not to play a very long scene behind a scrim. The fabric is never truly transparent, and looking through it for a long time can tire out an audience.

Another type of specialty drop is one that goes all the way across the back of the stage and is used to impersonate the sky—a **cyclorama**, or, a **cyc** (pronounced like "psych"). Cycs are often curved to increase the illusion. They also make use of scrims. In fact, a cyc is sometimes a combination of drops—a scrim hanging in front of a muslin drop. Light is then thrown on the muslin drop, while the downstage scrim "confuses" the audience's eyes, making it difficult to tell exactly how far away the muslin drop really is, or, in fact, if it is there at all. The whole effect, if done skillfully, can be quite convincing. For situations where the cyc is being used as a background for modern dance, many designers will add a black scrim in front of it. That way, they just turn off the cyc lights and they have an instant black background for the piece about old age and death. There's always a piece about old age and death.

In both dance and drama, cycs are often lit from below with a set of footlights. This might necessitate a **ground row**, a short wall of flats running across the bottom of the cyc to hide the lights. The ground row can be plain black (common in the dance world), or it can be designed as part of the scenery, looking like a distant hill, some shrubbery, a fence, or whatever.

If you are considering projections, you should know that there are drops specially designed for use as **projection screens**. These highly reflective drops come in two main varieties—front and rear. **Rear-projection screens** can generally be projected on from either side, while **front-projection screens** are really only good for what their name suggests (for one thing, they often have seams holding together the panels of fabric, and those seams will show when a projector comes on from behind). A rear-projection screen can also make an excellent sky; try colored light coming from the front and clouds projected from the rear. You can front-project onto a plain muslin drop painted white if need be, but nothing compares with the sharpness and brilliance of a rear-projection screen. Rear-projecting onto muslin doesn't work, you can see the "hot spot" of the lamp behind the screen.

Fabric

As a fabric for draperies, *velour* is both traditional and unparalleled. It has a deep pile that looks luxurious under stage lights, it drapes in deep, thick folds, and it moves majestically when pulled aside. It is also quite dense and will not allow light to pass through from backstage, something very few fabrics can claim. Finally, a black velour curtain positively *eats* unwanted spill light, making it the cleanest, sharpest masking drape available. It is no accident that velour has been the fabric of choice for stage draperies for decades. All of this wonderfulness comes at a price, however. Velour is one of the most expensive fabrics available for stage drapes, and one of the heaviest. A properly sewn velour grand drape can weigh hundreds of pounds and is not something you want to put up and take down on a regular basis.

Duvateen is another commonly used drapery fabric, but it is only really good for temporary uses. Although it is cheaper and lighter than velour, it is not very durable and doesn't hang in folds as well. The nap side is a pretty good light-eater though, so it is often used to cover openings in the scenery where a full drape is unnecessary or unavailable, say, behind a door where the audience can just catch a glimpse of the backstage area. Keep a roll of duvateen around to tear pieces off when you need a little bit of fabric to solve a masking problem.

There are literally hundreds of other fabrics that can be used for draperies. Velour and duvateen mark the rough boundaries of the choices, both in beauty and price. Anything more expensive than velour is too expensive for the stage. Anything cheaper than duvateen probably will not hold up. Other fabrics will be a trade-off between price on the one hand and thickness, durability, and attractiveness on the other. Talk to your theatrical dealer and look at samples. Make sure you hold the samples up in front of a lamp. You shouldn't be able to see any light through them.

Besides draperies, there are lots of other uses for fabric on stage. Covering a flat with a decorative fabric is an easy solution if you don't want to paint it. Many fabrics also add three-dimensional texture to walls, something a two-dimensional paint job can't always do.

Erosion cloth, which landscapers use to cover newly seeded areas, is a loosely woven mesh of twinelike threads. It is usually light tan, and looks sort of raglike and medieval on stage. You can use it for backdrops, ground texture, or anything else that you want to look beaten-up and lowlife-like. One hint: After you pick it up from the landscape supplier, hang it up outside and beat it with a stick to get some of the dust and dirt off before you bring it inside.

Felt is a cheap way to make a wall look snazzy. Felt comes in lots of colors and in several widths. **Industrial felt**, by the way, is a heavier weight of felt that can be used to make props and hats.

A good theatrical supplier will also carry a line of **designer fabrics**, many of which are put out by our friends at Rosco Labs. They range from the glamorous to the cheesy and are worth taking a look at, especially if your show tends toward the Vegas look. These fabrics also tend toward the expensive side, so consider combining them with something less pricey, like duvateen or felt.

Paint

It used to be that the world was nicely broken down into two kinds of paint: the oil-based *enamels,* which people used on furniture and shelving, and the water-based *latex,* which people used on walls. Low-budget theater artists generally preferred latex because it was cheaper and it could be cleaned up with water. Enamel lasted forever, but you had to have paint thinner (usually turpentine) to clean the brushes. In the theater world, however, there was a third type of paint. This paint was based on animal glue (what the grizzled old stagehands call "dope") and powdered pigment that was brewed up in the scene shop, off in a dark corner that smelled like a slaughterhouse. It had one major advantage, though: It could produce colors that were much more vibrant than ordinary latex paint (and it did not need turpentine to dilute or thin it). Most people don't want to paint their living rooms forest green or lemon yellow, but scenic artists aren't painting houses; they're painting sunrises and magic mountains, fields of poppies and mysterious forests. Antique white and eggshell blue just weren't going to cut it. So they brewed their own.

All of this changed when modern scenic paint became available. Finally, all of those magical hues were available commercially and scenic artists did not have to live with a witches' kettle percolating in the shop all the time. Life became more bearable.

Well, sort of. Life was certainly more bearable in the professional shops that could afford the good stuff. Companies like Iddings and Rosco Labs put out high quality, water-based scenic paint that rapidly became the industry standard. The rest of us, however—the high schools, the community theaters, and the hole-in-the-wall spaces—had to wait until the mid-1980s when Rosco Labs finally came out with a low-budget version called "Off-Broadway Paint." Since then, other companies have followed suit, and there are now several lower-budget alternatives. Of course, they don't last as long as the better stuff, and they lose vibrancy if you dilute them too much, but who cares? Leprechaun Green, Poppy Yellow, and Rocket Red at (a little above) the price of hardware store latex. Life is good again. So, when the time comes to buy paint, don't head for the hardware store if you need anything other than black, white, and beige. Get thee to a theatrical supplier and check out the paint that is specifically made for us.

If you do get in a pinch and have to go to the hardware store, go armed with a sample of the color you want. Show the clerk and tell her you want the cheapest "flat latex" that they have. "Flat" means it won't reflect light. This is very important on stage. "Latex" means you can wash out your brushes with water. "Cheap" means it won't last five years, but so what?

Now then, let's get ready to paint.

The Backstage Survival Guide to Painting: What to Buy or Borrow

- *Brushes:* Get brushes with bristles made for water-based paint (read the label). Get several different sizes, depending on what you are painting. Having the proper sized brush with the right kind of bristles is half the battle. Even if you are painting a large space with rollers, get a small brush or two to paint the corners and edges where the rollers can't reach.
- *Rollers:* If you are painting a larger space, get some rollers. In addition to being faster, rollers will put the paint down smoothly and without brush marks. Rollers come in different sizes, depending on the thickness of the *nap,* the fuzzy stuff that actually holds the paint. For most uses, a half-inch to one-inch nap is fine.
- *Paint:* As previously stated, get water-based theatrical paint unless you really only need house paint colors. One gallon of paint covers about 400 square feet so you have to do a little math. Come on, you can do it: Just multiply the width of the surface you are painting by its length or height. Guesstimate. Remember though, it is a far better thing to return unopened cans of paint to the store than to run out at midnight the day before opening. The corner Seven-Eleven does not sell paint.

- *Roller handles:* Get enough so that you can keep all your people working. Take care of them and they last a surprisingly long time. The rollers, I mean. Actually, the same is true of the people.
- *Roller handle extensions:* If you are painting walls, get at least one so you can reach farther up and you won't have to spend a lot of time on a ladder. If you are painting the floor, get one for everybody so nobody has to crawl around and get a pain in the back.
- *Paint clothes:* Do I sound like your mother here? I wouldn't bring this up except for all the people who show up to paint and then say, "Wow, I didn't know it was going to be such a mess." It *is* a mess and no matter what you do, it will always be that way. Sacrifice a set of old clothes and keep them in a closet at the theater so you know they are there when you need them.
- *Drop Cloths:* Same story. No matter what you do, etc. Cover everything. Paint has a mind of its own and that mind is constantly saying "Flee!" So catch those drops before they get too far. Paint stores sell plastic drop cloths but, personally, I prefer to sacrifice a piece of muslin or an old sheet, since the plastic ones are slippery and seem to always be bunching up under your feet.
- *A ladder:* Everybody seems to forget this one. A six-foot one is very handy.
- *A source of water:* Make sure you have access to a sink where you can pour water into buckets and wash brushes when you are done.

The key to successful painting is planning. Get the right materials in advance, set aside a time when nothing else is going on, get enough people, put the right music on, and olé! Painting is fun.

Painting is not just about color, however. Sometimes painting is about adding texture to a surface, or protecting it from harm, or making it shiny, or making it not slippery. Paint treatments can do all of these things when applied properly. Here are some possibilities:

Adding Texture to a Surface

This is usually done by adding some sort of material directly to the paint and then rolling it on. Sawdust works pretty well and you can't beat the price, but the best stuff is *stucco patching powder* (get it at the hardware store). This powder is used by commercial painters to patch stucco walls that have been plastered over and need to have their texture restored. It comes in three levels of coarseness, depending on how much texture you want. It is hard to get too much texture on stage, so go for the coarsest one. Stir it into the paint (follow the directions for amounts!) and roller it onto your flats. You will need two or three times as much paint to cover the same area so get extra. Get the really thick roller pads for this job (two-inch-thick nap).

Protecting a surface (such as a painted stage floor) is best done with clear acrylic glaze (a theatrical supplier will have it) or urethane. Urethane is a good deal tougher, but as for washing up the rollers afterwards . . . You might as well throw them out. It also takes longer to dry. Acrylic will take several coats over several days to really be strong. Both acrylic and urethane come in gloss, semigloss, or flat. Get the flat, unless you want the floor to shine and reflect light. Talk to the lighting designer before you create a glossy floor. He will have to make changes in how he lights it, so that the audience doesn't go blind from the glare.

For a truly Fred-Astaire, get-out-your-top-hat floor, use glossy urethane, which should be rolled onto the floor just like you would paint the walls in your home. There are lots of different varieties, so talk to the folks at the paint store. I used one kind that was marketed as "gym floor urethane," which produced the most incredible gloss I have ever seen. Get the opinion of the folks who sell the stuff before buying. As stated previously, if you use urethane, plan on throwing the rollers out, unless you want to spend the evening up to your elbows in paint thinner. Trust me, you would rather be watching *The Late Show*.

Getting rid of slippery surfaces. Plywood, masonite, and other common floor coverings are often slippery when first installed, so try to get them painted before you rehearse on them. This can be a problem, especially if you are in a situation where the technicians are building the set during the day and you are coming in for rehearsal in the evening. One night you will come in and the floor will look beautiful—wonderfully smooth and shiny with a brand new layer of raw masonite on it. Watch it! That stuff is very slippery and dangerous. Anyone in stocking feet or ballet slippers *will* fall. Try to find out ahead of time when the new covering will be put on the stage and then do everything possible to see that it gets a coat of paint before you rehearse on it. This is a sticky logistical problem for everybody, since the floor will need several hours to dry. It may mean rehearsing somewhere else that night. After all, paint crews are famous for coming to work in the middle of the night, but they're not famous for liking it.

Real Things: Doors, Windows, and So On

Okay, time for an exercise. Get your tape measure (you do have one by now, right?), take this book, and get up from wherever you are. Spend a few minutes walking around your house (your office, your friend's house, your cave, wherever you are right now) looking at each door that you pass. What's it made of? How big is it? Are there windows in it? Is there a doorsill across the bottom or is it smooth? Where is the knob? How many hinges are there? Which side are they on? Does the door swing into the room or out? Or is it a sliding door? A rolling door? A folding one? What do the locks look like? What other kind of hardware does it have? A peephole? A mail slot?

Take some time to get familiar with the doors that you encounter. Go through the questions above to remind yourself what you are looking for. Remember to *measure* each one. It is going to become increasingly important for you to become sensitive to how big things are, because technicians are going to constantly ask you, "How big do you want that to be?" and it will just impress the doggies out of them if you have a precise answer.

Once you have looked at the doors in your home, broaden your research. You don't have to go to the library, or buy a lot of copies of *Architectural Digest*. As you go through your day, just try to become aware of what kind of doors you go through.

And what about windows? They have just as much variety. They push up like sashes, swing out like casements, and slide open like French doors. Some of them are even round, for God's sake. Take your tape measure to a few, just to get an idea.

What's the point? The point is, if you are going to put replicas of real things on stage, you better take some time and start looking at what real things *look like*. Nothing is more valuable in the theater than the ability to keenly perceive the world in all its aspects: mentally, emotionally, and physically. There are people in the world who can help you with the first two. I'm here to help you with the third one. And although it may seem like an inconsequential thing to you, a little awareness of the infinite variety of everyday items like doors and windows can go a long way toward the creating of something beautiful on stage.

Designing and building doors and windows is a complicated process for two reasons: First, as I said, doors come in almost infinite varieties and finding the right one takes some effort, and second, because they are **practical**, that is, they have to really work. "Practical" is a general term for anything, from a faucet to a window, that is actually operated by a performer. Building something that has to work is a great deal different (and more expensive) than building something that is only decorative.

When you tell a technician that you want a door or a window, here's what he will want to know:

• *Is it really "practical?"*

Does it have to open and close or is it only decorative? A window that is built "nonpractical" is completely different than a practical one. A practical one is much more complex and expensive, so designating a window as nonpractical can save a lot of time and money. Unfortunately, once the

Fig. 7. Different ways to hang a door

window is built nonpractical, it cannot be changed without rebuilding the entire piece so, if you are in doubt, have them built practical. The worst thing that can happen is that the practical windows sit there unused during the run, a fact that won't make the guys in the shop happy, but they'll get over it. Of course, if you waste their efforts fairly frequently, they may stop asking you and start nailing the windows shut, so try and do your homework and give them the right information to start with.

• *What kind of door is it?*

As I said, there are lots of choices here: swinging, double, rolling, sliding, folding, screen, French, Barn-style, Cross and Bible, the list goes on and on. This is where you really benefit from your research. You don't have to know them all (there are thousands), but the more you know, the more the tech people can help you. When working with a set designer, try looking through some architectural books and magazines for doors and windows that fit your ideas for the show.

• *How big is it?*

Standard household doors are about two-foot-six-inches wide by six-foot-eight-inches high (have you measured yours yet?), but there is a great deal of variety out there. Doors were smaller in older houses, but that was partly because the people were smaller, so you may not wish to duplicate them exactly. You may also want to consider wider doors to accommodate period dresses, men with swords, actors in soap bubble costumes, whatever.

• *If it is a swinging door, which side are the hinges on, and which way does it swing?*

This is a really important question for everybody. A general rule is that *doors open up and off.* This means that the hinges are on the upstage side, and the door opens toward offstage. A door hinged on the upstage side will cover the sight lines better, and a door that opens offstage will not block an actor entering. Of course, you may decide to break this rule for some reason—a murder scene where an unidentified arm reaches out from behind the door with a pistol, that sort of thing—but as a general rule it holds. Which way the door swings also determines whether the door has be "finished," that is, painted and decorated, on one side or both sides.

• *What does it look like?*

This is where the designer really comes in, but as I said, the more you know . . . Does it have a window in it? What kind of doorknobs? Plain or ornate? You get the idea.

• *What kind of abuse will it get?*

Any carpenter worth her tool belt can build a stage door that can be closed good and hard, but I know a lot of carpenters who have seen their hard work slammed to smithereens because they weren't warned ahead of time that the door would have to put up with that kind of abuse. Actors can get very physical on stage and technicians can certainly accommodate them, but the shop needs to be told ahead of time what is expected. Saying, "By the way, Nora is really going to slam that door hard at the end," can save a lot of tech-week grumbling.

Moving Stuff Around: Rolling, Flying, and Gripping

Some of the time, your scenery will have to move during the play. In general, don't move something unless you have to but, if you have to, make sure that you take the time to decide which moving technique is most appropriate. No matter how beautiful your scenery is, if the audience has time to read the entire program between scenes, the effect of the show will be lost. A slick, well-choreographed scene change, however, can add life and vitality to a show, keeping the pace and emotion alive from scene to scene. When you think about moving scenery, keep asking yourself this question: "What is the fastest, smoothest way to get from this scene to that scene?"

Fast and smooth doesn't always mean elaborate or expensive. In fact, it often means just the obvious. In a world of motors, hydraulics, flying hardware, and automation, remember the scenic adage: *There's no tech like low tech.*

As suggested by the title of this section, scenery-moving techniques fall into three categories: **rolling** (moving horizontally on wheels), **flying** (moving vertically on cables), and **gripping** (moving any direction in the hands of a technician). Before we discuss the specifics of each technique, let's decide which one we need. Here are some questions to help you decide which way to go.

• *Do you mind seeing technicians?*

This is a stylistic question, and must be answered by the director. We depend on the audience's willingness to suspend their disbelief, and that willingness can be taxed by the sight of a technician gripping something offstage, even during a darkened scene change. On the other hand, let's not sell the audience short. The audience knows that they are sitting in a theater and they know that there are technicians backstage, so seeing one is not going to explode anybody's myth about what's really going on. Stylistically, however, during emotionally intense shows, it may be better not to force the audience to disconnect from the story. A visible technician may have that effect. Sometimes, the scene change can be choreographed into the show and the crew can be given costumes (be sure to warn your costume designer early on). This is particularly effective in big musicals, large-scale period pieces such as the Shakespearean plays, and musical revues. If you want the scene change to be truly "magic," however, and you don't want to see the crew, then you will almost certainly need rolling and flying scenery that is operated from offstage.

• *What kind of a theater do you have?*

It doesn't make sense to spend a lot of time talking about lifting scenery up when you don't have a flying system or a fly space. Or storing it back-stage when you don't have any wing space. Go take a look at the theater and talk to the technicians. Go through chapter 2 and answer as many of the questions about touring a new space as you can. Pay particular attention to what kind of machinery is hanging overhead, and how much wing space is available.

• *How big is the scenery?*

There is a limit to how big of a piece you can fly. Flying systems are generally set up with lots of pipes, or **battens**, hanging parallel to the proscenium arch, which means that they are very good at picking up scenery that is also hanging parallel to the arch, like drops. There have been a lot of attempts over the years to design more flexible flying systems, but all of their cleverness and flexibility has faded before a tough reality of show business: There is rarely enough time to make an entirely different setup for every production. In order to survive the pressures of money, time, and space, we live by standardization, and standardization means that battens are parallel to the proscenium. What you can fly also depends on how much space you have available above the stage. Remember, you have to have storage space overhead for anything that flies out. If you have a thirty-foot-high drop, you must have thirty feet available to put it in when it flies out. There are tricks that technicians use for folding, or **tripping**, scenery as it flies out, but those tricks can be complicated and time consuming.

> • *How fast does the scenery have to move?*

Flying is hands-down the fastest way to move scenery, so if speed is the greatest concern, think about taking the scenery up in the air.

> • *How heavy is it?*

There is a limit to the weight that a flying system can handle. There is also a limit to what a technician can move by gripping so, if your scenery is very heavy, consider rolling. Once in my life, I supervised the flying of an actual covered wagon, and I will never, *ever* try it again. Flying scenery should be *light*.

> • *What's the big picture?*

All of your decisions about moving scenery will be affected by other, larger concerns. How is the show designed as a whole? What other pieces are moving and how? Is this show part of a rotating repertory, where sets for other shows must be stored and played on in the same theater?

Gripping

Gripping scenery means just what it sounds like: Somebody walks out on stage, grips the scenery in her own hands and moves it. We spend a lot of time in the design process devising magic movements of scenery, trying to impress the audience with our cleverness, but it is not always necessary. Human beings are remarkably adaptable, capable creatures and they should be used whenever possible. I have spent countless hours devising effects, only to see the machinery get replaced with a stagehand walking out and picking up the scenery. Once again, "There's no tech like low tech."

Of course, gripping scenery is not without pitfalls. If you follow these simple rules, however, you can enjoy years of trouble-free gripping.

Walking up a flat (lifting it up to a vertical position) is a basic skill that every show person should know. First, tip the flat up onto its long side. Then, one person **foots** the flat by pushing his foot against the bottom corner, while the other person lifts the other end of the flat and walks toward the first person, lifting the flat higher and higher as she walks. The first person's foot keeps the flat from skittering away, and before you know it, the flat is upright.

Carrying a flat is just as simple but it has a critical rule, known among my friends as "Bernie's rule," since we all learned it from Bernie Works, the all-knowing teacher of technical theater at the University of Illinois, Urbana-Champaign. Professor Works is legendary the world over for his

Fig. 8. Walking up a flat

constant invocation of the phrase: "One hand high, one hand low! That's what makes the scenery go!" Each person should reach up as high as possible with one hand and as low as possible with the other. Furthermore, you and your partner should mirror one another. If you have your left hand high, then your partner should reach up with his right. If you both reach as high and as low as you can, and you mirror one another, you can move surprisingly tall flats with little trouble.

Beyond these simple rules, gripping scenery is a matter of common sense, but since we all know that common sense is not so common, here are some things to remember:

- Lift with your legs, not with your back.
- When you have to change direction, turn your whole body. *Don't twist.*
- Get enough people. Don't be a hero. Heroes sit around discussing old wars when they get old because they don't have the muscles left to do anything else. Stay young, stay mobile, get someone to help you.

Rolling

What if your scenery is too big or too heavy to grip? Answer: Consider using mankind's second oldest tool (after the flashlight): the wheel.

First, let's get our terms straight. A rolling scenic unit is called a **wagon** and the rolling thing you attach to make the wagon move is called a **castor**, not a wheel. A castor contains a wheel as one of its parts, but the whole piece of equipment is called a castor.

Castors come in lots of shapes and sizes, from the small furniture castors on a rolling desk chair to the giant ones underneath your garbage dumpster, but there are two distinct groups of them: **swivel** (also called rotating), and **straight-run** (also called fixed). The difference is just what it sounds like: The swivel ones are free to rotate and turn in any direction, while the straight ones are locked down and will not rotate. Stage techs often refer to swivel castors as "smart" castors (I guess because they can head off in any direction they choose), while straight castors are called "stupid" castors (because they can only move forward and backward).

Wagons can use straight-run (fixed, "stupid") castors if they only have to move forward and backward. This is called, not surprisingly, a **straight-run wagon**, and it is the easiest type of wagon to use because it addresses both of the two major problems with using wagons on stage: getting them to go where you want them to go, and getting them to stay there. Straight-run wagons, since they are relatively incapable of moving from side to side, are the easiest to steer into place. They roll out, they roll back. End of story. They are also easier to keep in one place, since you only have to keep them from moving in two directions: forward and back. Straight-run wagons sometimes have a metal blade, called a *knife,* which sticks down into a groove in the floor to keep the wagon on track.

Next time you go to a professionally produced, Broadway-style musical, take a look at the floor. Unless you're seeing *The Fantastiks* (the simplest musical ever produced), the floor will probably be crisscrossed with slots. These are the tracks that the wagons will be following. Try predicting where the wagons will end up. Amaze your friends.

Unlike straight-run castors, swivel castors can move in any direction you want. The bad news is, they can move in any direction *they* want. They are more difficult to drive and more difficult to keep in one place, but they offer you more flexibility.

You can also consider using both types of castors on the wagon, swivel castors on one end, and straight-run on the other. This produces a wagon that is only steerable on one end, like your car. Wagons sometimes have this combination for the same reason that your car does: It is easier to steer a platform that only has rotating castors on one end. Unlike your car, though, a wagon should have the rotating castors on the rear, not on the front. This makes the platform easier to steer when being pushed from the back, particularly when maneuvering in tight spaces.

There are other kinds of rolling wagons that show up from time to time.

Some shows switch back and forth quickly between scenes, and each of those scenes requires a full-stage set. For this situation, one rather expensive solution is the turntable, or **revolve**. Revolves require a major scenic commitment: Difficult and expensive to construct, they are notorious for bogging down tech rehearsals and breaking down at key moments. Nevertheless, there is a time and a place for them, so long as you have the money and, most important, the knowledgeable staff to handle them.

Of course, revolves don't have to take up the whole stage. They don't even have to be a full circle. One special kind of revolve pivots around one end: a *jackknife platform.* Some sadistic designers even put revolves in the middle of other revolves, but now we're getting out of hand.

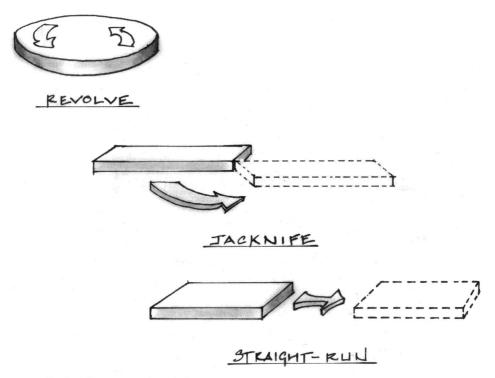

Fig. 9. Different ways that platforms move

Flying

As I said earlier, flying scenery goes back to the sailors who were brought in to rig the Italian Renaissance theaters in the 1500s. Actually, it goes back even further than that: right back to the Greek theater a thousand years before Christ. Some Greek plays ended with the entrance of a God who appeared to magically untangle whatever knots the mortals had tied themselves up in. These Gods often entered in a large scenic machine, called a *machina*. Basically, they were lifted over the back of the scenery in giant hand-operated cranes, an effect called the **deus ex machina** (literally, a "God in a machine"). The phrase survives today as a term describing any late-entering character who comes with near-divine powers to punish injustice and repeal injury.

The actual machinery that we use today, however, is descended from the Renaissance. The sailors designed a system, known today as a **hemp system**, which was extremely flexible and survived well into this century. In fact, it is still used today in a few theaters. The hemp system consisted of hemp rope lines running from the scenery up over pulleys, which are sitting on a grid high above the stage. The lines traveled across the grid, went over more pulleys, and then dropped down to the stage level where they were attached to sand bags and tied off to the **pin rail**. The sandbags provided weight to counterbalance the scenery so that it could be pulled up and down without difficulty. The hemp system was so flexible because the pulleys could easily be moved around and ropes could be dropped just about anywhere. Once all the ropes for a given piece of scenery were brought up to the grid and down to the pin rail, they were all tied together and attached to sandbags. The sandbags provided counterbalancing weight, allowing the stagehands to pull up very heavy scenery with less effort.

The problems with hemp systems were twofold. First, all that hemp rope had a tendency to stretch out, so things had to be readjusted all the time. If the theater was dark for a couple of days, all the lines had to be carefully tied off to prevent slippage. (Theater trivia note: All of this tying-off led to the creation of a special knot called a "Sunday," used to tie off the lines after the Sunday show, the theater being dark on Monday night. The term persists today—if a stage tech wants you to tie off a line temporarily, he will ask you to "put a Sunday" on it.)

The second problem with the hemp system was that it required highly skilled operators. Even with the best technicians, accidents still happened. (How many murder mysteries have you seen where the tenor is offed by a sandbag?) The problem was knots. A hemp system required the constant tying and untying of many different kinds of knots. Knot tying was a life-or-death skill to Renaissance sailors and they knew what they were doing. In the modern theater, however, a properly tied bowline knot is as rare as a clean-shaven poet. In the absence of this skill, hemp becomes a dangerous, accident-prone system. Furthermore, even well-treated rope degrades over time, becoming brittle and weak.

The first thing that had to happen, therefore, was a switch from rope to a stronger, more durable material: **aircraft cable**, so-called because that was the main use for it before theater came along. This switch, however, meant rethinking and redesigning the entire system. After all, cable couldn't be tied and untied all the time; it had to be permanently attached. And what about all those sandbags? How could weight be attached to the system without endangering anyone? It took some time, but, in the end, the thinkers and designers came up with what most theaters in this country use today: the **counterweight flying system**.

Conceptually, the counterweight system is built on the same idea as the hemp system: Tie a line to the scenery, send it up over a pulley, across the grid, over another pulley, and down to an operator who attaches some sort of counterbalancing weight to it. How all of that is accomplished, however, is substantially different.

First of all, the scenery is attached to a **batten**. This batten is lifted up by a group of cables called the **pickup lines**. Okay, get it out of your system: You always thought that a theatrical pickup line was something like, "Is this a dagger I see before my hand, or are you just happy to see me?" Small theaters may have only three pickup lines, a larger one as many as seven. All these lines go up to the grid where, as in the hemp system, they go over pulleys, travel across the grid, and then turn downward. Instead of sandbags, however, the lines attach to an **arbor**, a metal cage that travels up and down on a track. Rather than tying off sandbags to the lines, the technicians just pile **counterweights** (also known as **bricks**) into the arbor to counterbalance the weight. The battens and the pulleys that go with them are installed in permanent locations, and the arbor slides up and down a permanently installed track. No knots to tie and no rope to stretch.

There are two places, called **rails**, where the technicians go to operate a counterweight flying system. In a hemp system, the ropes were tied off at a **pin rail** off to the side of the stage. When the piece was first rigged, the call of "Meat to the Rail" went out, and everybody hauled out the piece. When the scenery was in the air, the sandbags were attached at ground level.

As the cables and arbors of the counterweight system were appearing, so was another innovation: the **loading rail**. Rather than bring the arbor to the technicians, the technicians now go to the arbor, climbing up to the grid while the batten is still on the floor.

———————————

Safety Alert! *While loading bricks into an arbor is less dangerous than using a hemp system, even the best technician gets sweaty hands now and then. When weights are being loaded above, keep everybody out from underneath the loading rail! Before loading weights, the technician above should shout, "Clear the rail!" Once everyone is safely out of the way, the technician in charge underneath should shout, "Rail clear!" Only then should loading begin. The rail should remain clear until the technician above yells, "Loading complete!" Stay alert! A forty-pound counterweight dropped from the grid will go through you, the floor, and anything else between it and bedrock.*

———————————

Once the weights have been loaded, the lines are actually operated from the pin rail, now renamed the **lock rail** because it holds the locks that keep the scenery from moving at the wrong time.

While cable has replaced rope on all the weight-bearing lines in a counterweight system, it is not much fun to grab onto. So, hemp rope is still found in one place: on the **purchase line**. "Purchase" is a strange word in the theater—it shows up all over the place. Besides the meaning that

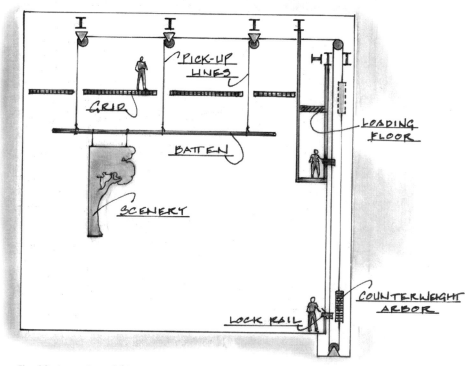

Fig. 10. A counterweight system

everybody is used to—heading for the mall with a credit card—it also
means being able to hold on to something. If you can "get purchase" on a
line, you can grab it hard enough to pull it. The purchase line, then, is the
part of the counterweight system that you actually grab onto and pull. The
purchase line is attached to the bottom of the arbor, so when you pull
down on it, the arbor comes down as well. Since the arbor is coming down,
the scenery will start going up and voilà! You're flying.

The purchase line is not just attached to the bottom of the arbor,
though. It is actually a loop from the bottom of the arbor, down through
your hand, through the lock, through a pulley on the floor, back to the
grid, and down to the top of the arbor.

This setup means that the counterweight system can do one trick that
the hemp system couldn't: It can pull the scenery *down* as easily as it can
pull it *up*, even if the counterbalancing weight is not exactly right. With the
hemp system, the counterbalance had to be kept a little lighter than the
scenery. Otherwise, when the scenery flew out, it wouldn't come back in.
When you look at the lock rail on a counterweight system, however, you
should see *two* ropes, one in back of the other. The *back* one is hanging

Dear Old Dad
Shift Plot

SHIFT A	FROM OFFICE TO PARK
Tim (fly rail)	1. (after Dean latches door) fly out wall #1 2. (after platform C clears) fly in trees #1
Denise (fly rail)	1. fly out wall #2 2. (after platform B clears) fly in trees #2
Valerie (stage right)	1. remove table unit stage right 2. remove two dining room chairs stage right 3. remove wing chair (with Craig)
Kirsten (stage left)	1. remove backing wall 2. set rock unit stage left (with Dean)
Dean (stage left)	1. latch door on wall unit #1 2. set rock unit stage left (with Kirsten)
Craig (stage right)	1. remove sink unit 2. remove wing chair (with Valerie) 3. clear books from floor 4. set kite and blanket

Fig. 11. A shift plot

from the arbor, so pulling that one brings the arbor down (and the scenery up). The *front* one is attached to the top of the arbor, so pulling that one brings the arbor up (and the scenery down). The rule is, *the front rope does whatever the scenery does*. If the front rope is going up, so is the scenery, and vice versa. Still can't keep it straight? Try this: "The Front rope Follows the scenery."

The whole kit and kaboodle—batten, lines, sheaves, arbor, and purchase line—is called a **line set**. Technicians often talk about the capacity of a flying system in terms of how many line sets it has: the more line sets, the more individual things that can be flown.

The Backstage Survival Guide to Scene-Change Choreography

Gripping, rolling, and flying are all possibilities when moving scenery around. No matter how you have it set up, though, you still need to take some time before tech rehearsal to work out who does what and when they do it. All this information should appear on a shift plot, like the one shown at left.

Scene changes don't just happen: They require planning, forethought, and as much choreography as a dance number, especially if they are done *a vista,* or in front of the audience. Here then, are some things to remember when choreographing your scene change.

• *Try not to use the actors.*

People are often tempted to get away with fewer technicians by having the actors move scenery around, but I try and talk them out of it. Having actors involved in a scene change can lead to mistakes. Actors aren't stupid; just preoccupied. After all, they have a lot to think about—lines to remember, characters to develop, movements to perform—all the time trying not to bump into the furniture and wondering if they remembered to zip their fly. I say, whenever possible, let the actors be the actors and let the crew be the crew. The exception? Actors with one-line, walk-on parts. Scene changes keep them from getting bored.

• *In general, move flying things first and last.*

The order should be: Old flying scenery goes out, then old rolling and gripped scenery goes out, then new rolling and gripped scenery comes in, then new flying scenery comes in. This way, the flying scenery is clear of the rolling scenery and the moving people for as long as possible, making it less likely that something will get tangled or somebody will get bopped on the head.

• *Don't run.*

Speed is important, but so are accuracy and safety. With practice, a good crew will achieve a swift yet controlled speed that never appears rushed, but gets the job done quickly.

If your scene change is *a vista,* keep something happening on stage all the time. "A vista" means visible, that is, the audience gets to watch. A well-choreographed shift can be a treat for an audience, giving them a "behind the scenes" feeling and, if the shift is really clever, adding to the magic of the show. If you are going to do it, though, give the audience something to watch throughout the shift. If there is nothing visible happening on stage, the audience will think the shift is over. When the action doesn't start right away, they will get impatient.

• *Never have anyone on stage doing nothing.*

An extension of the previous rule. Even if someone has to wait for something else to happen before they can do their job, have them wait in the wings. An idle person on stage makes the audience wonder: "Why is he just *standing* there?"

• *Don't take too long.*

Obviously, make it as short as possible. As a general rule, try and get your shift down to under thirty seconds. That's still a long time, but an audience will sit still for that, especially if they can watch (and you have music playing). If you are doing a musical and have a pit orchestra to play during the shift, you can get away with a little bit more time, but if the shift goes over a minute, you'd better be prepared to sell popcorn (if not drinks) between scenes.

• *Be sensitive to the pace and the subject matter of the show.*

This one is best illustrated by a story. One of the worst scenic mistakes I ever made was during a show called *For Benson, at the Height of His Career,* an original musical for which I designed scenery at Brown University. Toward the end of the show there was a funeral scene, complete with an ornate black casket on a marble slab center stage. The next scene was down left in a pool of light, where a narrator spoke, tying up the last threads of the show. During the narrator's monologue, the stage had to clear completely, since he was supposed to exit through the now-empty stage. The casket was big and bulky, but not too heavy. Since we did not want to see technicians onstage during the show, I decided to fly the whole thing out, slab and all. It sounded like a fine idea during the build and even through tech week. It wasn't until the resounding laugh from the audience on opening night that we realized that the sight of the casket "flying up to heaven" after the funeral just wasn't going to work. So, be aware of the moments before and after the shift as well as the general pacing of the show. You don't want to come on like gangbusters when the next scene is a lullaby.

• *Use your intermissions.*

They are gold mines of time—at least ten minutes when the audience is not really paying attention. You can also get away with making more noise during intermission. Don't just think about the next scene, either. Try and use the intermission to set up anything else that you can. Playwrights, take note: If you must have huge scene changes, try and put the biggest one during intermission.

Whether or not you are the scene-change choreographer, here's one rule that everybody in the theater should pay attention to:

• *If it doesn't work at first, don't freak out.*

It always requires several tries to get it right, and the shift will get faster every time. The crew and their chief should constantly be on the lookout for ways to speed things up:

- Is somebody standing around for a moment with nothing to do?
- Could something move faster if an obstacle were removed?
- Would it work better to do things in a different order?
- Could things that travel together be attached to each other?
- What else can we do ahead of time?

- How about attaching wheels to something that's being gripped?
- Can any offstage changes be put off until after the scene starts?

Listen to the crew, right down to the lowest ASM. They may have suggestions that will speed things up. Most of all, remember, there is not a crew in the world who will do it perfectly the first time, and some of them won't even come close. With practice, however, speed will probably increase dramatically. So, if it looks impossible at first, don't despair. Take a deep breath. This is fun.

Playing with the Audience: Special Effects and Illusions

Just in case you haven't yet picked up my feelings on the matter so far, let me say as clearly as I can here: There is no greater effect than a well-crafted script and no greater illusion than fine acting. No amount of fog or fire or strobe lights will ever save you if the basic show itself is faulty. So, don't look in this chapter for quick fixes, and for God's sake, don't *start* here. This stuff is the frosting. Make sure your cake is more than half-baked before you start choosing the decorations.

Now that I have that out of my system, there are several simple effects that people can (and do) use all the time:

Ultraviolet, or "Black" Light

Black light is somewhat of a outdated refugee from the seventies and is most often used these days for two rather opposite things: puppetry and strip joints. Black light will cause some colors, most notably neon shades of green, yellow, and orange, to shine brightly. It also makes white fabrics quite luminous. Very dark fabrics, such as navy blue and black, will not reflect black light at all, making anything covered by these colors disappear completely. Hence, puppeteers sometimes use it to bring focus down to a brightly colored puppet, while making a darkly dressed puppeteer invisible.

Designers of amusement parks, such as Disneyland, also use black light to hide machinery and bring focus to animatronic figures (the two-dollar word for puppets). Designers of strip-joint lighting (if there are such people) install it because it doesn't show skin blemishes, but it does highlight what there is of the dancers' costumes. It also seems to add to the "mystery" of a darkened room. You might also see black light used in some kinds of display lighting, making some neon-colored part of the display seem to "float" in front of a black background.

Black light usually comes in a long, skinny fixture like a fluorescent tube. The bulb puts out very little visible light, and provides almost no illumination by itself. What light it does provide comes from the reflections off other surfaces. Black light is also very annoying to look at for any length of time (as any stripper can tell you), so I don't recommend putting it anywhere the audience will be staring straight into it.

Strobe Lights

Any time you see a light that is flashing on and off very quickly, going from completely on to completely off instantly, without warming up or cooling down, you are probably looking at a strobe light. Strobes are useful whenever you want an instantaneous flash of light, or a quickly flashing, "moviola" type of effect. One of the most interesting uses I've seen was an imitation "supernova" in a planetarium. (That one was a BIG strobe light.) A strobe also makes a great lightning effect, either by itself or inside a specially prepared lighting instrument.

Safety Alert! *When using a strobe, you should warn your audience ahead of time. Some people, notably epileptics, will suffer severe physical reactions after seeing a flashing strobe. Put a notice in the lobby of your theater warning the audience that a flashing strobe light will be used during the show. What you lose in surprise, you will gain in audience comfort and happiness.*

Lightning

As I said above, a lighting instrument adapted for a strobe and fitted with a lightning-shaped shadow projection makes a great lightning bolt that you can project on the cyc, but if you don't have the time and expertise, there are other solutions.

If you are lucky enough to live somewhere that has great thunderstorms (I really miss them out here on the West Coast), watch one go by some time. You don't have to stand in a field and get electrocuted, just turn off the lights and look out the window. Look at the world around you when a bolt of lightning happens. What kind of light is it? A flash from a lightning bolt is instantaneous, much faster than an incandescent light. Try turning a room light on and off as fast as you can. See what I mean? An incandescent light, like the ones in your house, takes time to warm up and cool down, so it will never flash like lightning. What you need is either a very large strobe light, or a **lightning box**. Some rental houses have lightning boxes, but unfortunately, they are hard to find. A lightning box produces a large flash of light the same way a strobe does, by making a stream of electrons jump through the air from one pole to another. In fact, that's just what lightning is: a burst of electricity jumping from one spot to another. The best way to imitate it is to recreate it. Unfortunately, real lightning boxes are big and bulky, and, unless they are built correctly, they can be dangerous to use. Hence, they are disappearing.

Your best bet then, is a strobe light. But let's go back to that storm.

What else do you notice? You may notice that the light is bluish, and that it often seems to flash several times, sometimes from several different directions at once.

All these things can be recreated on stage. The best lightning effect is several large strobes coming from different directions, fired very quickly, one after another. You can get away with two, as long as you fire them off several times in a row at irregular intervals. Put some light blue filters in front of the lights to get the proper color. Sound complicated? Well, it can be, but persevere. Get two big strobes and put them on opposite sides of the stage. Strobes often come with a remote control at the end of a long cable so one person can operate both instruments by stringing the remotes to the same place. When the cue comes, fire one strobe and then the other, very close together. Experiment. Try firing one of the strobes more than once. Most importantly, get rid of as much normal stage light as you can.

If you can't get strobes, here's a *really* low-tech solution. If you have worklights backstage, try flashing them for the lightning effect. Worklights usually have very small bulbs, so they come on more quickly than stage lights. If you turn down the rest of the stage lights, you might get away with it.

Several lighting companies make metal patterns that can be inserted into lighting equipment to make a projected "lightning bolt" on the sky, but I would counsel against using them, unless you have the aforementioned strobe-light adapter for your equipment. As I said, incandescent lights don't flash quickly enough to imitate lightning. Rather than trying to project the lightning bolt itself, concentrate on the *effect* of the lightning on the ground.

Fire

Real flames, like real running water, seem to have an almost magical effect on an audience. It is almost as if, up until the flame is lit, the audience has just been playing along, like benevolent parents. Suddenly, the real flame appears and the audience realizes that the kids weren't just playing around: They actually put something *real* on stage.

Real fire on stage can range from a single candle to giant propane-fired torches. Unfortunately, I can't go into much depth in this area because of the great differences in fire regulations throughout the country. What is acceptable in one state may be unheard of in another. When I went to work at Seattle Rep, I was amazed to see a prop brazier on stage with flames a foot high jumping out of it. In Illinois, where I attended grad school, any flame at all (even a candle) required a fire inspector's visit and a crew member stationed on each side with a fire extinguisher. Local fire laws and their application are usually a function of history. If the theater business in a particular area has a good safety record, fire laws tend to be more relaxed. If, however, there has been a large disaster in the past, the laws (and the inspectors) are a good deal tougher. In the case of Illinois, the Iroquois Theater fire of 1903, which killed over a thousand people, caused all the Illinois fire laws to be strengthened. Even now, nearly a century later, the fear of another disaster remains deeply rooted in the local consciousness.

The reader should not interpret the above, however, to mean that fire safety should only be maintained to the limit of local regulation. On the contrary, it is up to us to protect the performers and the audience at all times. If you are thinking about using a flame on stage, contact the local fire authorities to find out what the regulations are. Any time a flame is used, fire extinguishers should be readily available on both sides of the stage, with crew members standing by them.

In any case, it is highly recommended that you maintain a positive relationship with your local fire department inspectors. Remember, they do have the ability to shut you down, a possibility that should not be taken lightly. More than that, though, you should consider this relationship to be a partnership, the outcome of which should be the safety of everyone in the theater. There is no compelling reason whatsoever to put performers or audience in a potentially dangerous situation and the fire department can help you avoid doing that.

Smoke and Fog

I treat these two different effects together because they are so often confused with each other. When theater people say "smoke," they mean something that hangs in the air; fairly evenly distributed throughout the stage. When they say "fog," they are talking about a colder-than-air substance that hugs the ground. Smoke rises and fills the air while fog stays on the ground. The two effects require radically different processes to create.

Smoke is fairly easy. Rent or buy a commercial **smoke machine**, fill it with fluid (often, confusingly, called "fog juice"), plug it in, wait for it to heat up, and then push the button. Whoosh! Smoke fills the air. Smoke machines come in different sizes, and they are rated by how many cubic feet of smoke they put out. For most applications, a 1500 smoke machine will be adequate, unless you want a *lot* of smoke. There are smoke machines large enough to fill a gymnasium, but these are used more often to train firefighters than for the stage.

If you are using a smoke machine, make sure you allow yourself enough time to let it warm up. Some machines take up to an hour to really get up to speed, but for most, ten to twenty minutes should be adequate. Make sure you test the machine in rehearsal with all of your air-handling equipment (heating, ventilation, air conditioning) operating as they will be during the show and with all the stage lights on. Lamentably, between the ventilation blowing through the house and the hot lights over the stage, smoke has a tendency in most theaters to flow out into the audience. You may want to consider using fans to keep it on stage, or even a low-tech solution like a stagehand waving a sheet of cardboard in the wings. Also, try opening a few doors backstage. Experiment. Adjust the airflow any way you can until the smoke goes where you want it to. Most machines also let you alter the rate at which smoke comes out, so play with that as well. Smoke is tricky stuff sometimes, and it can have a mind of its own. Of course, when you get a full audience of people in the theater, the smoke may decide to go someplace else entirely.

There is another, older smoke-making technique that you may run into: the heating of chloride-containing powders. The most common powder, sal ammoniac (aluminum chloride), is also the safest, but all of these powders may cause respiratory problems and I don't recommend them.

When you are buying fog juice, be aware that there are different kinds. Stay away from the fogs that contain petroleum distillates (they can be flammable) and, whatever you buy, pay attention to any warnings printed on the label. Look for organic fogs, preferably with a high concentration of water. This kind of fog is not toxic on your skin, but some people do report throat irritations after long exposures. Singers, in particular, may want to avoid heavy concentrations of it. There is also an unconscious reaction that sometimes happens when people are surrounded by smoke. Whether or not it is actually harmful to them, the sight of smoke makes people want to cough. There doesn't seem to be any way around this (it even happens to people who understand the psychosomatic nature of it), and experienced performers simply learn to overcome it. The audience, however, won't be able to overcome that urge, so do your best to keep the smoke out of the audience. Otherwise, the actors will have trouble making themselves heard over the chain-smokers' convention in the house.

Finally, a trick: If you are using smoke for the beginning of a scene and the curtain is down before it, pump the smoke into the air a few seconds before the curtain opens and then have a technician run through it right before the curtain goes up. The audience will be treated to a swirling cloud of smoke that will seem to have a life of its own. Pretty cool.

Unlike smoke, fog lays on the ground, well away from the eyes and mouth, so it won't prompt the coughing reaction. It does, however, have

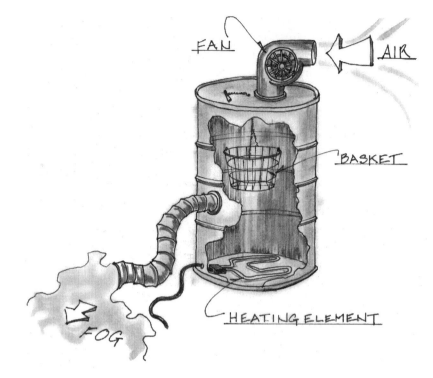

Fig. 12. A fog machine

problems of its own. Fog is created by heating up a container of water and then dropping **dry ice** into it. The dry ice, which is actually frozen carbon dioxide, vaporizes in the water and produces a colder-than-air fog that flows out of the machine and crawls across the floor like a passing vampire. A **fog machine** (which you can rent, build, or buy) is a fifty-five-gallon drum with a heating coil in the bottom to keep the water warm and a fan on top to blow the fog out. A fog machine is bulky (usually about the size of a large oil drum) and must be kept plugged in since the water must be constantly heated. If the water is not constantly heated, the effect will last just a few seconds because the intense cooling effect of the dry ice will cause the water to rapidly lose all its heat. If you only need a few seconds, you might be able to get away with dropping the ice into a pan of hot water, but the effect will be ultra brief. Even with a proper machine, the effect will gradually fall off since the heater coil in the bottom of the drum can't keep up with the dry ice. Fog is best used to create an impressive opening to a scene, and then to add a little atmosphere as the scene goes on.

Besides getting the machine, you will also have to get hold of the ice itself. There are two places to get it: ice companies and welding supply houses (dry ice is used to quickly cool metal that has been welded). Dry ice is not expensive, but you usually have to buy it in thirty-pound to fifty-pound blocks. Even though you'll only need a few pounds every time you do the effect, you'll need to buy a new block every two days or so, because the remainder will melt away. You can slow down the melting process a little by placing the ice in a cooler or some other insulated space but, basically, dry ice is so cold that, no matter where you put it, it won't stay cold enough to prevent melting. Don't put the dry ice in your freezer, either, or everything else in there will become a solid block of ice and be ruined. Believe me. I've tried. If you are going to use dry ice, plan on getting a fresh supply every other day or so.

The other problem with dry ice is handling it, but I'd better say this emphatically.

Safety Alert! *Dry ice is much colder than ordinary ice and it can adhere to your skin and burn you. When handling dry ice,* never let it touch your skin! *Use gloves whenever handling it and keep it away from children and animals.*

Okay. So you've bought or rented a fog machine, you've filled it with water, and you've turned it on at least an hour before the show to heat up. You've gotten the dry ice and you're ready to set up the fog-effect. Take out a chunk of dry ice about the size of a cantaloupe and break it up into golf-ball size chunks. The more surface area you provide, the faster the ice will vaporize and the more fog that will be produced. *This theory should not be taken to extremes.* I know of one technician who completely chopped the ice into dust and threw it into the hot water. It produced so much fog that it blew the fog machine's heavy metal top thirty feet straight up in the air. It became known as the "Orville Redenbacher" effect and was not repeated. Keep the chunks between golf-ball and baseball size and things will go smoothly.

The fog machine should have a wire cage where you put the ice, as well as some way to lower the cage into the water once the top has been put on the machine. The machine should also have some hoses to direct the fog where you want it to go. Dryer hoses work best (if you rented the machine, they should come with it). Load the cage up and close the top. Now, before you drop the cage, take a minute to survey the situation, because once that cage goes down, things are going to start happening in a hurry. First, make sure that the hoses are going where you want them to go. Next, be aware that some condensation is going to happen wherever the fog goes, but particularly right at the end of the hose. Often, a small puddle of water collects there. This can be a problem, particularly in dance, which is one of the big places fog is used. Put a towel under the end of the hose, covering the floor for the first foot or so that the fog travels across it. This will catch most of the moisture.

All set? Well then, drop the basket and be prepared for a big "whump!" as the machine begins to spit out fog. Depending on how small you chopped the ice, and how hot you are keeping the water, the result could be anywhere from an anemic little puff of fog to a ground-eatin', actor-chillin', Hunchback-of-Notre-Damein' fog fest that folks will talk about all year. As with all effects, E-X-P-E-R-I-M-E-N-T.

It is possible to use a smoke machine and dry ice together to produce ground-hugging fog for a longer period than can be achieved with a fog machine alone. Go to the convenience store and buy a Styrofoam™ cooler and cut holes in either side for dryer hoses. Make some baffles with lumber or rocks. This will help the smoke stay in the cooler longer, cooling it down even more. Fill the cooler with dry ice. Then, pump some smoke into the cooler. If you have enough ice in the cooler, and you have created some good baffles, the smoke will come out the other side hugging the ground. It won't however, stay close to the ground forever. As soon as the smoke feels the heat of the stage lights, it will start to rise. This effect is less messy than a fog machine and the smoke will stay onstage longer than dry ice fog. Plus, you need less dry ice. It is also a good trick for theaters that already own smoke machines and want to get more usage out of them. Remember, though: Fog produced this way will never lay completely down on the stage like dry ice fog.

Breakaway Glass

Breakaway is a general term for anything that has to break, or appear to break, on stage. _Breakaway glass_ bursts easily into hundreds of tiny pieces without sharp edges. For some reason, breakaway glass (also called "candy glass") is always depicted in the theatrical supply catalog as beer bottles being broken across a cowboy's head. I guess the barroom brawl is a necessary part of every Western. Breakaway glass, however, is available in lots of different styles, including bottles, glasses, and plates, and can be purchased from a theatrical supply house. It has two problems: cleanup and expense. Because it bursts into so many pieces (sometimes almost like dust), it is tiresome to sweep up (particularly during a darkened scene change). As far as the expense goes, be sure to check out the price before you commit yourself to the effect. If the expense is too great, _do not be tempted to use real glass._ I spent one rather unpleasant evening driving to the hospital with an actor who had sat on real broken glass on stage. The sight of this poor guy kneeling on all fours in the back seat, bloody rump to the sky, made me determined never to make that particular mistake myself (even if it did lead

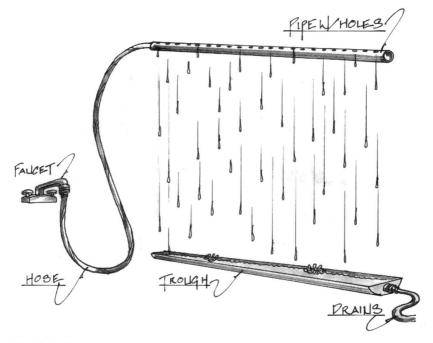

Fig. 13. Making rain

to the longest continuous string of butt jokes I have ever heard in my life). Don't skimp. If you cannot afford the breakaway glass, then cut the effect, fake it, alter the scene, or do without. It is not worth the risk.

Rain

Ninety-five percent of the time, rain on stage is done with just a sound cue. The sound of a thunderstorm outside can go a long way toward giving the audience the idea that it is raining. (Does everybody know that you can get the sound of rain by recording bacon frying?) Now and then, however, you do need real rain, either because a scene takes place outside (*Singin' in the Rain*, *Night of the Iguana*), or the set has a window and the rain needs to be seen through it. Either way, the effect is basically the same. A pipe is perforated with lots of holes on one side. Then, the pipe is installed over the stage with the holes facing upwards. A hose is connected to one side and a catch basin is put underneath it. Water is pumped into the pipe, where it flows up out of the holes, dribbles around the pipe and rains off the bottom. Because the holes are pointed up, the water flows everywhere over the pipe and comes down in irregular drops, instead of steady streams like a shower head.

Large-scale installations, like *Singin' in the Rain* on Broadway, use recir-

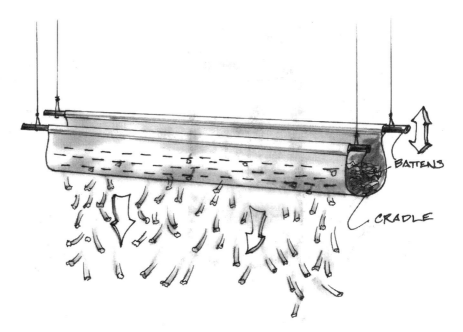

Fig. 14. A snow cradle

culating pumps to send the same water back up and through the system. Great care must be exercised with water effects on stage since they will easily short out lighting and sound systems.

Snow

Okay, so you're doing *The Nutcracker* and you've got to deal with the "Waltz of the Snowflakes." A good snow effect requires a flying system, so if you are in a theater without movable battens, you can't do this one. Do the "Waltz of the Sunspots" or something. People will marvel at your creativity.

If you do have movable battens, then you need a **snow bag** and two adjacent battens. A snow bag is not really a bag, it is a piece of canvas about two feet wide and as long as your battens. The canvas has holes cut in it about a foot from one side and tie lines along both long edges. Tie the bag between the two battens like a long cradle (some people refer to this as a "snow cradle").

Next, the bag is filled with snow. (I recommend that you spring for commercial snow: It is flameproof, it flutters beautifully, and it even looks good sitting on the stage.) Then the cradle is gently rocked, causing the snow to sift through the holes on one side of the cradle and gently float down to the stage.

By the way, keep in mind that cleaning snow up takes some time and is almost impossible to do during a fast scene change. If you really *are* doing *The Nutcracker,* you're in luck: Tchaikovsky was no fool about technical theater. The "Waltz of the Snowflakes" is the Act One finale, and you've got the whole intermission to clean it up.

Most scenic effects have two things in common: First, they work best if other distractions are reduced, and second, combinations are the most effective. Take away as much other stimulus as you can: Get rid of all the unwanted light and sound so that attention is focused on the effect. Then, try combining the effects—sound with light, smoke with projections, and so on. Unlike virtually everything else in the theater, in scenic effects, more is more.

CHAPTER 5

Lighting Design: Illumination, Mood, and Focus

Because our society is becoming increasingly oriented toward movies and television, it often works to think about stage lighting in terms borrowed from those media. One of the main differences between the theater and movies is that, in the movies, there is a huge piece of technology between the performer and the audience: the camera. The camera directs our view of each scene; it tells us when, where, and how closely to look. Not surprisingly, the person who decides where the camera should go is called the "director."

In the live theater, it is the lighting that performs this "direction." It can broaden to include the whole stage, or focus in (just like zooming a camera lens) to bring our attention to one person or thing. The lighting can also affect our mood, determine time of day or season, and move the play forward by separating the scenes and telling us when the show has begun and ended. Lighting also discriminates between where the show is happening and where it is not. Lighting is the opposite of masking. It says, "Look here. This is the show." If you are a director, you should know as much about lighting as Steven Spielberg knows about the camera.

Of course, the most important job that lighting does is to provide *illumination*. The audience must be able to see the performers and the scenery clearly. Once we can see clearly, we can think about time, place, mood, atmosphere, and other luxuries.

Illumination: First and Foremost

With all the things that lighting can do, as well as all the training we have from watching music videos, it is not surprising that we sometimes forget the basics: *We have to be able to see the performers clearly and comfortably* or we are not going to care what they do. Watching a dark or unevenly lit show can cause eye fatigue. Your eye muscles are like any other muscles in your body—they get tired when you overwork them. Peering through the gloom at a dark stage wears them out, making you want to close them or go to sleep. The opposite is also true: Looking at a stage that is unremittingly bright can wear out your eyes as well. What the eye wants is even, comfortable illumination with some slight variations to keep it interested. If you give the audience a brief blackout, for instance, they might be able to watch the next scene with more energy. Conversely, bringing the lights up bright "stresses" your eyes a little, making it more relaxing to watch darker scenes afterward. Of course, all this should be looked at within the context of the script. Lighting must conform to what the script, the director, and the action require.

Many people believe poorly-lit actors are also more difficult to hear. In other words, when our eyes are working harder, our ears suffer the consequences. This may be a psychosomatic reaction, or it may be that actors speak more softly when lit less brightly. Whatever the case, many people swear by this phenomenon so it is worth taking note of it. Lighting is the art of perception: People see whatever they think they see.

Good illumination, besides being the most important thing that lighting does, is also one of the most difficult things to achieve. Even the best lighting designers still struggle with it, and most of them spend years developing techniques.

Why is it so difficult? Why do directors find themselves looking at the same spot on the stage night after night, the spot where they *told* the designer they needed more light, and it never seems to get any better? Why do designers put their heads in their hands every time an actor hits a dark spot, the same dark spot that has been there for the last three rehearsals and refuses to go away?

Well, like most things, there is not one central reason. A lighting designer is fighting a battle against the senses: As I said, people see what they think they see. No matter how much light you are pumping into a scene, if people think it is dark, then it is dark. The lighting designer is a slave to the human eye.

Time for an exercise.

Go out to your living room, your lobby, or your reception area—anywhere with natural light. Look around. Notice how the light flows evenly over all the surfaces. Notice how all the colors look pure and clean. Notice how the shadows are sharply defined, but also notice how you can see objects that are not directly lit. Look up at the ceiling. It probably is not getting any direct light at all, but chances are you can still see it clearly. Look at the features on people's faces—they will probably be easy to make out.

The sun is one heck of a lighting instrument. It is the lighting instrument that lighting companies have been trying to imitate for years. They make progress all the time, but they are still light years (sorry) away from imitating Mother Nature.

Why is the sun so terrific?

Well, first of all, the sun is an *extremely* bright light source.

Brightness is measured in "foot-candles," a pretty straightforward unit of measurement. The amount of light produced by one candle, measured from one foot away, is one foot-candle (in theory anyway). A sixty-watt bulb in the ceiling of a light-colored room produces out about 25 foot-candles. The sun, on a clear day in summer, produces about 250 foot-candles, ten times as much. If you have ever walked out of a bright, sunny day into a room with no windows, you know that your eyes need a moment to adjust to the new space, regardless of how brightly the room is lit. The sun is putting out a lot more light than our stage lights.

It does not help that the light coming out of a lighting instrument falls off very quickly as you move away from the instrument. This makes it hard to create an even amount of light everywhere on stage. Imagine that there are two actors, one standing ten feet from a light source, the other standing twenty feet away. Due to something called the "inverse square law," the person standing twice as far from the light source only gets one-quarter as much light. Since the sun is so much further away, it really does not matter if one person is ten feet farther away (or ten miles, for that matter). The light on them will be the same. On stage, however, people can get different amounts of light depending on how close they are to the lighting instrument.

Unfortunately, there are difficulties with using the sun to light our shows. For one thing, it is outside, and we are in. For another thing, a lot of our shows have scenes that take place at different times of the day, and the sun doesn't respond very well to commands like "Proceed to five o'clock, please," let alone, "Fade to black."

What to do then? How do we provide all of the benefits of the sun—its brightness, its evenness, its accurate rendition of color—with the equipment we have available?

Back in the infancy of lighting, when most of the theaters we now refer to as "Broadway" were built, theater designers were only concerned with providing a place for lighting that had as direct a shot at the stage as possible. Therefore, they installed a pipe running across the front of the balcony and put all the lights there. Because of the shape of the theaters, the **balcony rail**, as it is known to this day, was almost level with the stage, providing a horizontal angle of light. The performers were brightly lit, but they looked flat, like animals caught in the glare of oncoming headlights. With light only coming from one direction, their faces were not "modeled," that is, they had no three-dimensionality, and features were hard to distinguish. The actors had to wear very heavy makeup so that the audience could make out their expressions.

This situation persisted until the fifties when a new movement appeared in stage lighting. This movement was best encapsulated by a man named Stanley McCandless, who published a book called *A System of Stage Lighting,* which, quite simply, changed everything.

The Forty-five Degree Concept

McCandless pointed out, as artists and photographers have known for years, that the most attractive angle of light for the human face was about forty-five degrees up, much higher than the balcony rail. Furthermore, the face was best illuminated by two lights, one to each side, both coming in at a forty-five degree angle.

McCandless also took note of the fact that, when illuminated by any light source, faces take on two different colors, one on the side toward the light source and another in the shadows on the side away from the light source. He felt that the audience should see light on the stage looking like real sunlight, moonlight, or room light. Whatever side the "real" light was coming from was called the **motivational side**. The color hitting the actors from that side would be the color of the "real" light source: bright and warm for the sun, cool and blue for the moon, yellow for candlelight and so on. The color coming from the other, "nonmotivational" side would be the color of the light bouncing off the walls, the trees, the ground, the sky, and so on. Does this phenomenon really hold true in reality? Opinions about the McCandless theories vary widely. One good place to look is in paintings. Rembrandt knew a lot about the color of shadows. Remember, however, lighting is subjective. The audience sees what it thinks it sees.

Anyway, McCandless's book gave birth to the "warm/cool" idea in stage lighting. The two forty-five degree lights that we talked about previously would be colored with filters: one warm, one cool, depending on which one was on the motivational side. The contrast between the two colors, along with the more attractive angles, would provide the modeling effect on people's faces that would help the audience distinguish features.

There have been a lot of changes over the years since McCandless's book first appeared in print, and these days his system is viewed as somewhat dated. Nevertheless, the forty-five degree angle is still considered the most flattering angle for front light, and we still try to choose a motivational side. Most designers stay away from a strict interpretation of the "warm/cool" system, since it tends to make actors change color as they turn and move on stage, but the general idea of using groups of lights placed at forty-five-degree angles is still in constant use, as is the use of color to create modeling.

Rim Light

Front light is only the beginning of illumination. If you think back to your field trip to the natural light laboratory, you will recall that in a well-lit room, there is light coming from many directions. The same is true of a well-lit stage.

When performers and the scenery behind them are only lit from the front, they will tend to fade together. When viewed from the front, the performers will melt into the scenery, particularly if the colors are similar. It is necessary to add some **rim light**, that is, light that comes from the side or the back to illuminate the "rim" of the actor—the shoulders, the top of the head, and the sides of the costume. This "halo" of light will help separate the performer from the background, and give the stage more depth. Back light and side light should be applied to the acting areas just like front light, so that each acting area has its own instruments.

Acting Areas

McCandless also suggested that the stage be broken up into **acting areas**. The designer divides the stage into small blocks of space and designs a set of lights to illuminate one area—two front lights, a back light, and two side lights, for example. Then, he will replicate that set of lights for every area on the stage. This way, the light on every part of the stage would be coming from the same angle, plus, the actors would always be about the same distance from a light. This idea is still very much in use.

How do you decide how many instruments to use for each acting area, and which angles to put them at? Now you know how lighting designers earn their fees. Most designers have their own favorite formulas, systems, and magic books for determining the best arrangements of lights, but you can fake your way through it.

The simplest system for an acting area would be two front lights, evenly placed forty-five degrees off the center line and a single back light. This gets the job done in a basic way. By adding two more front lights, you have a second set of colors for the night scene. Adding side light gives you more rim light and better illumination. These are only some of the possibilities.

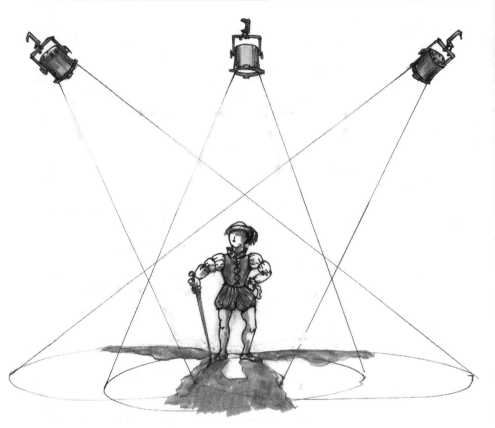

Fig. 15. Lighting an acting area

What about a light coming straight down? Very dramatic. You might decide to emphasize light coming from one direction (perhaps the scene is in a dungeon, and the only light is from a high, barred window), or your theater may not have the right positions, or there might be scenery in the way, or you may simply discover a system that you like better.

How do you decide? And what do you do when you just want to survive? A few simple guidelines will help. Here are the three rules that I use:

- Each acting area should be lit from at least three different angles. By using three different angles, you can achieve the modeling effect, and give the audience something comfortable to look at. You can, of course, use more than three (something I would highly recommend), but three is the absolute minimum.

- At least one of those angles should be *downstage* of the performer. Whether or not you choose to use the flattering forty-five degree position, you should light the performers from downstage so that the

audience can see them. If you are going for a "realistic"—not styl-
ized—look, then you will probably want to use at least two different
angles of front light. You may wish to only light performers from the
back for an "effect" moment, but be aware that the audience will
quickly tire of looking at an actor with no front light, so do your
moment and then show the performer's face to the audience.

- At least one of those angles should be *upstage* of the performer. As I
said above, you need to get some "rim light" on the stage in order to
make the performer stand out from the scenery. This can be straight
from the back, from the side, or anywhere in between, but you will
need it to keep things from looking flat.

So far you have divided the stage into acting areas and devised a system
of lighting each area. Now what?

Wash Light

While the acting area system outlined above will cover most of the bases, it
is not enough in most applications. For one thing, lighting instruments are
not perfect. The beam of any instrument (especially those with a few miles
on them) will be uneven, with hot spots and dark spots. Even brand new
instruments will be brightest at the center and dimmer toward the edge of
the beam. Furthermore, the designer may want the light from some
instruments to be limited with **shutters**, movable metal blades inside the
instrument that cut off part of the light. He may do this to keep the light
off the scenery or the proscenium, or he may do this so that light from one
area doesn't spill into another. Shutters cut off the light, but they often
create hard shadows, which will show up as **shutter lines**, dark shadows
crossing actors' faces as they move from area to area.

In order to smooth these ills, as well as a hundred others, it is a good
idea to include some **wash light** in a lighting plot. A wash is a set of soft-
edged instruments, all pointed in the same direction, that provide a
smooth, broad wash of color over all the areas. Washes can be used to
regulate the overall color of the scene as well as blending the acting areas
into one another, covering the gaps.

The combination of well-designed acting areas and appropriate wash
light will provide comfortable illumination.

Motivational Light: Time, Place, and Season

By now you know that motivational light is not the head speaker at a lamp
convention. Actually, "motivation" is a term stolen from acting. Actors use
it to refer to whatever is happening in their character's life that "motivates"

them to take whatever action they are taking. For us, motivation refers to the light source that is apparently causing the room to look the way it does. **Motivational light** is the light that would be illuminating the scene if it were in a real place: the moon for a forest scene, for example, or fluorescent lighting in an office scene. Whenever you are working with a lighting designer, one of the first questions she is going to ask is: "Where is the light coming from?" The set designer may provide part of the answer by incorporating lamps, overhead lights, a fireplace, or some other light source into the set. The playwright may help by choosing when and where the scene is taking place. Here are some of the things that the designer will want to know about the motivational light:

• *Where is the light in the room supposed to be coming from?*

Sometimes the answer is easy. If the scene is outside, then you are primarily interested in the sun or the moon. There might also be streetlights, neon signs, Joan of Arc burning at the stake, or other types of additional light. If the scene is indoors, the sources may be lamps, candles, fluorescent lights, and so on. Sometimes the lighting will be a combination of indoor and outdoor sources, as sunlight or moonlight may be coming through the window.

• *What time of day is it?*

This is a critical question, as lighting conditions change all day long. Sometimes they will need to change within a scene, as the sun goes down, for instance, or a character turns a light switch on.

• *What time of year is it?*

Like time of day, time of year determines a great deal about lighting. The sun is cooler and lower in winter, brighter and higher in summer and sometimes playwrights use this for dramatic effect. Chekov's *The Cherry Orchard,* for instance, uses the approaching fall as a dramatic device to comment on the impending "winter" that is about to befall the Russian aristocracy. A good lighting designer can do a lot with this sort of detail.

• *Where is the play taking place?*

Light is different by the seashore than in the mountains, different in the city than on a farm.

A good lighting designer spends a lot of time looking at the world, and so should you. What color is the light in the room where you are sitting right now? What is the "motivation" for the light in the room?

Mood and Atmosphere: Angles and Color

Angles in lighting are divided into five categories: front light, side light, back light, down light, up light and they all have their uses and meanings.

I say meanings because each angle seems to come with a certain emotional baggage, which you can either exploit or ignore.

- **Front light.** The best light for illumination, the most "natural light," best delivered from around forty-five degrees up. When delivered from straight ahead, it is "deer-in-the-headlights" light, useful for sudden realizations or the arrival of the police.

- **Side light.** The best light for illuminating the body and for giving the figures on stage sharp outlines. Side light builds excitement and "show value."

- **Back light.** Essential for separating the figures from the scenery. Used alone, it is great for sinister villains and dark shadows in the door. A subset of back light is the **silhouette**, where figures are seen against a brightly lit background without any light on themselves. This seems to have a connotation that is more "dramatic" than "sinister."

- **Down light.** "God" light. Makes for awkward rim light, as it not only lights the rim, but also the nose. Better to use it alone for a dramatic opera procession or an unusual dance. Good scene-change light. Will get you a laugh if used alone with a booming, divine voice.

- **Up light.** Light coming up through a grating gives the "industrial" look. Foot lights can give an olde-time theatrical look or a bizarre, Fellini-esque glare that is distinctly ominous.

Color in lighting is often more difficult to talk about than color in scenery or costumes. Color in lighting is rarely seen in isolation. Designers use a combination of colors to achieve a "balance" of color on stage—a general, overall range of colors that center around a particular part of the color palette.

Color is part of what makes each lighting moment distinctive. Light changes color continuously throughout the day, more pink in the morning, tending toward yellow in the afternoon, a warmer orange in the early evening, falling off towards blue as night falls. Light changes color when it reflects off objects as well. Light in a forest is a different color than at the beach.

Like everything else about lighting, color is subjective: An audience sometimes expects to see something that is not really there. Firelight is one of the better examples of this. Next time you are sitting around a campfire, look at the color of the light that hits people's faces. If you are burning normal, dry wood, the light will be a yellowish white. Any good lighting designer, however, knows that audiences expect to see *red* light coming from a fire, and will filter it accordingly. People see what they think they see. As a theater artist, you have the choice of whether to play the game or not.

Color in lighting is also at the mercy of sets and costumes. There is a common belief, basically true, that it is easier to change the color of the lights than those of the set and the costumes. Sometimes, a lighting designer will choose a color that (pardon the pun) shows a costume in an unflattering light. In *Hedda Gabler,* Hedda kneels over the stove and, page by page, burns the manuscript written by her rival. Because of the glowing fire, I lit her in deep amber. Unfortunately, the costume designer had dressed her in purple. Purple cloth plus yellow light equals brown dress. I lost that battle, as lighting designers invariably do. It's easier to change a lighting filter than to make a new dress.

The colors in the lights need not be stagnant throughout a show. In fact, in many cases, it is essential that they change over time, just as the color in real light does. Colors will change as the motivational light changes, as the sun goes down, for example, or as the room light changes. Sometimes color will become less saturated, as in the famous confrontation scene between Stanley Kowalski and Blanche DuBois in *A Streetcar Named Desire.* Blanche tries to hide her suffering behind a mask of gaiety and nonchalance, choosing a colorful Japanese lantern to light her dingy room. Stanley rips the colored paper off the light and holds the stark white bulb up to Blanche's makeup-smeared face.

> *Stanley:* There isn't a damn thing but imagination, and lies, and conceit and tricks. Take a look at yourself in that worn-out Mardi Gras outfit, rented for fifty cents from some rag person.

The absence of color in the light makes a powerful point about Blanche's refusal to confront reality.

One final note about color: Since the primary job of a lighting designer is to provide illumination, and what we are illuminating primarily is people, it is very useful to know which colors are best for which skin tones. Most of the time, for most actors, the oddly-named "Bastard Amber" is a good bet. Bastard Amber gets its name because it is not really amber—more of an orangey pink. (There is also a color called "Surprise Pink," because Surprise! It isn't pink.) Very light blues are all right as well, but they will make actors look a little pale. If you are lighting for video, however, stay away from saturated colors entirely. That romantic blue moonlight that looked so good on stage will look like little blue men from Alpha Centauri on television. Keep it white for TV.

Creating Focus: Specials and Follow Spots

Okay, so you are doing *When Ya Comin' Back Red Ryder?* a tense but quirky drama that follows a pile of offbeat characters playing out their lives in an Arizona diner. The waitress in the diner—a shy, portly girl named Angel—never leaves the stage during the show and the director wishes to make the point that, after all is said and done, all these people have really been living in her world.

You decide to leave Angel in a pool of light for a brief moment after all the other characters have gone. A brief, lyrical moment. A blackout. Applause.

Enter the **special**, a single lighting instrument that lights one particular place on the set. Specials are generally a less saturated color than the rest of the lighting, allowing them to "punch through" the rest of the color. Often, they have no color at all. Specials are usually ellipsoidals because you want to have precise control over where the light goes.

When you really want to add emphasis and your subject is moving, there is nothing like a **follow spot**. A follow spot is any lighting instrument that is capable of being moved by an operator to follow an actor on stage. They come in all shapes and sizes. Follow spots may be hard-edged, super bright spotlights, or they may be more subtle and soft-edged, almost blending into the rest of the lighting. The subtle, soft-edged spot is very popular in opera, where the designers want to emphasize the lead singers without destroying the overall ambiance.

Generally, choosing to use a follow spot means choosing to enter the visual style of musical theater. An audience is usually unwilling to accept that light is following an actor unless that actor is singing. I guess two departures from reality cancel each other out. The image of an actor standing in a follow spot is so strongly associated with musical theater that putting a follow spot on stage virtually declares, "We are doing a musical show." An actor standing in a follow spot is one of our cultural icons, so make sure that icon fits your show before you do it. I welcome rule break-ing, but be sure you know which rule you are breaking before you do it.

Lots of theaters have a built-in position for a follow spot toward the rear of the theater. Unfortunately, this creates a flattened-out look that can be unattractive. Follow spots are just like acting area lighting—the most attractive angle is around forty-five degrees. Of course, if your spots are built in, then you must live with what you have.

Spots do not come only from the front. Back light spots occasionally show up as well. Look for them in large musicals and rock-and-roll shows.

Where the Show Is (and Isn't): House Lights and Actors in the Audience

House lights serve a practical purpose—they help the audience to find their seats and read their programs. They also serve an aesthetic purpose—they tell the audience when the show is starting (by turning off) and ending (by turning on again). The line between house lights and stage lights also helps the audience to know where the show is taking place. Sound like I am stating the obvious? Not necessarily. Sometimes, a director wants to have an actor go into the audience area. It can be problematic to light an actor walking through the audience because the lighting positions are in the wrong place. (Lighting positions are designed to light the *stage,* after all . . .) In this case, someone usually makes the suggestion that the house lights be used to light the actor. This is a difficult issue.

In the first place, there are very few theaters that have specifically focused house lights that can be turned on individually. Usually, when you hit the house light switch, the entire house is lit. Right away you lose the primary raison d'être of lighting—to provide focus. Once you have brought the house lights up, the audience has a lot to look at—namely, itself.

When the house lights come up, the audience becomes part of the show. Fair enough, but the reverse is also true: The actor becomes part of the audience. That is, the actor ceases, in some ways, to be his character and he becomes a real person who is trying to portray a character. The audience's willingness to accept the actor as the character is strained. It is no longer clear what is the show and what is not.

Some productions want to do exactly that! Some directors want to play with these issues, and that is fruitful ground. As with follow spots, it is important to be aware of the conventions before you break them. Unless you are trying to make a point, however, use stage lights, with their capacity to be focused and directed, to light an actor in the audience. Of course, if you are in the musical theater style, you can always use a follow spot.

If you are using a space where you have to hang your own house lights, keep these suggestions in mind:

Use very unfocused lighting instruments, like big scoops, without lenses. If you are using fresnels, take the lenses out (be sure that you store them carefully). Add soft orange filters to give them warmth. Dim them down halfway. Hang them slightly behind the audience, pointing a little toward the stage. This keeps them from getting in the audience's eyes, yet allows easy reading of the program.

Moving the Show Forward: Cues, Timing, and Blackouts

Besides helping the show move around the stage by steering the audience's eyes, lighting also helps the show move through time by separating the scenes and defining the beginning and the end.

Every time the lighting changes, it is referred to as a **cue**. Cues are numbered, starting with cue number one, the lights that are on stage when the audience enters. Cue two is usually the light change that happens as the show begins, often a blackout. Cue three is the light that begins the first scene, and so on.

Each cue is a list of which lights are on and how bright they are. Besides these levels, each cue has a time. This time tells how long (in seconds) it takes for the lights to fade to the levels written in the cue.

The timing of lighting cues is critical, and it is one of the most important things that a designer does, along with providing clear, steady illumination. The most important times are the ones at the ends of scenes, particularly if you are going to a blackout. A long slow fade at the end of a scene can cause the emotions of the scene to become deeply internalized by the audience, as they slowly take in what has just happened on stage. Fast blackouts, or **snap outs**, can be a stunning punctuation, leaving the audience with an after-image impressed on their retinas. Of course, in comedy, the blackout is a critical part of the show's timing. A second or two can be the difference between getting the laugh you so richly deserve and actors stumbling off the stage in uncomfortable silence.

Unfortunately, lighting equipment does not always go to black as quickly as we would like. Even with a snap out, there is always a slight glow on stage for a few seconds after the lights go out. The problem is the filaments in the lights. When the lights are on, they are glowing white hot (that's what makes the light, after all). When the power to them is cut, it takes a moment for them to cool enough to stop putting out light completely. This takes longer for a stage light than it does for a household light because the stage light has a much bigger filament.

Actors should always hold their positions on stage for a few seconds after the lights go to black. Look at the filaments in the lighting instruments. If they are still glowing, the audience can probably see you. Count to three before you move. If you are not sure if you can be seen after blackouts, ask someone who is sitting close to the stage during a rehearsal if they saw you move.

In some cases, a scene will be followed by a scene change. The crew moving the scenery will need some light, so the designer will create a dim **scene-change light** (typically some blue lights or a dim back light) to allow them to see. This cue needs to be dim enough so that the audience recognizes it for what it is and does not believe that there is a scene going on. If you are doing a scene-change cue, make sure you "button up" the previous scene by going to black first. Once you are in blackout, the actors can exit, the audience knows the scene is over, and the scene-change cue can come on. Likewise, do not fade directly from a scene-change cue to the lights for the next scene. Go to black first. It buttons up the scene change and tells the audience that the "show" is starting again.

Lighting for Dance

Lighting actors means lighting faces. Lighting dancers means lighting bodies. Some time after the middle of the century, somebody (lots of people take the credit) figured out that lighting dancers from the front, like actors, did not fully reveal their bodies in three dimensions. Sure, it was great for their faces, but dance is less about facial expression than the shape of the entire body. That discovery, along with the need to keep light off of the large fabric backdrops that dance used, brought dance lighting around to the side of the stage. The wings became full of instruments stacked up on tall booms from the floor to high in the air, offering a variety of angles to light the dancers from the side.

All these angles have names: The lowest light is called a **shinbuster**, because that is what it does when you run into it. Next up is the **crotch light**, which is just what it sounds like. After that come the **mids**, so called because they are in the middle of the side-lighting boom. Above that are the **heads**, or **tops**. Above them are instruments called **pipe-ends**, because they are actually hanging on the end of the batten and not on the boom at all. (Pipe-ends are somewhat romantically referred to as "high suns" or "high moons," by the old-school ballet designers.) All of these instruments may be doubled or tripled to give the designer more color options. Dance lighting is literally composed of a wall of side lighting. A side-lighting boom in a first class company may have fifteen or twenty instruments on it.

Another way to get more colors is to change the filters between numbers, either by manually changing the ones that can be reached from the floor, or by using mechanical **color scrollers**. These little wonders have long scrolls of different colors in them, allowing crew members to change from one color to another by remote control.

As a more abstract medium, there are far fewer "rules" in dance lighting than in straight drama. Basically, you can get away with anything that the choreographer lets you try. Lighting designers tend to like doing dance because of this freedom.

With more freedom, however, comes more pitfalls. Lots of lighting

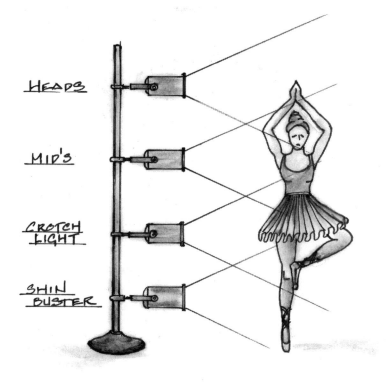

HEADS

MID's

CROTCH LIGHT

SHIN BUSTER

Fig. 16. Lighting instruments on a dance boom

changes can distract from good dancing, and it will *never* save bad dancing. Dance lighting should amplify and reveal the movement, and the designer should pay close attention to the music. If you are a choreographer working with a designer, send him the music first. Let him play it and have reactions to it before you begin discussing the dance. Let him know if there are specific moments in the music that you would like to emphasize. You do not have to be overly specific—it is okay to talk in generalities, even metaphor. As in the spoken-word theater, it is always helpful to show paintings or photographs that are in line with the message that you are seeking to create. As a side note, since so many choreographers ask me, I must tell you no, it is *not* possible to light your dancers to make them look thinner.

Dance productions tend to have little scenery, both because they need the stage space to dance and also because, in dance, the human body acts as its own scenery. Dance will often have a single backdrop or a cyc behind the dancers. Hence, one of the biggest decisions that the designer will have to make is what color to make the background. Of course, it does not have to be a single color. It can change over time. It can have patterns or slides projected on it. In theaters with cyc footlights, the bottom and top of the cyc can be different colors. Do not be afraid of white! Or black, for that matter. It is very dramatic to have dancers perform in front of a black drape, particularly if a show has many separate pieces. Staging a dance in front of a black drape is a dramatic break from all those other pieces that simply pick a new color for the backdrop.

What dance productions *do* have is costumes. Lighting designers will often lobby for costumes that have more fabric in them than just the leotard. Having folds of fabric on the dancers creates more interesting lighting surfaces. I encourage all choreographers to explore fabric, not only as a costume but also as props or scenery. Give the lighting designer a surface on which to perform her magic.

Lighting for Musicals

Musical theater is a peculiarly American art form. In the classic fifties-style show, there is dialogue, which furthers the plot and leads up to some sort of conclusion. Then the action stops and someone turns to the audience and sings about what just happened. It makes no sense. It shatters every theatrical convention about acting as if the audience were not there. And everybody loves it. Why not? It's fun, it's emotionally cleansing, and you can walk out humming the tunes.

This alternating structure affects the lighting choices. When the dialogue stops and the singing begins, the lighting should reflect the change. Because you are already shattering the "reality" of the show, it is possible to make more "unrealistic" choices in lighting the number. The stage as a whole can get brighter (for an upbeat dance number) or darker (for a ballad) for no apparent reason. Pools of light or follow spots can appear out of nowhere. The idea that you must pay attention to the "motivational" light can be put aside. Musical theater lighting can be more emotionally expressive than lighting for spoken-word theater.

Musical theater lighting is full of conventions. I present them here to alert you to the presence of cultural stereotypes, not to tell you what to do. You must decide whether you will follow them, thereby making your audience comfortable, or ignore them, thereby challenging your audience's perception.

Follow Spots

Perhaps the most traditional part of musical theater lighting, follow spots, are used during musical numbers to focus attention on the characters who are singing. If the number is upbeat and several different characters are singing at once, the spots may be omitted, since there is no need to single out one performer. The size of the spot depends on how much the character is moving (bigger spots for characters that move more) and how upbeat the number is (smaller spots focused on the head and upper body for slower, more introspective numbers). The size of the spot may change through the number as the character dances or as the number becomes more introspective. This is called **irising in** or **irising out**.

Generally, follow spots do not come on when the music is not playing. This is in line with the convention that the musical numbers are expressions of inner thoughts or emotional states and therefore subject to dramatic liberties.

Level Changes

The overall light level on stage will change at the beginning and ends of numbers. For slower numbers, the lights will drop (allowing the follow spots to be more obvious). Big, upbeat dance numbers generally require an increase in light. For a song that alternates between verses sung by a single character and choruses sung by the entire ensemble, the light levels may bounce up and down.

In any case, most upbeat numbers end with a **bump cue** that pushes the lights just a little bit brighter for a little flourish at the end (often on the last note). Quiet numbers often end with the lights fading gently to black. For extra tears, try irising in the follow spot as the lights fade away.

If the number doesn't end the scene, the designer will do a **restore** after it. This means that the lights come back to the "reality" level they had before the number started.

Side Light

For shows that have big choruses and/or lots of dancing, you will want lots of side light for emphasis. Costumes with lots of glitter and sparkle need side light to really shine. Dancing bodies, as we noted in the "Dance" section above, are also best illuminated from the side.

The "God" Light

Singers need to see the conductor. So do musicians in the orchestra pit. In order to make him visible, the designer may have to hang an instrument straight overhead to light the conductor. Putting white gloves on the conductor helps, too.

Lighting Fashion

Lighting fashion means lighting clothing, and it almost always means lighting a runway. Ordinarily, lighting clothing and the body would mean a generous use of side light, as in dance. On a runway, however, side light is out of the question because it would blind the audience on either side. Even forty-five-degree light, as in straight drama, will end up flinging light into somebody's eyes. The only way to avoid it is to light from directly above, but that will create ugly shadows on the faces of the models and will not show the clothes to best advantage.

What to do?

Deal with it. The fact is, no matter what you do, if you have a runway, you are going to have light get into the audience's eyes. Accept it. Embrace it. Love it.

And try and minimize it. Put the lights at about fifty degrees—far enough down to give the clothes some sparkle and make the faces look good, but far enough up to spare all but the first few rows.

Fashion calls for lots of bright, clear light. When lighting clothes, it is not a good idea to put lots of color on the them. Let them be what color they are. If you want lots of color, throw it on the set.

Models: Be aware that the lighting designer is pumping in lots of light to make the clothes look good, and adjust your makeup accordingly.

Video Lighting

Video lighting means lighting to serve the camera, and the camera is a greedy master. It wants light, and I mean LIGHT! Video cameras require almost three times as much light as the human eye to get a good image. Not only do they need a lot of light, they need a very specific color of light. Television **lighting directors** (note the different job title) spend a lot of time talking about **white balance**. Contrary to what you might think, there is no clear standard in lighting about what "white" light is, especially since your eyes are capable of identifying lots of different colors as white, depending on the surrounding visual context. As countless detergent commercials have shown us, you may think you have a white shirt on until you see one that is "whiter and brighter." In stage lighting, you may think that you are looking at white light until you see it on a video monitor and it looks pink or orange or blue. Video cameras must be told "this color is white." Once they have identified "white," they can adjust the rest of the colors appropriately. This process of training the camera is called "setting the white balance" and videographers must do it before they shoot.

Lighting directors also talk about **color temperature**. They are not talking about how hot the lights are—once again, they are talking about white light. The term "color temperature" comes from the way a piece of metal changes color as it heats up. It starts yellow, then becomes orange, then red, then finally blue-white and "white-hot." The color temperature scale goes by the temperature of the metal. Normal incandescent light is around 2500 degrees Kelvin, by the color temperature scale. Sunlight is around 5300 degrees. Video likes anything over 3500. To change a lower color temperature light to a higher one, you don't heat it—you put a special color filter in front of it. Watch the video people as they set up— they will be putting sheets of light blue color in front of some of the lights. They are trying to make all the lights the same color temperature.

Remember: Video takes *lots* of bright light, so be prepared to have more lights burning than you would for a normal stage production. If you are videotaping a stage production, prepare for the stage to be much brighter. If you have scenes in dim light, be prepared to lose some of the intimacy that low light levels can produce. Video cameras can be set to pick up the image even in low light, but the picture will be grainy and low-quality. If you only remember one thing about lighting for video, remember this: lots of Light.

Rock-and-Roll Lighting

When I say "rock-and-roll," I do not mean only head-banging, blood-spitting, guitar-raging rock-and-roll. I mean any kind of live music that is not classical. The visual style of rock-and-roll music has spilled over into country, jazz, pop, funk, rap, and everywhere else.

For years, the primary instrument in the world of rock-and-roll has been the **PAR can**. Basically an automobile headlight with a color filter holder in front of it, the PAR can is very bright and very durable. You can knock it around in the back of a truck for five hundred miles, throw it up over the stage with some color in it, point it roughly in the right direction and you're rocking. Subtle it ain't. It has no shutters and it cannot hold a template. The beam is rough-edged and not even round. It's a lot of light and that's about it.

While we still rely on PAR cans, many other kinds of exotic instruments have appeared to make rock-and-roll one of the most visually exciting shows around. One of the most sweeping changes was the introduction of moving spotlights by the Vari-light company in the mid-eighties. Vari-light created a spotlight that could spin, zoom, tilt, and change color on cue. Pretty cool. It caught on because rock-and-roll is extremely dynamic. The Vari-light allowed the lighting to respond to the music in a heretofore unattainable way—it allowed the light beams to move in time to the music. The beams of light could actually dance. The rock band Genesis was so taken with the idea that they bought the Vari-light company outright and equipped their entire touring rig with movable spotlights, completely dispensing with PAR cans. It was radical, beautiful, and very, very expensive. Since that time, other companies—most notably a northern California outfit called Mobius—have built and marketed other kinds of movable spotlights that have challenged Vari-light's dominance in the field.

Large-scale touring rock shows carry their own lighting instruments (unlike touring theater shows that use whatever is there or rent locally). This is primarily because rock shows do a different venue every night and there is no time to set up the house system or deal with a rental company. The lights will be pre-hung on a trusswork of pipes that gets pulled off the truck and hung over the stage the day of the show. This kind of a setup is essential for movable spotlights since the lighting instruments are pre-programmed to hit particular parts of the stage. As long as the truss is in the same place relative to the stage, the lights do not have to be repro-grammed every night.

Today, most large-scale rock shows carry a combination of the cheap, simple PAR cans and the expensive, movable spotlights.

Besides movable lights and PARs, you will also see some other exotic lighting instruments in large-scale shows, including **lasers** and **ACLs**. You probably know what a laser is, but ACLs might be less familiar to you. They shouldn't be. You see them all the time. They are *AirCraft Landing* lights—headlights for planes. If you see a plane landing at night, look at the lights stuck in the wings. That lamp appears in rock-and-roll all the time. You can recognize it by its bright, narrow beam. ACLs are often used in groups to create a spray of light beams.

But what if you are doing rock-and-roll on a smaller scale and you don't have the money or the staff to handle movable lights and lasers? What if you have a band coming to your convention's closing dinner, or you are trying to light a small club stage? Never fear. You can have exciting rock-and-roll lighting on the cheap.

Rock-and-roll lighting rule number one: Get as much light on stage as you can. Get as many instruments as you can afford. PAR cans are cheap to rent. Rule number two: Use lots of color. Hang sets of colored light, like a group of red back lights, that you can turn on together. Try and get as many different sets of color as you can, to increase the variety. Rule number three: Use lots and lots of back lighting and side lighting. You will not need much front light—just a few white lights to hit faces. If there is a drum set, make sure that you get lots of side and back light on it. All those brass cymbals will really shine. Back and side light will provide dynamic color and you can flash them to the beat to create an exciting stage show. Speaking of flashing the light, Rule number four is: Get a control board with **bump buttons**, buttons that flash individual lights up full when you hit them. Use the buttons along with the other control features of the board (presets, masters, etc.), to follow the flow of the songs. You don't have to be flashing and bumping continuously, but try to emphasize beginnings and endings of songs, as well as marking verses and choruses with appropriate changes.

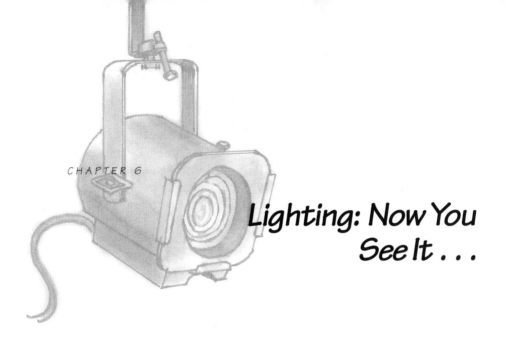

CHAPTER 6

Lighting: Now You See It . . .

Lighting is really just electricity made visible, so we will start by trying to understand what electrical power really is. Then we will follow the flow of electricity through the theater, past the dimmers and the control board, through cables and plugs, and into the instrument itself, where it will change to visible light inside the lamp. Then we will bounce off reflectors, pass through lenses and color media, and finally land on the stage and provide illumination for the show.

The Birds and the Bees: Where Does Power Come From?

What is electricity?

Okay, an analogy: When I lived in Seattle, we used to go down to the fish market where all the tourists hang out and buy fresh fish. The shops had these long tanks full of fish and whenever somebody wanted one, the sales guy would reach in with his bare hands, yank one out and toss it over the heads of some surprised tourists right into the hands of another guy by the cash register who would wrap it and sell it, singing in Sicilian the whole time. It was pretty impressive, but even more impressive when you consider that is how electricity works. Imagine a long tank full of fish. I mean, really full. Imagine a tank so full that you could not put one more fish into it. Absolutely jammed. Now imagine that the sales guy down at one end reaches in and pulls one fish out. With one fish removed, there is room for another fish. Now imagine that there is a fisherman who pulls up to the other end of the tank with his catch of the day. He sees that there is room for one more fish in the tank, so he dumps a fresh one in. Only he does not stop there. He keeps trying to force more fish into the tank. No matter how hard he pushes, though, he will not be able to get another fish in the tank until the sales guy down at the other end pulls one out. The fisherman keeps trying, though, and every time the sales guy pulls a fish out, the fisherman succeeds in getting a new one in. Sometimes, the fisherman pushes so hard that, when the sales guy reaches into the tank, he comes up with not one fish but two, or three. In fact, if the fisherman pushes really, really hard, the sales guy might be overwhelmed by fish when he reaches into the tank.

This is electricity.

Confused? Of course! Okay, the fish are electrons, and they are swimming around inside the fish tank, which is a cable. The fisherman is the source of the electricity, which means that he is the power company. The sales guy is the **load**—the thing that is using the electricity. He could be a stereo, a toaster, a clothes dryer, or a theatrical lighting instrument. It does not matter. A load is a load. The load (the sales guy) is pulling electrons out of the cable. He is using electricity. (The guy at the cash register singing in Sicilian does not figure into this analogy. I only put him in for local color.)

This analogy breaks down in one place. Power requires a round-trip ticket—a circuit. There must be a complete path from the power source to the load and back again to make a circuit, and there must not be any breaks along the way. If the circuit is broken at any point, no power will flow, no matter how hard the fisherman pushes or the sales guy pulls. The simplest way to break a circuit is something we do every day—turn the light switch off. Turning a switch off creates a physical break in the circuit and interrupts the flow of power. I could improve the analogy, I guess, by having the sales guy throw the fish back into the ocean for the fisherman to catch and bring back to the market, but let's not split hairs.

There are three terms that we use to describe how the fish move through the tank, or how the electrons move through the cable. The **wattage** is how many fish (electrons) the sales guy (load) can pull out at a time, and it is a function of how big he is. All loads, whether they be lighting instruments or toasters, are rated in watts. A small load cannot pull out as many electrons as a big load. A two-hundred-watt lamp cannot pull as many fish as a five-hundred-watt lamp.

The **voltage** is how hard the fisherman (power company) is trying to push fish into the tank. Voltage describes how much pressure is being put on the electrons in the cable and, in turn, on the load. More volts mean more pressure. If the voltage is too high and the load is not strong enough to deal with it, it may be overwhelmed, as the sales guy could be overwhelmed by the fisherman pushing too hard. When this happens, the load

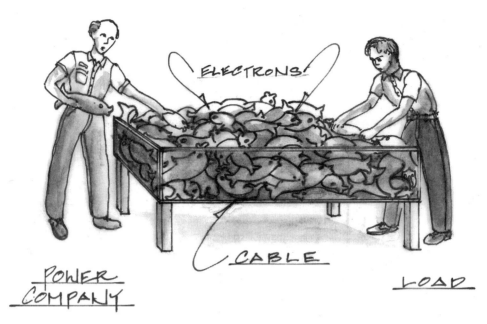

Fig. 17. How electricity works

may burn out. All lamps will burn out sooner or later, but higher voltage shortens their working life. If the voltage goes really high, the load will burn out instantly.

Every load is designed to work with a particular voltage. In the United States, the power company is pushing around 115 fish, uh, volts, so lamps sold for use in this country are designed accordingly. In Europe, the power company is pushing around 220 volts, so the lamps must be built to handle more power. This is also why you have to take a voltage adapter with you when you travel with appliances that are made for use in the United States. The adapter sits between the power company and your hair dryer and takes some of the pressure off.

The third term describes how quickly the fish are moving through the tank. This is **amperage**. The cable (the tank) is rated by how many amps it can handle at one time. If the voltage goes up (the power source is pushing harder), so will the amperage. Likewise, if the wattage goes up (the load is pulling harder), that also forces the amperage up. No matter how far up the wattage goes, the power source will just keep throwing more electrons into the cable as fast as the load pulls them out. This can lead to an overload situation, where the power company and the load are pushing and pulling so hard that the cable itself is in danger of being damaged. This can result in the cable breaking down, and it is a major cause of fires. That is one reason why we have **circuit breakers** and **fuses**. These two devices work differently but they basically do the same job: They monitor the flow of power and, if the flow of power gets too high, they shut down the system by breaking the circuit. We will talk more about fuses and circuit breakers in a minute, but for right now just remember that fuses and circuit breakers, like cables, are rated in amps.

These three terms: wattage, voltage, and amperage, are related to each other by a simple formula known as the "West Virginia" law. It says: Wattage equals Voltage times Amperage, or: $W = V \times A$.

Let's try a few problems. Say you have some 100w lamps plugged into a circuit with a 15a fuse (a common size in most houses). How many of the lamps can you plug into the circuit before the fuse blows? Fill in the formula (remember, the power company in the United States provides 115 volts):

$$W = V \times A = 115v \times 15a = 1725$$

You can put 1725 watts into the circuit, so you can plug in seventeen 100-watt lamps with a few watts to spare. The eighteenth one will trip the fuse.

How about trying it from the other direction? Say you have three 250w lamps and you want to know what size cable you need. First, add up the loads:

$$3 \times 250w = 750w$$

Now, solve the formula for amps. (Come on . . . you did it in tenth grade):

$$W = V \times A$$
$$A = W/V$$

Fill it in:

$$A = 750w/115v$$

Do the math . . .

$$A = 6.5217391304$$

Yeesh! Save me from that kind of number. Of course, you can round off your answer to find you need a seven-amp cable, but you still have to carry a pocket calculator around to do the long division (at least, I do).

Or, you can do the whole problem an easier way.

You still have to use the West Virginia law, but with a slight change. If you are in the United States, just assume that the power company is putting out 100 volts. It will make the numbers come out a little high, but that is okay, since it will make us a little more conservative. Look what substituting 100 volts does to the problem above:

$$A = 750\text{w}/100\text{v} = 7.5$$

When you divide by one hundred, all you have to do is move the decimal two places to the left, and you are done. Now your answer says that you need a 7.5a cable, which is a little bigger than before, but we can call the difference a safety margin. So, we now know that, rather than bothering with the formula at all, we can just add up all of our loads and move the decimal place two spaces to the left to get our answer. Try it again. Let's say that you have two 500w lamps and you want to know how big a cable you need:

Add up the loads:

$$2 \times 500\text{w} = 1000\text{w}$$

Now, move the decimal over two places to the left. Your answer is 10 amps. 1,000 watts equals 10 amps.

So, if you know how many watts you have, just move the decimal over two places and you will know how many amps you need. Likewise, if you know how many amps you have, just move the decimal two places to the *right* to find out how many watts you can plug in. You can also just say "hundred" after you say the amperage, that is, if you have an 18-amp cable, you can plug in 18 "hundred" watts.

Of course, like any kind of mathematical formula, this one gets much easier after you work with it for a little while. Besides, lighting is standard-ized, so there are some amounts that you will get used to. For example, most stage cable is 20-amp cable, so you can plug 2,000 watts into it. Or how about this one? Many stage lights are 500 watts, so that means they need 5 amps apiece. Are you with me? Great!

Last one: Suppose you are doing a show in a hotel ballroom and the hotel electrical guy tells you that he will put a 30-amp power strip out in the room for you to plug your lights into. You call the lighting rental com-pany and they say that they have lots of 500w instruments and how many do you need? Using the "West Virginia" rule, figure out how many instruments you can plug in that power strip. The answer's at the bottom of the page.*

Enough math! (Don't worry, it comes easy with a little practice.)

Protecting Yourself

Time for another field trip. This time we are going to a **circuit breaker panel**. If you live or work in an older building, you might have a genuine

_____

*Using the simplified formula: $W = 100$ volts $\times 30$ amps $= 3,000$ watts, so $3,000 \div 500 = 6$ instruments.

Fig. 18. The power commute

fuse box. Otherwise, you have a circuit breaker panel. You can tell immediately when you open the box. If it is a fuse box, there will be rows of round metal fuses with little glass windows staring at you. If you have breakers, there will be rows of switches, usually black. Let's talk about fuses first.

The old-style round **fuse** is the original no-brainer electrical device. It consists of a thin wire built into a metal and glass enclosure that screws into a socket in your panel. This wire is carefully designed so that a power surge above a certain amount will cause it to melt. When the wire melts and separates, the circuit is broken and no power will flow. There are two things that will cause a fuse to blow. The first thing is a **short circuit**. A short circuit means that the wires going to the load somehow get connected, or "shorted" to the wires moving away from it, thereby cutting the load out of the circuit entirely. This means that there is now an uninterrupted path from the power company, through the cables, and right back to the power company—without any of the power being "used" by a load. This can happen if a cable gets damaged, or if you stick a paper clip into both sides of an electrical outlet. (SAFETY NOTE: *Do not do that.*) Electrons are like Ferraris on the Autobahn—they do not pay attention to speed limits. When a short circuit is created, the jubilant electrons start whipping through the circuit at light speed, causing an unrestricted, almost infinite, flow of power. If the circuit is not cut off, *right now,* you are in danger of the wires heating up and catching fire. The wire in the fuse is built for just such a contingency, and it will immediately sever, breaking the circuit. Whew.

The second thing that will fry your fuse is an overload—when you have too many things plugged into one circuit. Remember our West Virginia formula? Most household fuses are 15 amps, so how many watts can you plug into the circuit?* If you try to plug too many things into the circuit, the wire will heat up and, eventually, melt. The fuse can save you in this situation as well.

Fuses are a one-shot deal, however. Once they blow, they have to be replaced. This is one reason why electricians moved on to circuit breakers. Here is another one. Fuses are not as precise as circuit breakers. Even though you may have a 15-amp fuse, if the power is brought up gradually, a fuse may let it stay on a little higher before cutting off the circuit. Because of this lack of precision, electricians prefer circuit breakers for most applications. Fuses do have one advantage: Once they decide to blow, they blow more quickly than circuit breakers—an important consideration when short circuits or other massive power surges are happening. This is why you still see a few of them around—inside your stereo, for instance. There is probably a big fuse buried inside your breaker panel as well. Look up toward the top for a tube shaped like a small soda can. This protects your house from a massive power surge if, for example, a telephone pole down the street gets hit by lightning.

A lot of theatrical equipment (dimmers, for instance) have both fuses and circuit breakers. The fuse protects against short circuits (when you need a fast cutoff), while the circuit breaker watches for overloads (because it can monitor them more precisely).

Aside from the one big fuse, however, your panel at home probably has circuit breakers. Take a look at the panel now. A breaker panel is like a freeway interchange. It is a way to split up the incoming traffic into lots of different, smaller roadways. Most breaker panels have a door that you can open to see the breakers, but to really see the insides, you have to unscrew the front of the panel. *Do not remove the cover yourself.* There is more than enough power inside the panel to kill you if your fingers do the walking down the wrong streets. Either get someone who knows what she is doing to open it for you, or wait until an electrician is doing repair work and peek in.

Whether or not you are looking inside the panel right now, let's talk about what happens there. There are three big wires coming into most breaker panels (four or five if you are looking at a large industrial panel).

*100 volts × 15 amps = 1,500 watts

These are the hot line, the common line, and the ground line. (In large panels, there are sometimes additional "hot" lines.) The hot line brings the power in and the common line takes it out. The ground line is there to "soak up" extra power that might be released by a short circuit.

The hot line, which can be upwards of 200 amps (quick: how many watts?), runs right down the center of the panel. Sticking out from it are a number of "exits," little metal tabs that are connected to one side of all the circuit breakers. The circuit breakers are smaller (15–30 amps), so each circuit can only handle a small portion of the available "traffic." The power leaves the hot line, passes through the breaker, goes out of the panel, travels through the walls of your house, and finally hooks up to one side of an electrical outlet. When you go into your bedroom and plug in your clock radio, the plug takes the power and sends it up to the clock where it passes through a bunch of electronics and makes those little numbers change. Then the power goes back down through the cord, into the other side of the outlet, and back to the breaker panel. All of these returning lines are collected together at a long metal strip, where they are attached to the common line that is heading back to the power company. As long as the breaker in the panel and the clock radio in your bedroom are on, there is a complete circuit from the power company, into your house, through your clock radio, back to the panel, and out to the power company. Just one big power commute.

You also might notice a few breakers that are double-size, that is, twice as big as the rest. These breakers take up two "exits" from the power freeway, and they are there to provide power for some of the big power eaters in your house, like your hot water heater, or the dryer. You might also have a really big breaker that shuts off the whole house.

Circuit breakers and fuses are not the whole protection story, though. If you have electronic devices like computers, stereos, televisions, and so on, you should also include two other kinds of protection in your system: **surge protection** and **spike protection**.

While the level of power coming from the power company is pretty reliable, there are inconsistencies, and sometimes the power will float a little above or below 115 volts. Circuit breakers guard against fluctuations in amperage, not voltage, so they won't guard against this problem. Surge protection guards against these annoyances. If you have a lot of really critical electronic equipment, you should explore **power conditioners**, which take whatever is thrown at them and put out a steady, precise 115 volts. This is unnecessary for most of us, but critical computer installations, sound studios, and other highly electronic environments should invest in them.

Besides these small fluctuations, there might also occasionally be a large, fast, jolt of power caused by a lightning strike or some other momentary problem in the power grid. These "spikes" can go as high as 10,000 volts, if only for a fraction of a second, and they can easily take out a computer, so a spike protector is a good investment.

Surge and spike protectors usually come bundled together in the same device and often are built into a multi-outlet power strip. Their quality and reliability varies, however, so spend some dough and get a good one. It does not make sense to trust a thousand-dollar stereo to a ten-dollar spike protector.

Highways and Byways: Outlets and Plugs

We can get this one out of the way in a hurry, and a good thing too. Boring.

Plugs and outlets go together, so let's deal with both at once. In the modern American theater, there are three types of plugs. The first one—the **Edison plug**—is the one you see in your house. It is easy to plug in, commonly available, and cheap. It lacks toughness, however, and it cannot handle a huge amount of power, so it is limited to smaller uses, like toasters and televisions.

Most theater applications use one of the other two kinds of plugs. If you are using rental equipment, it is important that you get all of one kind, because they are not compatible. The first is the **stage pin plug**, also called the "three pin" or "stage plug."

Stage pin plugs are tough, durable, and can handle lots of power. I highly recommend taping stage pin connectors together with gaffer's tape. Do not use duct tape or masking tape—it will melt, and then you'll have gooey glop all over your pretty black plugs.

The third and, in my opinion, best kind of plug is the **twist-lock plug**. These are durable, can handle large amounts of power, and best of all, they do what the title says: They twist and lock into place, so they will not come apart. No taping required.

One caution about twist-locks: They did not come onto the market with the same degree of standardization that Edison and stage pin plugs did, so there are several different kinds of twist-lock out there. If you are renting or buying instruments to use along with your existing equipment, make sure the plugs match. You may have to take one of your plugs down to the supply company to be certain. It is easy to get cynical about these kinds of compatibility problems until you realize how amazing it is that all the electrical outlets in all our different houses fit all the electrical plugs on the ends of all the different clock radios that are sold all over the country. Now that is something to be happy about. I can deal with the occasional odd twist-lock.

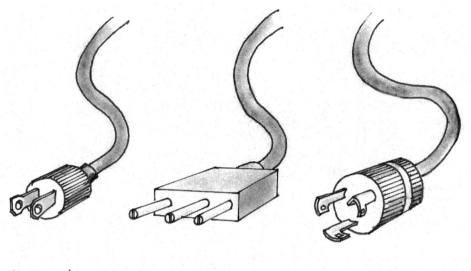

EDISON

STAGE PIN

TWIST-LOCK

Fig. 19. Different kinds of electrical plugs

One final note about plugs and outlets: The end of the cable where the prongs of the plug stick out is called the male end. The end that has the holes that the prongs stick into is called the female end. That is what they are called—I did not invent it and I do not want to get any letters about it.

Taming the Beast: Dimmers and Control Boards

As useful as electricity is, sometimes you want a little less of it. In fact, sometimes you do not want any of it at all.

There have been a lot of schemes over the centuries to make lights dim up and down on stage. Back when they used candles to light the stage, some clever entrepreneur invented little cans that slipped down over the candles to partly cut off the light. When gas lighting came in, technicians invented complicated mechanisms called gas tables that routed gas to little burners all over the stage. Most of the gas-lit theaters burned down, and now you know why.

Dimmers

When theaters went to electric power, the first dimmer that took over was the **resistance dimmer**, so called because it dimmed the lights by creating resistance to the electricity. Basically it just wasted the extra power. Resistance dimmers were mounted in big piano-sized modules with Frankenstein-style levers on them. Every six dimmers had its own "piano box" and it took a score of technicians to run them all. (The crew at Radio City Music Hall are reputed to have worn roller skates.) All that resistance created a lot of heat as well. Legend has it you could cook breakfast on the dimmers after an all-night rehearsal.

Today, through the miracle of science, we have solid-state, electronic dimmers, called **SCR dimmers**, to do the job. (That's Silicon Control Rectifier, and aren't you glad you asked.)

In most lighting setups, the dimming is handled in two different pieces: The dimmers themselves sit in a closet backstage, while a control board sits in the light booth and tells the dimmers what to do. If you are renting dimmers, they might come in two separate units—the dimmer pack and the controller—or as an all-in-one dimmer/controller combination.

Dimmers are rated in watts. The most common size is 2400 watts, often abbreviated as "2.4K." You will also find 1K (1,000-watt) dimmers. Dimmers often come in packs of six. Control boards are listed by how many dimmers they can control and, since dimmers come in sixes, so do control boards. Look for six-, twelve-, twenty-four-, or thirty-six-dimmer boards. You also get to choose between manual or computer boards, but we will talk about that in a minute.

Time to Plug It In

Okay, so you have some lighting instruments, you have a theater, you have some dimmers, and you want to plug it all together and make it work. Great. What now?

Well, the next part is kind of like that children's game, the one that goes: "The hip bone's connected to the thigh bone. The thigh bone's connected to the knee bone," and so on. It goes like this:

The instrument is connected to the circuit.

The circuit is connected to the dimmer.

The dimmer is connected to the channel.

The channel is connected to the master fader.

From the top: A theater is full of *circuits*. A circuit is an outlet, a place to plug the instrument in. A theater might have only a few, or it might have hundreds. These circuits are connected to a cable that travels through the walls of the theater back to a panel in a room somewhere, not unlike how the cable from your clock radio travels back to the circuit breaker panel in your house. The panel in the theater, however, is slightly different. It's called a **patch panel**, because it is here that circuits are "patched" together with dimmers. Most theaters have more circuits than dimmers, so you use the patch panel to determine which dimmers will send power to which circuits. Some fortunate theaters are wired **dimmer per circuit**, which means that there is a dimmer plugged permanently into each circuit. In this case, there is no patch panel. The rest of us, however, must slog through patching.

There are several kinds of patch panels, but they all serve the same purpose: They let you decide which dimmers are going to control which circuits. You may decide to let all the odd-numbered dimmers control all the lights on stage left and vice versa, or you may decide to have all the dimmers that end in "0" control special effects, or whatever. Every designer has his own system. If you are using a rental system, the patching is done by plugging the cables from the instruments right into the side of the dimmers themselves. Inhouse patch panels sometimes look like those big telephone patch panels that old-time operators used to use, or sometimes they are rows of little sliders that you slide across to make connections, but the principle is the same: You take a cable that leads to a particular circuit and plug it into whatever dimmer you want to control it. Of course, you should be keeping track of what you are doing. Here's one example of a chart, called a **hookup chart**, that stores all of the information.

In a larger theater, or in a theater that is wired dimmer per circuit, you will end up with a lot of dimmers, maybe even hundreds. For this reason, many computerized control boards have another level of organization—the **channel**. With these boards, it is possible to assign groups of dimmers to a single channel and control all those dimmers at once. For example, let's say you have a large group of instruments set up to look like sunlight flooding through a window. They are all the same color and you know that you are going to want to bring them all up and down together. They are plugged into circuits all over the place and controlled by a whole bunch of dimmers. By assigning them all to the same channel, you only have to remember one number. Every time you bring up that channel, all the dimmers will bring up all the instruments at the same brightness. Magic.

One confusing thing about this setup is that, while dimmers and circuits are real physical objects, channels only exist in the computer's brain.

The final step in the control process is the **master fader**. Every control board in the world—computerized or made out of yak skins—has a master fader that controls all of the dimmers or channels. Fade the master down, and all the lights fade out. This is the best way to create a blackout on stage.

Many control boards have a **blackout switch**, which turns all the lights off with a flick of a tiny switch. I suppose light board manufacturers include it for those people who want really quick blackouts, but for my money, it is not much faster than just slamming down that master fader. Plus, it has "problem" written all over it. Brush against it, and the stage

Sweet Matilda! Hookup Sheet

POSITION	NUM.	TYPE	CIRCUIT	DIMMER	COLOR	FOCUS
1st Beam	1	6x9 ellipsoidal	3	1	Lux 03	Acting Area 1
	2	6x9 ellipsoidal	6	2	Lux 03	Acting Area 2
	3	6x12 ellipsoidal	2	30	No Color	CD special
	4	6x9 ellipsoidal	3	1	Lux 08	Acting Area 1
	5	6x9 ellipsoidal	3	3	Lux 03	Acting Area 3
	6	6x9 ellipsoidal	11	2	Lux 08	Acting Area 2
	7	6x9 ellipsoidal	3	3	Lux 08	Acting Area 3
1st Electric	1	8" Fresnel	21	4	Lux 03	Acting Area 4
	2	8" Fresnel	27	5	Lux 03	Acting Area 5
	3	8" Fresnel	29	6	Lux 03	Acting Area 6
	4	8" Fresnel	26	4	Lux 08	Acting Area 4
	5	6x9 ellipsoidal	23	31	No Color	phone special
	6	8" Fresnel	32	5	Lux 08	Acting Area 5
2nd Electric	7	8" Fresnel	24	6	Lux 08	Acting Area 6
	1	8" Fresnel	34	11	Lux 54	backlight
	2	8" Fresnel	37	12	Lux 54	backlight
	3	8" Fresnel	35	13	Lux 54	backlight
	4	8" Fresnel	41	14	Lux 54	backlight
3rd Electric	1	Borderlight	45, 46, 47	34, 35, 36	Lux 27, 81, 90	cyclorama
	2	Borderlight	45, 46, 47	34, 35, 36	Lux 27, 81, 90	cyclorama
	3	Borderlight	45, 46, 47	34, 35, 36	Lux 27, 81, 90	cyclorama

Fig. 20. A hookup sheet

goes black. People are always calling rental companies to say that their rental board does not work, only to find out that the blackout button was down. If I was in charge of worldwide theatrical lighting, I would ban blackout switches. My advice? Tape it over. Next time you take your board in for service, have them remove it.

The Control Board

The control board sits in the light booth and communicates with the dimmers through a thin control cable. The power that is flowing to the dimmers never goes through the control board itself. The control board is not controlling the power, it is controlling the dimmers, and the dimmers are controlling the power.

As I mentioned earlier, the moment-to-moment operation of lighting is organized into **cues**. Every time a new cue comes along, it may mean that dozens of dimmers are all moving at the same time. On a manual control

Abby and the Alderman   Lighting Cue Sheet

CUE #	PRESET	TIME	1	2	3	4	5	6	7	8	9	10	11	12	13	14	15	16	17	18	19	20	21	22	23	24
1	x	3	7	7	7	7	7						F			3	3	3						8		4

CUE #	PRESET	TIME	1	2	3	4	5	6	7	8	9	10	11	12	13	14	15	16	17	18	19	20	21	22	23	24
2	y	5					B	L	A	C	K	O	U	T												

CUE #	PRESET	TIME	1	2	3	4	5	6	7	8	9	10	11	12	13	14	15	16	17	18	19	20	21	22	23	24
3	x	0	8	8	8	8	8	8	8	8	8		5	5	5	8	8	8			F			8	4	8

CUE #	PRESET	TIME	1	2	3	4	5	6	7	8	9	10	11	12	13	14	15	16	17	18	19	20	21	22	23	24
4	y	3					5	5	5	5			F			3	3	3							F	

CUE #	PRESET	TIME	1	2	3	4	5	6	7	8	9	10	11	12	13	14	15	16	17	18	19	20	21	22	23	24
5	x	7	8	8	8	8	8	8	8	8	8					3	3	3			F	F	F	8		4

Fig. 21. A cue sheet

board, there is a slider for each dimmer, but unless you have dozens of fingers, you're not going to be able to move them all at the same time. That's why, on manual boards, we use **presets**.

Let's say that your theater has thirty-six dimmers (a fairly common number). Your control board will have thirty-six sliders on it to allow you to control each of the dimmers individually. Underneath those thirty-six sliders, though, there are thirty-six more sliders, identical to the first set. Down to the side, there will be a big slider marked "X" on the top and "Y" on the bottom. As long as the big slider is up, the top row (the "X" row) of sliders is controlling the dimmers. If it's down, then the bottom row (the "Y" row) is controlling the dimmers. This big slider is called a **crossfader**.

Why bother with all these sliders?

Well, if the top row is on, then you can set up a new group of dimmer readings (a new cue) on the bottom row. Then, when the time comes, you can slide the crossfader from the top to the bottom, thereby gradually shifting control from the top group of sliders to the bottom group, and changing all the dimmer levels simultaneously. Then, when the bottom line is on, you could reset the sliders on the top one and, at the appropriate moment, fade back to it. This kind of a board is called a "two-scene" preset, and it is the foundation of how we control lighting equipment. Back before computer control came into operations, it was not uncommon to see five- or even ten-scene preset boards that would allow an operator to work several scenes ahead of the action on stage.

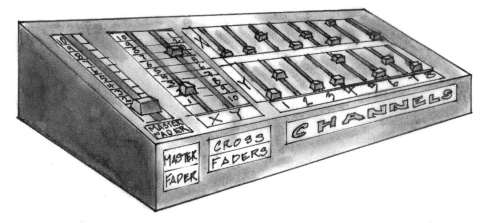

Fig. 22. A two-scene preset lighting control board

Computer control simply automates this process. Instead of having to set up all those dimmer readings by hand every night, you simply set them up once and the computer remembers what they were. It also remembers how fast you want the lights to change. When you want a cue to occur, you push the bright green button that says "Go." The computer changes all the levels from the previous cue to the next one. Because it's a computer and it doesn't have anything else to do with its brain, it will run the cue the same way every night. In addition, it can do a few tricks that a human would find difficult or impossible:

- **Split fades**, which means that the cue fading out is fading at a different rate than the one fading in. You might decide, for dramatic reasons, to fade up the lights for a scene in a new part of the stage, before an earlier scene in another part of the stage is done.
- Run multiple fades at once, such as when you have a sunset going on outside, plus an actor comes in and turns on an overhead light switch, plus car headlights appear in the window, etc., etc. . . .
- **Chase effects**, like movie marquees, or the slowly changing flickers of a fireplace. A chase cue is a series of cues that the computer will cycle through, one at a time, at whatever speed you choose.
- Run cues really fast, as in a rock-and-roll show or an up-tempo musical. A computer can run cues as fast as you can hit the "GO" button.

If you do not have a computer board, you will suffer some limitations about what kind of cues you can run and how fast you can run them. You may encounter particular difficulties when you try to run cues too close together or if you are trying to have two different things happen at once. Some operators are better than others. Of course, having a computer board will not make your life a bed of roses. Any computer anywhere comes with its own set of problems. It is important to remember that a computer will not save you time. It will simply allow you to do more things.

If you use a computer, this is the most important rule I can tell you: Back up your files. Right now. I repeat, *back them up* or, I guarantee— beyond any shred of doubt—you will be sorry. Maybe not today. Maybe not tomorrow. But someday, you will be. It's not a question of whether your board will crash, it's a question of when. There are two kinds of computer operators, those who have lost large amounts of data and those who are about to. Enough said? Probably not.

The Real Workers: Lighting Instruments

At last, something that puts out light!

Contrary to what you've been told all your life, all of those metal things hanging up there above the stage are not called lights. Light is what comes out of them. The things themselves are called *lighting instruments,* or simply, instruments. People do call them "lights" now and then (even I say "bring up the lights!"), but I recommend the term "instrument" when you talk about them individually.

Inside the instrument is a glass and metal assembly that actually puts out the light. Contrary to what you've been told all your life, this is not called a bulb. This is a **lamp**. The glass part of it, exclusive of the metal base and the filament, is the bulb. The whole thing is a lamp.

Lighting instruments are usually mounted on pipes. The standard mounting clamp is called a **C-clamp**, because it looks like one. The C-clamp is attached to a U-shaped **yoke**, which straddles the instrument and attaches on either side. To turn the instrument left and right, you loosen the bolt on the side of the C-clamp. In newer instruments, there is a little handle you can grab onto, but on older ones, you have to put a wrench on it. Be careful! It's easy to twist that little sucker right off and then the clamp will be frozen forever.

To move the instrument up and down, loosen the bolts that hold the yoke to the instrument itself. Newer units have handles, older ones have bolts. Regardless of what you are working with, the tool of choice (and one of the things that all show people should own) is an eight-inch adjustable Crescent wrench.

On the front of the instrument, there is a color frame holder. It's nothing complex—just a slot in front of the lens. Some instruments will have a little spring-loaded flap that you have to pull open to slide the frame in.

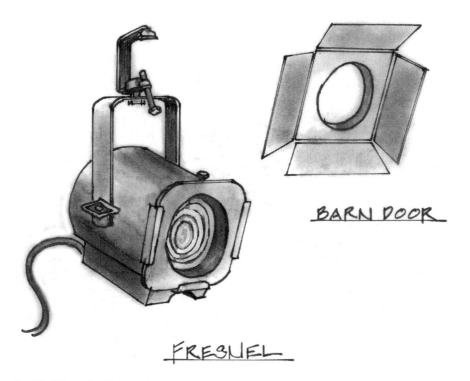

Fig. 23. A Fresnel with barn doors

Other instruments will only have a slot on three sides, so be careful that it is pointed the right way when you hang the instrument. The open side should point up, or the color frame will fall out.

Lighting instruments generally fall into two categories:

Soft-edged Lights

Everyone has seen the image of the crisp, hard-edged spotlight piercing the dusty air to light the emcee downstage, and a lot of people believe that all stage lights look like that. A lot of them do, but many do not. When you are using a lot of instruments to light a stage, you do not always want that sharp, clear stab of light. As a matter of fact, more often then not, you want the lights to blend together as seamlessly as possible, forming a smooth wash of light. For this kind of application, a soft-edged light is the instrument of choice. By far the most common kind of soft-edged light is the Fresnel (pronounced "fur-nell"), named after the distinctive ridged lens invented by Augustin Fresnel, a French physicist who spent his life developing a number of important optical formulas and preparing the way for the theory of relativity. You can always tell a Fresnel from any other kind of

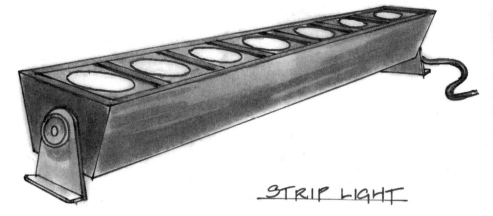

Fig. 24. A strip light

instrument by rubbing your hand over the outside of the lens. A Fresnel
lens will have ridges in it. Anything else will be smooth. Actually, Fresnel
developed his famous lens for lighthouses.

Besides its impressive pedigree and unusual lens, the Fresnel has a
number of other positive features. It is a cheap way to get a lot of light on
stage and its beam has a nice soft edge that blends with the light from
other instruments. The Fresnel beam is also adjustable in size, from a large
circle to a small one. Making the beam larger is called **flooding** it, making it
smaller is called **spotting**. These adjustments are made by sliding the lamp
closer to or farther away from the lens.

Fresnels come in lots of sizes but the two most common in the live
theater are six inch and eight inch (the number refers to the diameter of
the lens). Film sets use lots of Fresnels as well, in larger diameters. A Fresnel
is great for lighting stages where you still might need to isolate smaller
areas. Sometimes, however, you have a large expanse, like a drop or a cyc,
and you need a large, smooth wash of light. For these uses, the best choice
is a **strip light**, also known as a **border light**. Strip lights are long, narrow
metal enclosures with rows of lamps set into them. They provide large
amounts of unfocusable light, usually in several colors. A strip light may
have one circuit of red, one of green, and one of blue, for instance. Since
the lights are soft focus, it all mixes together on the drop, creating one solid
color. By varying the mixture, the designer can change the color on the
drop. This is how designers create sunsets, for one thing. They light the top
of the cyc with various shades of dark blue, while lighting the bottom with
everything from red to orange to lavender. With a computer board or a
skilled human operator, those colors can be changing and blending con-

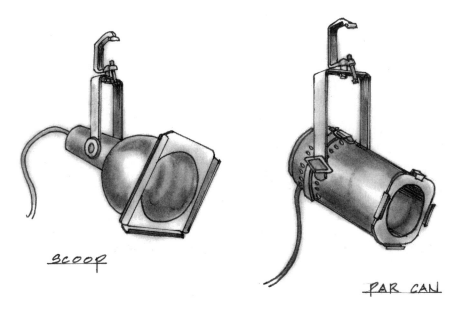

Fig. 25. A scoop light

Fig. 26. A PAR can

tinuously, giving the audience a visual treat. When the sun finally goes
down, you could turn on the stars that are sewn into the cyc and then . . .
whoops, sorry. Got carried away.

There are two other types of soft lights you might run into. First, you
may encounter **scoops**, which are just what they sound like, big ice cream
scoop–looking things with a large lamp in them. Since they have no lens
and no optics to speak of, they are cheap, but the light that comes out of
them is difficult to control. They are best used to light large areas (in a
single color) or as work lights.

Finally, there's the instrument that has changed the face of rock-and-
roll: the **PAR can**. Basically an automobile headlight mounted in a metal
can, the PAR can (it's written in all caps because it's an abbreviation—
Parabolic Anodized Reflector—and no, you don't need to know that) is
bright, intense, and durable. It is not a subtle instrument. It cannot be
focused, spotted, or given any kind of sharpedge. Even so, many theater
and dance designers have been lured to it by the intensity of the beam. It
makes great sunlight, among other things. As I said before, most rock-and-
roll shows are packed with PAR cans.

With all soft-edged instruments, it is good to remember that the light
from them is more difficult to control than that from hard-edged instruments. This can be significant if, for instance, you are using them in a

front-of-house position, where it is important to keep the light off of the proscenium arch, or if you need a tightly focused pool of light. A small piece of equipment, like **barn doors**, which fit into the color filter slot on the lighting instrument, can help you control the light better. Barn doors have two or four little wings that can be swung in front of the lens, masking off part of the light. This masking does not produce a sharp edge, but it will get a lot of light off of the scenery, the audience, or whatever. (If you are hanging Fresnels pointing anywhere near an audience, barn doors are a necessity.) If possible, all Fresnels should be hung with barn doors. One good reason not to use barn doors: If you are hanging the instruments on battens that have scenery moving next to them, barn doors are notorious for catching draperies, corners, moldings, and just about anything else that goes by. I swear, they reach out and grab them.

Hard-edged Instruments

When you need to have greater control over the light, the instrument of choice is usually an ellipsoidal reflector spotlight, also called an **ellipsoidal**. The ellipsoidal is sometimes referred to as a **Leko**, but this is actually a "Kleenex" word—a brand name that has become the general term for something. Like Kleenex, Jello, and Muzak, these words have entered the dictionary in a way that brings great joy to the original manufacturer. People will know what you mean if you say "Leko," but I recommend that you use the more general term "ellipsoidal," both for the sake of clarity and in fairness to all of the other fine manufacturers of stage lighting equipment.

Ellipsoidals are actually capable of being either hard- or soft-edged and, all things being equal, I would usually prefer to use them over the more finicky Fresnels. All things are not equal, however, because the ellipsoidals, with their more complex optics, are considerably more expensive to own and rent than their soft-edged counterparts.

Not that an ellipsoidal is some kind of rocket science. An ellipsoidal reflector spotlight is so called because (are you sitting down?) it has a reflector shaped like an ellipse. This style of reflector has the useful property that it focuses the light more precisely, making it easier to manipulate. From there, a slightly more complex lens system collects the light and sends it out the front.

One way that light is manipulated in an ellipsoidal is with **shutters**, little metal blades that push in from the side of the instrument and cut off part of the beam. Using the shutters, you can give the beam a sharp edge that, for instance, follows the line of a drape, the bottom of a flat, or the edge of a podium. Ellipsoidals are also designed so that you can slide in a **template**, a piece of metal with a design cut out of it. The template, or

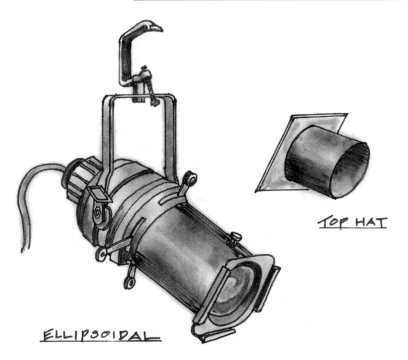

TOP HAT

ELLIPSOIDAL

Fig. 27. An ellipsoidal with a top hat

pattern, or **gobo** (short for "go-between"), allows the instrument to act as a sort of shadow projector, projecting whatever shape is cut out of the metal. Templates are a great way to get creative with lighting. You can cut your own simple patterns out of pie plates, or you can select from the constantly growing selections offered by several different companies. Ask your dealer for a catalog. Remember, though: If you are going to use templates, you must have an ellipsoidal spotlight. Fresnels cannot handle templates.

I mentioned earlier that an ellipsoidal is capable of being either hard or soft edged. This is possible because an ellipsoidal has all of its lenses mounted in a movable barrel that can be slid back and forth. If you want to make your ellipsoidal more "fuzzy," that is, get rid of the sharp line, just "run the barrel" forward or backward until you like it. Likewise, if you are inserting a template and you want the image to sharpen up, run the barrel back the other way.

Ellipsoidals are referred to by two numbers: the diameter of the lens and the **focal length**. The focal length is the distance between two mystical points in the optical system, and the only thing you need to know is that the longer the focal length, the narrower the beam that comes out the front.

There is also a class of ellipsoidals called **zoom ellipsoidals**. These handy instruments have an adjustable focal length, so you can make fairly radical changes to the size of the beam without hanging a different instrument. Why not use them all the time and have more flexibility? There are two trade-offs: cost (predictably, zooms are more expensive), and amount of light—zooms tend to be less bright than the fixed focal length units, because they waste some light inside the instrument.

Follow Spots

Follow spots come in many shapes and sizes, but there are some things that are common to all of them. Follow spots are designed to put out a bright, crisp circle of light, much like an ellipsoidal (in fact, you can bolt a handle onto the back of an ellipsoidal and have yourself a low-tech follow spot). The size of the circle of light is determined by the **iris**, which is operated by a sliding handle on the top or the side. A spotlight will also have **shutters** that shut off the light by sliding in plates from the top and bottom. Many spots can also dim the light out gradually with a **douser**, two plates that swing in from the sides to gradually block out the light. These controls— the iris, the shutter, and the douser—are often right next to one another. On most spots, they are on the top.

A follow spot will generally have a number of different **color frames** that may be pushed in one at a time or together to put a color filter in front of the light. These color frames are controlled by a series of levers on the side of the follow spot. Pushing one color frame in knocks the previous one out.

Finally, many spots have a lever, called a **trombone**, that you can push back and forth to adjust the focal length, just like a zoom ellipsoidal. Pull it back to shorten the focal length and produce a wider beam. Forward to do the opposite. Unlike the iris, shutter, and douser, the trombone is a "set it and forget it" control that the operator will only need to mess with once.

Different size theaters need different size follow spots. In order to determine which spot you need, you need to know the **throw distance**. This is the distance from the follow spot to the stage. Thirty feet is quite short; a good distance for a converted ellipsoidal or a "club" spotlight. These spots use lamps similar to those in regular lighting instruments. Some of them even use "MR-16" lamps, the low-voltage slide projector lamp I mentioned before.

As spots get bigger, the light sources start to change. For throws approaching one hundred feet, use a metal-halide, or **HMI** lamp. This highly specialized lamp has no filament. It produces light by forcing electricity to jump a tiny gap, sort of like a miniature arc welder. It packs a real wallop though, and it is often used for rock-and-roll. If you go to a rock concert and see follow spots mounted on the truss directly above the stage, they are probably HMIs. They make excellent spots for clubs, fashion shows, and theater as well. An HMI spot comes with a twelve-pack–size piece of equipment that sits on the floor under the spot. This is called a **ballast**, and it is required to keep the lamp burning, so make sure you do not forget it when you rent the spot. One caution about metal-halide: Once you turn it on, do not turn it off until the end of the show. HMIs will not restart if they are hot, so if you turn it off at the beginning of intermission, forget about getting it back on for the second act. You must let it cool for a couple of hours before you can use it again.

For extra long throws (200 feet and up) in large theaters or stadiums, technicians use another type of spot. This kind of spot uses an arc like the HMI, but the arcs are much bigger and the light is much brighter. There are two varieties: the **carbon-arc spot** and the **xenon arc spot**. Both of these spots require permanent installations and external venting to accommodate their large size and noxious fumes. Carbon-arc is a much older technology and is gradually disappearing. It requires a fair amount of skill to operate because the light is produced by arcing the light between two carbon electrodes, called **trims**. These trims slowly burn away, increasing the gap between them. If the gap gets too big, the arc will stop and the light will go out. If it gets too small, the trims will fuse together and the light will go out. If the gap is only slightly too big or too small, then the light will smoke, flicker, and look terrible. It requires a skilled operator to maintain the proper amount of space between the two trims. Furthermore, the trims only last about forty-five minutes to an hour, so right in the middle of the show, they have to be replaced with fresh ones, which is called "retrimming." It used to be that rock-and- roll shows had a period of about a minute built right into the show when all the spots could be shut down to retrim.

There is a general trend in theatrical equipment toward making things easier to use, and the carbon-arc spot is a welcome casualty of this movement. Replacing it is the more sophisticated xenon arc spot. The concept is the same: Force an arc to jump across a sizable gap and it will produce light. The xenon arc, however, is enclosed in an airless glass envelope and the electrodes do not get used up in the process. Xenon lamps do occasionally have to be replaced or adjusted, but the adjustment happens every few years, not every few minutes.

Movable Spotlights

Ah, rock-and-roll. Not since the invention of the motion picture has one aspect of show business had such an effect on all the others. The growth of music videos and their lightning-fast editing style has deeply affected all of us in show business.

Along with this change in style came a change in technology, led by the introduction of the **movable spotlight**. The first movable spot that really had any success was put out by the Vari-light company in the early eighties. Since that time, other companies have been suffering the Kleenex syndrome, as all movable spots became known, erroneously, as "Vari-lights."

Movable spots do three things. First of all, they pan—they turn in a circle. Most movables can do a 360-degree turn. There are two ways this is accomplished. One is to mount the lighting instrument on a rotating platform, which is what Vari-light, Mobius, and most other rock-and-roll-oriented companies do. The other, cheaper way is to permanently mount the instrument pointing straight up into a mirror. Then, the motor turns the mirror and the beam of light appears to rotate. This scheme is more common in disco lighting. It is a better approach when the instrument is going to be permanently mounted. The mirrors tend to get shaken around when you put them on the road. The rotating mirror scheme also makes it hard to do the next thing that movable spots do, which is tilt. Besides the motor that turns the platform, a movable spot has a second motor that moves it up and down. The tilt and pan motors work together to make the instrument point in whatever direction the designer wants.

The third thing that a movable spot does is change color. There are various ways to do this (not all of which the companies will reveal) but basically there is a set of color filters inside each instrument that rotate and line up in different combinations to produce a wide range of colors. The colors are brilliant and varied—just the thing for rock and roll. A movable spot can also make a smooth transition from one color to another, which is a pretty neat trick. Some of them are also capable of irising in and out (making the beam larger and smaller) or changing templates. All in all, a pretty nifty little instrument.

Color, movement, irising, and any other tricks performed by movable spots are controlled from a remote console that is usually separate from the main lighting console. Lots of show people get excited when they watch movable spots and they start trying to figure out ways to use them in other applications.

"Wow," they say, "we could hang fewer lights since the same light could do different things in different scenes." Or, "Hey, we could use them as follow spots and not have as many operators." Or simply, "Wouldn't it be great to have movable spotlights in our dance/play/fashion show/beauty contest/awards ceremony?"

To which I reply, yes, it would be great. More power to you. But have a serving of reality soup before you order the main course.

Movable lights are *expensive*. In 1991, I lit a beauty contest in San Francisco and the choreographer, fresh from watching too much MTV, said she wanted movable spots and (my favorite lie) "I don't care *what* it costs!"

Yee-ha! I thought. I get to play with all the toys.

I sent out a bid for twelve (only twelve!) instruments and the control board to run them. The company promptly informed me that they would be more than happy to accommodate me, for just under $9,000.

Needless to say, the show's producers *did* care what it cost, and I did not get to play with the toys that time. I have since checked out this figure with other lighting technicians and their response was universal: "How'd you get such a great deal?" Just my charm, I guess.

Why is it so expensive? Besides the fact that movable lights are complicated, expensive technology in and of themselves; they also come as part of a package. You cannot just rent the lights, you have to hire the technician that comes with them. Since that technician may not be local, you may have to pay travel, lodging, and per diem expenses. You also have to pay shipping for the instruments, complete with their motors, cables, truss, and control board. Then you have to pay the technician to set them up, program the computer that runs them, and take them down afterward. Big money all the way around.

The second big problem that comes with movable spotlights is noise. In a quiet theater the noise of the motors is clearly audible. Obviously, noise is not a concern in a rock-and-roll show, but in most theatrical applications you will hear them.

Sorry to be the bearer of bad news, but it is important to know what you are talking about when you start complicating your backstage life. As I said before, though, there is a general trend in technical theater toward making things easier to use, so expect the technology to become more and more accessible as time goes by.

Fluorescent Lighting

Time now to talk about a few kinds of lighting that you will find in the "real world." Fluorescent light is produced by sending an electrical current through a gas contained in a tube. The gas is excited by the current and begins to glow, or "fluoresce." They are cheap to operate and they put out an even glow in all directions.

Fluorescent lighting has several major drawbacks when used on stage. First of all, it is impossible to dim: It has only two settings—full on and full off. For that matter, if it is slightly out of adjustment, it may not even turn on instantly, but may flicker a couple of times before snapping on to its full brightness. An undimmable light may be a major stumbling block onstage, since you generally want to begin and end your show with a nice smooth fade to a blackout.

Besides the dimming problem, it is difficult to control where the light from a fluorescent light falls on stage. Since the light comes from a long tube, without the benefit of a lens system, the light tends to splay out in all directions, hitting people, scenery, and everything else.

Finally, most people find fluorescent lighting hard to look at for long. It has a harshness that can be difficult to withstand. Of course, if this is the effect you are trying to achieve, then go for it, but think it over carefully before you commit.

Because of these three reasons, fluorescent lighting is generally avoided on stage unless the designer is seeking a specific effect.

Sodium Vapor and Mercury Vapor

I have always had a deep appreciation for the 1973 oil crisis. During America's campaign to use less power, most cities switched from fluorescent street lighting to sodium vapor or mercury vapor. Almost overnight, travelers flying over cities saw them change from bright white to soft orange and green. A definite improvement.

While these instruments were a boon for our streets (and our electric bills), they are a horrible thing to inflict on a theater. The reason is simple: They take too long to turn on. When you flip the switch, you will see a tiny glow in the heart of the lamp right away, but it takes *forever* for that little flicker to become usefully bright. It can take up to fifteen minutes for the lamp to come to full bright. This is acceptable in a streetlight or even in a gymnasium, but not in a theater.

You may be stuck with some of these lights if you are doing a show in a gym or a cafeteria, so take note of them. You may have to rig another set of houselights unless you want the audience to sit in the dark for five or ten minutes after the curtain call.

Color My World: The Joy of Filters

The last thing the light beam sees when it leaves the instrument and heads out on its trip to the stage is a color filter.

Terminology time: Color is produced by stripping away a part of the light. To the physicists, this is called "subtractive mixing." To us it means that filters do not add color to a light beam—they take it away. If you put a red filter in front of a beam of light, that filter will strip away all the light that isn't red. It is sort of like that old joke: How do you make a sculpture of an elephant? Just get a piece of rock and carve away everything that does not look like an elephant.

The first color filters that appeared were actually made out of gelatin, an animal byproduct. The term **gel** has persisted to this day, even though filters are now made out of various types of high-tech plastic. Likewise, the piece of metal that holds the filter is often referred to as the **gel frame**. Since we are in search of accuracy here, let's give them their proper names: the **color filter** and the **color frame**.

Color filters are available from lots of different companies. Filters are always referred to first with the name of that company and then with a number. For instance, Lee 120 is a dark blue filter put out by the Lee company. RoscoLux 27 is a primary red from Rosco Laboratories. GAM 385 is a light amber put out by Great American Market, and so on. All of these colors have names as well, but those names mean about as much as the names people give paint or lipstick. "Steel Blue" for example is a color that everyone carries, but Rosco's Steel Blue is a different color than Great American's. There are thousands of colors available from many different manufacturers and they are all unique. Each company puts out sample books (persistently called "gel books") and lighting designers spend a lot of time experimenting and keeping track of what is available. In the end, most designers develop a palette of favorite colors that they use whenever they design a show. This list of favorites is part of what gives each designer her distinctive style. As you learn more about lighting, you may also develop favorites. You may learn, for example, which colors look good on your own skin, and then you can really drive designers crazy by insisting that they use them.

Color is sold (you cannot rent it) in large sheets, usually about eighteen-by-twenty-four inches, which will give you six pieces for a six-inch ellipsoidal or Fresnel, or four pieces for an eight-inch Fresnel or a PAR 64. Excess scraps can be taped together with Scotch tape to make more pieces if you're strapped for cash.

Color will fade over time, especially darker colors. Dark blue is particularly short-lived. It's a good idea to poke some holes in the filters to let the hot air pass through them. Make short, quarter-inch long cuts with a razor blade or, to be truly cool, buy a "pounce wheel" from a fabric store. A pounce wheel is a little spiked wheel that you can roll over the filter to make a series of tiny holes. (The costume shop uses it to mark fabric, but do not steal theirs unless you want the crotch in your next costume sewn shut.) Do not worry about white light sneaking through the holes—unless the holes are huge, the light beams will mix together and hide any white light.

To install color in a lighting instrument, get a color frame for the instrument you are coloring. (Make sure it's the right one—color frames from different manufacturers are frustratingly incompatible.) Using the frame as a guide, cut a piece the right size. Open up the frame and insert the color, making a filter sandwich. Most color frames have a small hole punched in them so you can insert a brass paper fastener through the whole assembly to keep it from coming apart as you carry it up the ladder. Otherwise, put some tape around the edges to keep it together. Slide the color frame into the little shelf on the front of the instrument. It does not matter which side of the filter faces front.

Besides color filters, lighting companies also make a line of **diffusion filters**. These highly useful filters look just like color filters except that they are white and frosty, sort of like the glass in your bathroom window. They are designed to spread out the light in various ways. Some of them just soften the light a little bit, getting rid of shutter lines and hard edges, while others spread the light out over a large area. Some diffusion filters only spread the light out in one direction. This is useful if, for example, you are trying to spread the light across a drop. You can combine diffusion with a color filter in the same frame, but be sure to put some holes in both filters so the heat can get out (otherwise the filters may melt together). Diffusion comes in lots of varieties, so play around.

Color filters are especially fun to use with templates. Try cutting two different color filters in half and taping them together in a single frame. This is called a split color and it can do fun things with an intricate pattern.

This may be stating the obvious, but since I have seen people try it, I must tell you not to try putting color into the slot where the template goes. It will melt faster than you can say . . . too late, it's gone.

Putting it in the Theater: Lighting Positions

There are probably instruments hanging all over your theater, in a number of different **lighting positions**. The **batten** (remember? the long horizontal pole hanging over the stage) that instruments are hanging from is called an **electric**. Electrics are numbered starting at the proscenium arch and moving upstage, so the closest one to the proscenium is called the **first electric**. Out over the audience, the lighting positions are called **beams**, or sometimes, **coves** (particularly if they are built into the ceiling). Any vertical lighting position, whether out front or backstage, is called a **boom**. Beams are horizontal, booms are vertical. Still with me?

Depending on the theater, there are lots of other kinds of lighting positions that have names that are peculiar to individual theaters. For instance, there was a set of short booms in the auditorium at San Francisco State that happened to be located over a set of speakers. They were always referred to as the "Speaker Box" lights. There was probably more than one student who went to his first professional job looking for the Speaker Box position. That term, however, was unique to that particular theater.

Many theaters have lights in a small position to the side of the apron, pretty much where our speaker box position was, and that position goes

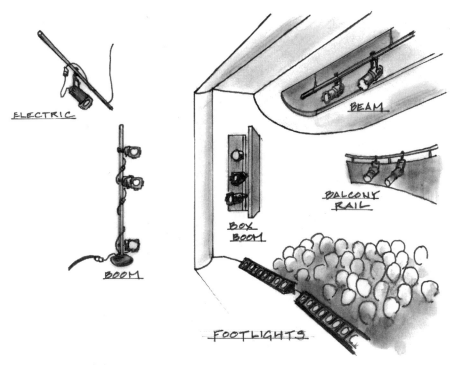

Fig. 28. Common lighting positions

under a number of pseudonyms: **side coves**, **juliets** (because of their resemblance to the famous balcony), and often **box booms**. That last one is relatively common and is descended from the old Broadway theaters. When the theaters were built, the architects included box seats in the side wall of the auditorium for the gentry to sit above the madding crowd. These boxes were well to the side, almost over the stage itself, and they didn't have much of a view. They did, however, give the audience a great view of whoever sat in them, which was more the point. As time went on (and the price of theater tickets went up), people became more interested in seeing the show than being seen by the audience, and that, combined with a greater emphasis on lighting, caused the boxes to be overtaken by lighting equipment. Today, any lighting boom in that position, regardless of whether or not there was ever seating there, may still be called a box boom. Incidentally, if you ever buy Broadway show tickets that are labeled "restricted view," they might be selling you seats alongside the lighting booms in the old boxes.

Take a look at the diagram if you need to get oriented.

Okay, you've selected your instruments, you've hung them, you've plugged them in, you've got your color ready to go, and you're ready to try and do something useful with the light. The job of getting the instruments pointed in the right direction is called *focusing,* and it is an art. It will take you some time to get used to this process, so do not get frustrated. It's time for:

The Backstage Survival Guide to Focusing

Prepare, prepare, prepare. Take the time before you start to figure out what you are doing.

- Make sure your paperwork—the instrument schedule and the hookup sheet—are complete and accurate.
- Get all the lights hung in the right place, get all the color cut and put in, and plug the instruments in to the right dimmers.
- Make sure you have all the ladders you need, enough wrenches for everybody, and spare lamps to fix the burnouts.
- Get enough people to help you. Focusing takes at least four people: somebody on the ladder or catwalk, somebody to hold the ladder, somebody to run the dimmerboard, somebody to tell everybody what to do (generally the designer).

• *Keep it quiet.*

Lots of people, including me, like to work with the radio on. Focusing, however, is a time for quiet. The designer will need to talk to the technician and people are usually doing things high in the air. For safety and clarity, keep the music off and conversation to a minimum. Above all, no power tools should be in use. Focusing is best done when nothing else is going on in the theater. Sometimes the painters can work while you are focusing, but they should know that you may have to move scenery around to get to the instruments.

• *Have a plan.*

Make a decision before you start about what order you are going to focus the positions in. A good designer can alternate between two crews working in two different places in the theater. For example, one crew might be working out front over the audience while a second crew works over the stage.

- *When you get to the instrument, prepare it for focusing.*
- If it's an ellipsoidal, pull all the shutters out.
- If it's a Fresnel, pull it to full spot.
- Take the color out.
- Loosen the three adjustment bolts: the one on the side of the C-clamp, and the ones on the side of the yoke. As you get used to the process, these first actions will become second nature to you.

• *When you start to focus the instrument, first get it pointed in the right direction.*

With the designer directing you from the stage, point the instrument in the proper direction. Many designers will simply stand in the right place and tell you to "hit me." Look at the beam of light coming from your instrument—there is a bright spot near the center. This is called the **hot spot**, and you should put it right on the designer's face. After all, the face is what we want to see most clearly—unless you are doing dance lighting. For dance, you should put the hot spot in the center of the body. Above all, listen to the designer.

• *Lock it off.*

Once the instrument is in the right spot, tighten the bolts. Do this before you move the shutters or put in the color. Otherwise the instrument will move, and you'll have to go back to the previous step.

• *Insert the template, set the shutters or adjust the spot/flood knob.*

Again, follow the designer's instructions. Once the designer is satisfied, drop the color in. Then, move on to the next instrument. It's helpful if the dimmerboard operator turns the next instrument on "at a glow," or at a very low level. This makes it easy for you to see which one it is. While you are moving to the new position, the designer can go work with the other crew. Continue this way, alternating between crews, until you are done.

• *Take breaks.*

Focusing is hard work and it is easy for the designer on the floor to get wrapped up in the work so make sure that the crew gets to rest every couple of hours.

Once a crew has worked together for a while, they will build up a rhythm and be able to work quickly. Professional crews can focus hundreds of instruments in a single day, but even an amateur crew can become really productive with practice.

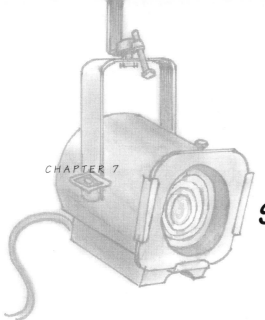

CHAPTER 7

Sound: Audible Atmosphere

Sound is the most mysterious backstage technology. Something about it seems mystical and strange. You speak into a microphone and somehow that sound goes down a cable, goes into some black boxes, changes, gets louder, and comes out of a big speaker over your head. Magic.

People often assume that theatrical technology is more complicated than it really is. People shy away from scenery and lighting because they appear overly complex. People assume there are lots of complicated things they would have to learn when, in fact, the actual process is fairly simple.

With sound, however, the opposite is often true: People underestimate the complication. They don't realize what it takes to produce really good sound. What makes this especially tragic is that good-quality sound is absolutely critical to a successful production. In its ability to stir emotions, sound has no rival. Furthermore, for a budget-conscious theater company, sound can be the financial miracle worker, producing the deepest experience for the least amount of money.

We'll start this discussion with an overview of the entire sound system, known as the **signal chain**. Then we will enter the system at the microphones, explore the mixer, get pumped up by the amp, and head back out into the air through the speakers.

The Signal Chain

"Sound" is something you hear. It is what your mouth produces and your ears pick up. When a sound enters a sound system (through a microphone, for example), it is translated into electrical energy, an energy that goes up and down as the sound gets louder and softer. This energy is called a **signal**. The signal continues through the system until it gets out the other side, where it is changed (in a speaker) from electrical energy back into audible sound. While it is inside the system, however, it is an inaudible electrical force—a signal.

Every sound system is a set of links, a chain that this signal moves through. This **signal chain** has four major links, and every sound system has all of them. Sometimes, one piece of equipment may do more than one thing. In a portable tape player or "boom box," for example, one piece of equipment does all four. Regardless of size or purpose though, all sound systems have all four pieces. They are:

- *A Source:* The sound has to come from somewhere. If the sound is something audible in the outside world, then the source is the microphone used to capture it. If the sound is already recorded, then the source is the tape deck or the CD player that is playing it back. Somehow, the sound must enter the system.
- *Routing:* The signal has to be sent to the proper place at the proper volume. This is done by some sort of **mixer**. On your home stereo, you choose "tape" or "CD player" on the front panel and turn the volume up. Believe it or not, that huge mixer at the back of a theater does not do much more than what you did by hitting "tape" and raising the volume. It just does it better, more quietly and with more options. On a mixer, for example, you can have input from several sources playing simultaneously. Plus, you can set the volume for each one separately. Imagine that your home stereo allowed you to play the CD player and the radio at the same time, while also letting you talk over a microphone, setting a separate volume control for each one, and you can start to see what a mixer does.
- *Amplification:* The signal coming from the source (the microphone, the tape deck, whatever) is not powerful enough to drive the speakers. If you were to plug your CD player directly into your speakers, you would not hear anything. For the signal to be loud enough, you need amplification. On your home stereo, this is usually built into the same unit that routed your signal. In most theater sound systems, however, it is a separate unit that takes the output from the mixer and pumps it up to a strong enough level for the speakers.
- *Output:* There must be some way for the sound to get out of the system so that people can hear it: speakers.

As the signal travels through the sound system, it goes through some changes. Some of the most important changes it goes through are changes in strength, or **signal level**. A signal may appear in various places in the system at various levels. Let's look at the different levels:

- *Mic* (pronounced "mike") *Level:* When you speak into a microphone, the air pressure from your voice causes a small magnet inside the microphone to move, creating a tiny electrical charge. This electrical energy travels down the microphone cable to the mixer. This is an extremely low-level signal, a sort of electronic whisper. This "mic level" signal must be boosted by a **pre-amp** before it is useful to the sound system. That is why you cannot take a microphone and plug it in to the tape input on your stereo and expect it to work. The tape input has no pre-amp. If there is an input on your stereo marked "mic," then that input is equipped with a pre-amp, which boosts the signal up to a higher level. On a mixer, there is generally a switch by each input that allows you to make that input a mic input. Turn it to "mic" if you are plugging in a microphone and the pre-amp will boost the signal properly. If you are plugging in a tape or CD player, however, you should leave it set at . . .

- *Line Level:* Tape decks, CD players, and electronic musical instruments all put out line-level signals, so they do not need to be boosted when they get to the mixer. In fact, line level is the level that all electronic devices use to talk to each other. If you are plugging two electronic devices together, the signal that is traveling down the wire is at line level.

  The mixer may adjust the volume up and down, but the signal level that it puts out remains the same. This distinction may be hard to understand, because sound people sometimes use the terms "level" and "volume" interchangeably. Just remember, both mic level and line level refer to a range of volumes. A high mic level is still less powerful than a low line level. Think of it this way: A high school teacher's salary may fluctuate up and down over the years, but it is still in the range of high school teacher salaries. The CEO of General Motors has a much higher salary, which may also fluctuate up and down. The range of the teacher's salary, however, will never be anywhere near the CEO's. (Then again, the CEO doesn't get three months of summer vacation. Some things are better than money.) In the same way, mic level, though it may fluctuate, will always be lower than line level.

- *Speaker Level:* Once you are done combining the signals and adjusting their volumes, the resulting signal gets sent to the amplifier. Here, it is pumped up to a level that will actually drive the speakers. This level is *way* above either line level or mic level, so you definitely don't want to plug the output of an amp to anything other than a speaker. If a line level signal is a CEO's salary, then speaker level is like the budget of the Pentagon. During the Reagan administration.

Microphones: The Testy Toddlers of Sound

As I said above, the first thing you need in a signal chain is a source. The world of signal sources can be divided into two distinct groups: microphones, and everything else.

If it were not for microphones, sound design would be the easiest dollar in show business. It is not that the rest of the equipment lacks complication. It is simply more predictable. Microphones are unpredictable to the point of rebellious. A sound engineer who can keep microphones happy is a valuable person indeed.

What's the deal? Why are microphones so skittish? Well, first let's explore what they are and how they work, and then talk about how to keep them happy.

At the heart, microphones are simple machines. Sound is created by movement. When an object (like your vocal cords) vibrates, it creates waves of air pressure—sound waves. The greater the pressure, the more volume the sound has. This wave of sound pressure bumps into everything in its way, and if the object it bumps into is delicate or light, the air pressure will cause it to move. In your ear, there is a sensitive membrane called your eardrum. When waves of sound pressure hit it, it vibrates. Those vibrations are transmitted to your brain as electrical impulses. This is how you hear.

A microphone is a mechanical ear. When sounds arrive from the outside world, they move a sensitive membrane called a **diaphragm**. The diaphragm is connected to a magnet. As the diaphragm moves, the magnet turns these vibrations into electrical impulses and sends them to the rest of the sound system.

A microphone is the ear of the sound system. It is how the sound system "hears."

Like your ear, the microphone converts sound from a wave of pressure into a series of electrical impulses. The mixer and the amp amplify the sounds in turn and pump them out to a set of speakers. The problem is, the microphone is innocent and naive, like your basic toddler. And just like a two-year-old who doesn't know Cheerios from rat poison, a microphone will pick up whatever is around and happily put it in its mouth, sending it off to be amplified and broadcast. And, just like a toddler, some of the things that it will pick up are not good for it. If the sound system gets a taste of these unappetizing tidbits, it may respond with anything from persistent static to an ear-splittin', equipment-fryin', I-want-my-mommy wail. It is not without logic that Jimmy Thudpucker (Doonesbury's fictional rock-and-roll star) considered naming his new baby "feedback." If you don't go out of your way to feed your microphone only what is good for it, the whole sound system is going to call you a bad mommy.

Choosing a Microphone

If you have ten dollars, you can buy a microphone and still buy lunch. If you have ten *thousand* dollars, you can buy a different microphone and not have a quarter left for the parking meter. Microphones come in an almost incomprehensible variety, from the inexpensive ones at Radio Shack to the multithousand-dollar ones that studio engineers treat better than their girlfriends. There are microphones specifically designed to amplify guitars, drums, or saxophones. There are mics that attach to your body, to your clothes, and in your hair. There are even mics that sit on the floor and look like mice. Let's talk about what makes them all different.

Dynamic versus Condenser Mics

Dynamic mics are simple and robust: These mics have a lightweight, suspended diaphragm that vibrates when sound hits it. Dynamics are the tougher style of microphone and will put up with more abuse than the other kinds. Live music shows and speeches rely heavily on them and virtually every rock-and-roll show uses them exclusively.

Condenser mics are more sensitive and reproduce sound more accurately, but are less durable and convenient. Condenser mics use a more complicated mechanism that involves generating an electrical field inside the mic. Incoming sound creates disturbances in this electrical field, generating a signal. Because the electrical field is easier to disturb than the physical diaphragm, the mic is more sensitive. Condenser mics also require a power source, so they will usually have a power cord hanging off them. Some condensers can get power through the audio line, through a trick called **phantom power**, but the mixer must be equipped to handle it. Because of their fragile nature, as well as their need for external power, you will find fewer condenser mics backstage.

Low Impedance versus High Impedance

Impedance is a fairly mysterious audio phenomenon that even some professional sound engineers do not understand. They do understand its importance, however. Put simply, impedance is the amount of resistance an electrical circuit puts up to an incoming signal.

Why is impedance significant? Three words: Noise, noise, and noise.

Remember how I said a microphone is like a toddler crawling around stuffing sound into its mouth? Well, one of the unsavory things that it will wrap its chubby little fists around is electrical noise. Lots of backstage gear creates electrical noise: extension cords, lighting equipment, fluorescent lights, even wall sockets. Video monitors are particularly notorious, as are refrigerators. Where there is electricity, there is electrical noise. This noise isn't audible to us, but it can be deafening to a microphone circuit. Remember: Everything the microphone sends to the sound system is going to be amplified; first by the pre-amp, and then by the amplifier. Silent electrical noise will become clearly audible by the time it gets through the amplifier.

Here is a little secret, however. Electrical noise does not create sound pressure, so it is not really the microphone that picks it up. It's the cable. A mic cable operates like a big radio antenna, sweeping up any kind of electrical impulse it can get its hands on. Actually, it is not *like* an antenna, it *is* an antenna (the radio antenna on your car is just a cable), so do not be surprised when passing police cars start broadcasting into your theater.

Audio engineers shut out noise by using **balanced lines**. A balanced line is a microphone cable that sends the signal out on two wires at once, one running from the mixer to the mic and one running from the mic to the mixer. Any noise that the cable picks up gets sent in both directions at once, effectively canceling it out. An **unbalanced line** sends all the noise in a single direction: toward the mixer. Result: The noise enters the sound system.

The catch is, you have to use a low-impedance microphone to use a balanced line. Better-quality mics are always low impedance and it's easy to tell the difference. Look at the plug coming out of the end. A low-impedance mic will have a three-pin **XLR plug** coming out of it. This kind of plug is required for a balanced line, because a balanced line has three wires: one running in each direction, plus a ground wire.

A high-impedance mic will generally have a **phone** (or **quarter-inch**) **plug**. This kind of cable only has two wires, ergo it is unbalanced. Without the balancing effect, the cables will tend to pick up extraneous noise.

Bottom line:

Low impedance = balanced line = XLR plug = better.
High impedance = unbalanced line = ¼" plug = cheaper.

Don't understand it? You are not alone. Electricity boggles a lot of people's minds, including mine. Here's the *real* bottom line:

All mics should run on balanced, low-impedance lines using mics and cables with XLR plugs.

And don't try to beat the rule by putting an adapter somewhere in the stretch of cable between the mic and the mixer. Any piece of unbalanced line will cause you trouble. Maybe not today, maybe not tomorrow . . .

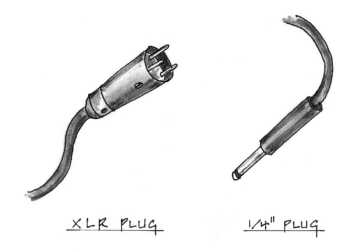

XLR PLUG   1/4" PLUG

Fig. 29. Different kinds of audio plugs

All of this impedance and balanced-line nonsense only applies to microphone lines. Tape decks, CD players, keyboards, and many other kinds of sound equipment can be happily plugged in with quarter-inch plugs on unbalanced lines. Because this equipment operates at line level, it tends to wipe out the noise.

Types of Microphones

Here are some questions to help you decide on a mic, whether you are renting or buying. Knowing the answers to these questions will help you talk intelligently to a salesperson or a sound designer:

- *What are you micing?* Some mics are specially designed to pick up voices. Some are better for instruments. Some are better for picking up sound from a large group, such as an orchestra or a chorus. Some mics are built for specific uses, like **lavaliere mics** that attach to your clothing, or mics that are designed for a particular musical instrument.
- *How much do you want to spend?* The eternal question. You may not have to spend an incredible amount to get what you need, but skimping will come back to haunt you. A run-of-the-mill, solid microphone will cost you at least a hundred dollars to buy, and unless you want to be climbing the walls later, you should put the money out. A dime-store mic can be had for five dollars, but it won't be worth the aggravation. I heavily recommend, if at all possible, that you spend the money for a low-impedance mic.
- *Does it need to be wireless?* Sometimes the mic cord will get in the way of something. Sometimes you just want the performer to have more

mobility. In situations like these, you may want to get a wireless mic. Wireless mics have their own set of problems, though, so read the section on them before you decide.

- *What do you like?* You probably won't be able to answer this one right off, but spend some time listening to mics. Some will pick up sound more accurately than others. Some will produce more low end, or bass sound. Some will produce more high end, or treble sound. If you find a favorite mic, ask for it by name.
- *What are other people using?* I steal other people's secrets whenever possible, and I suggest you do the same. Ask people what they use. Get the benefit of their experience.

Once you know the answer to these questions, you can look at specific types of microphones. When in doubt, however, go for...

The Regular Old Mic

If you don't ask for a specific mic by name, people will assume you want a mic shaped like an ice cream cone. It will not be wireless and it will be designed to stick into a holder or be carried around with the cord trailing behind. The most common R.O.M. is the Shure SM-58. If you are ordering a mic for a podium, an emcee, or a vocal performer, you can just tell the rental company that you want a "SM-58 style" mic and they will know what you mean. A Regular Old Mic.

Wireless Mics

Wireless microphone systems continue to improve and more theaters can now afford to rent or buy them. Wireless mics work by producing a radio signal that is picked up by a receiver offstage or in the back of the house. The receiver then creates the electrical signal that is sent to the mixer. Each microphone requires its own receiver and its own radio frequency. This can get pricey if you have a lot of mics, so many theaters try to get by with just a few.

Wireless mics come in two varieties, **hand-held** and **body**. Hand-held mics are the ones you see on MTV all the time being carried around by rock-and-roll singers. They are now so accepted by audiences that it is surprising to see a performer with a mic cord any more. This is especially helpful in situations when the performer is lip-syncing, or in less polite terms, faking it. It's gotten so you don't even have to run a cord to a lip-syncing performer any more. You just put something approximately mic-shaped in his hand and the audience will believe that it is a wireless mic. Some people don't even realize that a mic cord actually has a purpose. I had a student recently who was singing into a regular wired mic mounted on a podium. Once he got rolling, however, he decided that he needed some freedom to move, so he whipped the mic out of the stand, pulled the cord out of the mic, and dropped it on the floor. Of course, the mic quit working, a fact that confused him mightily.

Even with all the advances in technology, sound designers still lose a lot of sleep over wireless mics. They are battery-operated, so the batteries must be constantly checked and changed. The radio frequencies they use can pick up interference, and it is not uncommon for police and fire department radio transmissions to slip through from time to time. On Broadway, where the use of wireless mics has reached epic proportions, there are now specific frequencies assigned to each show. New show openings can be delayed until another show closes and frees up enough radio channels.

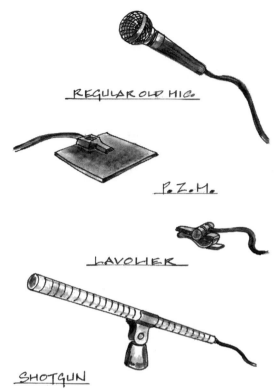

Fig. 30. Different kinds of microphones

Body Mics

The human voice is an incredible instrument, and it is capable of astounding depth and volume when properly trained. Unfortunately, the trend in the modern theater is toward amplifying actors artificially, particularly in musicals. The demands on a modern musical theater performer are huge. Modern pit orchestras are louder than ever before and actors must be able to perform up to eight times a week. Furthermore, as I said in the opening chapter, the modern, film-oriented audience is more demanding about being able to hear the performers clearly. Small wonder that today's actors depend on small, nearly invisible mics mounted on their bodies in order to be heard.

Still, I would like to encourage theater artists everywhere to approach body mics with caution and reluctance. No sound system in the world is a match for the nuance and persuasion of the human voice. Actors should make vocal training a high priority for their careers, and they should seek to develop a voice that will fill a large house without amplification. Though the task is difficult, the rewards are immense.

Having said that, we can begin exploring this rather touchy technology. Wireless body mics were developed to be hidden on actors in musicals. They consist of two pieces: a pencil eraser–sized microphone and a pack of cigarettes–sized belt pack. The two pieces are connected by a cord that runs underneath the costume. The mics are generally concealed in the actor's hair or over the ear. The over-the-ear placement is used if the actor is balding or if a hat is put on or taken off during the show. In a pinch, the mic can be put on the collar of the costume, although designers tend to avoid that one because it may pick up too much of the low frequencies and lead to a sound that is unnatural. They can also sound hollow if two actors are close together. Plus, a good hug will produce an earth-shaking thump, as the mic gets banged around.

Other circumstances might influence mic placement as well. If you are doing *South Pacific*, for instance, you've got to deal with the "I'm Gonna Wash That Man Right Out of My Hair" scene when the character actually washes her hair on stage, precluding any kind of a mic placement above the neck.

Besides the mic itself, you also have to hide the **belt pack**, which contains the batteries and the **transceiver**, the part that actually sends out the radio signal. Despite its name, the belt pack rarely goes on the belt. In a perfect world, the mic is clipped in the hair, the cord runs down the back of the neck, and the belt pack rides in a pocket in the costume in the small of the actor's back. This isn't always possible, however, since a close-fitting or revealing costume may not cover the pack. In fact, belt pack placement may take some ingenuity. Sometimes a costume modification is necessary. Shoulder holsters, which place the pack underneath the arm, are fairly common, as are hip, butt, breast, and, I kid you not, codpiece packs. "Find the Mic" and "Find the Pack" are two games you can play the next time you go see a show with body mics.

Even if you find good places for the mic and the belt pack, you're only halfway home. Heavy physical action, such as a fight or dancing, can work the mic loose. Perhaps the biggest killer of body mics, though, is sweat. The mic itself is quite tiny, and a single bead of sweat will cover it. If this happens, the mic will begin to sound like someone has his hand over it and soon after, it will go out altogether. This is called *sweating out a mic* and there isn't much to be done except get the actor offstage and dry it out or change it.

If you are wearing a body mic and you think your mic is out, you aren't lost. If you can't get offstage, try standing right next to another actor and say your lines into *her* mic. It's not perfect, and it may make for some interesting blocking, but it will get you through a scene.

PZM Mics

PZM stands for "pressure zone modulation," but who cares? Not me. The PZM is specifically designed to sit on the floor, where it picks up not only the sound coming directly from the source, but also the sound that bounces off the floor right in front of it, making the microphone more sensitive. You can grasp this by standing in front of the apron during rehearsal and leaning down within an inch or two of the stage. When you get within an inch of the stage floor, you should hear the actor's voices get louder. While you may have to put up with Indian guide jokes, you will understand why PZMs are so efficient. You often see PZMs lined up across the front of the stage, looking like little black cigar boxes. Sound people sometimes refer to them as "mice." Careful, don't kick them. That's a bad thing.

Lavaliere Mics

Lavaliere, or lav, mics are those black, marble-sized mics you see clipped to people's lapels on talk shows. Lav mics pick up voices quite well, and they are useful in situations where you don't want to see a mic in front of someone, or when you don't want the speaker to be tied to a microphone mounted on a podium. If you are doing video interviews, this is your boy. Meeting planners, take note. Lav mics are great for speakers because they can walk around the stage and gesture up at overheads and so on. For true mobility, get a wireless lav. They still have all of the radio frequency problems, but at least they don't sweat out like the tiny body mics. Of course, they are harder to hide than body mics, but you usually use them in situations where you don't care about concealment anyway.

Shotgun Mics

In placing a mic on the stage, proximity is everything. The best way to pick up any sound is to get close to whatever is making it. If you are not using hand-held or body mics, then you may have to get creative about where you put mics onstage. Sometimes you just can't get a mic close to the source and it must be mounted farther away. In this case, you want a mic that will only pick up what is directly in front of it, rejecting the sounds to either side, even if the target sound is far away. Enter the shotgun mic. It's often used by television camera crews when they can't get close to some-thing they need to record. In the theater, they are used when the only good mic placement is far away: for example, when you have to put a mic high above the stage on an electric pipe. A shotgun mic will tend to reject sounds to the side even if they are closer than the target sound, minimizing unwanted noise.

Even with a shotgun, you may not have the solution. Depending on the quality of the mic, it may only work ten to thirty feet away, and the sound quality may be questionable. At best, this can be a real problem solver. At worst, it's a low-quality stop-gap.

The Backstage Survival Guide to Keeping Microphones Happy

- *Turn the mic on.* Many mics have switches, so if your mic isn't working, look for one. Wired mics have them on the side, wireless on the bottom.
- *Use low-impedance mics on balanced lines.* It will help you to eliminate noise.
- *Do not run mic lines next to power cords, video cables, or lighting equipment.* Ditto.
- *Don't blow into a microphone.* Hey, we don't blow into each other's ears to see if we're listening, do we? If you want to keep sound people happy, don't blow into the mic. It may damage the diaphragm. If you need to check if a mic is on, tap it gently.
- *When speaking into a mic, put your mouth about a hand's width away from the mic and keep it at a constant distance.* The mic's ability to pick up your voice drops radically when you move away, even a few inches. Likewise, don't "eat" the mic. The low frequencies in your voice will be unnaturally amplified and your voice will be distorted. Plus, you'll slobber on it.
- *Don't point the mic at a speaker.* This will create **feedback**. Want to become the least popular person in your theater? Take a live microphone, and stick it right in front of a speaker. If everything is on, you will be rewarded with a deafening squeal that the Brits call "howlround," the Americans call "feedback," and everybody else calls annoying.

Feedback is the audio version of a short circuit. It happens when a sound comes out of a speaker and immediately reenters the sound system through a microphone. These nearly instantaneous round trips cause the sound pressure level to build rapidly on itself until it reaches the crisis point and wango! Feedback.

Besides being painful to listen to, feedback is also not a good thing for equipment. It can fry electronics and blow speakers. When feedback starts, you should deal with it immediately, like *right now*. If you are holding or

Fig. 32. Where feedback comes from

speaking into a mic, turn the mic away from whatever speaker is closest to you. If there are several speakers, or you do not know which way to turn the mic, then just leave it. There is nothing you can do. The person on the mixer will have to solve it. There is a common myth that, if feedback starts, you should put your hand over the mic. *Do not do this.* It will actually make it worse. If you are running the sound system when feedback starts, turn the volume down. Try to figure out which mic is the culprit. If the feedback has just started, you may be able to drop the volume just a little bit and no one will be the wiser. If a feedback cycle really gets going, though, you may have to turn the volume all the way down to break it up.

The most important thing is to listen for it. Except in extreme cases, feedback starts softly, either as a high-pitched whine or as a little ringing sound at the ends of people's words. Listen for it, and back the volume off before the crisis begins. The best way to fight feedback is to have a good *equalizer* in your sound system, as well as somebody who knows how to run it. More about that when we get to "signal processing."

Other Sources: Tape Decks, CDs, and DAT

Microphones are fine for amplifying voices or other "live" sounds but, at some point, everyone wants to play back prerecorded sound. These days, there are two familiar formats (cassette tapes and compact discs), two older formats that are still around (reel-to-reel tape and vinyl LPs), and two new formats that are rapidly growing in usage (DAT tape and samplers).

First, the familiar:

Cassettes are the most common, most readily available, and best understood of all sound playback formats. The blank tapes can be bought in any record store, drug store, or grocery store, and the machine itself is probably sitting in your house. They are easy to operate, and the tapes can be banged around (to a certain extent) and still work. Many nonprofessional companies use them exclusively. Pro companies shy away from them, however. Why? Three reasons: fidelity, editing, and cueing.

Fidelity means truth. In the audio world, we want the tape to be "true" to the original sound, or to have "high fidelity." Cassette tapes are an **analog** recording medium (see sidebar) and that means lower fidelity than a **digital** format, like CDs or digital tape. The real problem, however, is the size and speed of cassette tape.

Digital versus Analog

The difference between analog and digital forms the great divide in the world of audio. Analog means continuous. An analog signal continually varies, up and down, and is not broken into pieces. Your old vinyl record player is analog. The sound was recorded by actually shaping the grooves on the record. The needle slid through the grooves, moving up and down with the tiny hills and valleys, using the continuous movement of the magnet in the needle to "read" the sound. Digital means that the sound is broken down into numbers as it comes into the machine. If the noise gets louder, the numbers get bigger, and vice versa. This conversion process, known as **sampling**, happens very fast. In a CD player, it happens at a rate of 44.1 kilohertz (abbreviated KHz), which means that the computer assigns a numerical value to the sound a little over forty-four thousand times a second. That number is known as the **sampling rate**, and 44.1 KHz is about as fast as it gets. Some people claim that digital recording actually degrades the sound, but they have better ears than I do. Digital media, like CDs, do not suffer from noise problems. Because the music is stored in numerical form, it cannot be harmed by dust or scratches, the way a vinyl record album can. In general, digital media have much higher fidelity than analog.

A piece of analog tape, like the cassette in your tape deck, is composed of microscopic pieces of iron bonded onto a long thin piece of plastic tape. A tape recorder has two little heads that the tape runs over, both of which are basically magnets. As the strip of tape passes over the first head (the recording head), the magnet in the head puts out tiny magnetic charges that correspond to the audio signal. These magnetic pulses make those iron fragments spin around and form a pattern. If the signal is strong, then the magnet turns a lot of iron fragments. If the signal is weak, fewer bits get re-oriented. The pattern is invisible to the naked eye, but it is crystal clear to the other head, the playback head. When you play the tape back over that head, its magnet "sees" the pattern and sends out the corresponding signal. In this way, the sound is "printed" onto the tape in a sort of mosaic of iron fragments, and then "read" when you play it back.

Now imagine you were going to make a mosaic portrait with a bunch of colored chips. If you had a hundred chips, you could probably make an acceptable likeness of someone's face. However, if you had a thousand chips and a much larger space, you could produce a picture that had much greater detail. The same is true of recording tape. The more iron fragments you have to work with, the greater the detail that is possible in reproducing the sound. We get more fragments by making the tape wider, and by passing it over the recording head at a greater speed.

Cassette tape is about one-eighth of an inch wide, and it travels at one-and-seven-eighths inches per second. In the world of audio recording that is the size of an ant and the speed of a tree sloth. Most reel-to-reel tape players that are used in the theater, for example, use quarter-inch-wide tape (twice as wide) running at seven-and-one-half inches per second (four times as fast). The result is eight times as much tape passing over the head every second: eight times as many chips in the mosaic. A studio recording deck might use half-inch wide tape running at fifteen inches per second: thirty-two times as much tape as a cassette. Some decks even use one- or two-inch-wide tape. Cassette audio fidelity, then, is much lower than that of other kinds of tape. For that reason, cassette tapes rarely reproduce all the nuances of music or recorded speech. This loss of fidelity might not be a problem for a low- to medium-budget production, but theaters with high production values may not be satisfied with it.

The second problem with cassettes is **cueing**. In order to start a tape at exactly the right place, sound technicians like to actually mark the starting place on the tape itself. Since cassette tape is hidden inside a case, it is impossible to mark the tape exactly where you want to start. If Darkly Sinister is tying Sally Purebright to the railroad tracks and his next line is "Look, there's the train!" you'd better be able to make the train blow its whistle at the right moment. Otherwise, the actors will be stuck improvising until the train finally arrives, courtesy of an unreliable tape. With reel-to-reel tape, you can actually mark the starting place on the tape. Then, you can line up that mark by the playback head, hit the "play" button, and *Woo, Woooo!* The cue plays immediately.

Accurate cueing is not always important. If you are playing a twenty-minute-long tape with the sound of crashing waves as background ambiance for a scene, then the exact starting place is not critical. Start the tape anywhere, bring up the volume, and—voilà!—splendor on the beach. Other examples include wind, rain, background music, and crowd noise. Cassettes are ideal for this kind of cue because you can get really long tapes (up to sixty minutes without having to flip the tape) for cheap. Cassette tapes also work well for dance because each piece in a show can have its own tape. Cueing is less of a problem, since the dancers just wait for the music to start.

The third problem is editing. Let's say that you have recorded a piece of music to cover a scene shift. You think that the shift will take about a minute, so you find a piece that is a minute and ten seconds long. Unfortunately, the shift crew gets their act together and trims their time to thirty seconds. Now you've got forty seconds more sound than you need. You could just fade the music out whenever the shift is done, but you like how the song ends. What you want is the beginning and the end of the music, but not the middle. If you have a cassette, you are out of luck. With a reel-to-reel tape, however, you can physically cut out the part of the tape that you don't like. Then, you paste the other two ends back together, and—presto!—the music is shorter. Of course, this only works if you can find two places in the music that can be cut together without sounding strange, but this is easier than you think. Radio stations do it all the time.

Once you realize you can do this kind of "cut and paste" editing, you will want to do it all the time. It's like faxing: It is one of those things that you never knew you needed to do until you found out you could. At least, you can do it if you have reel-to-reel tape. This is why reel-to-reel tapes have hung around in the theater long after the rest of the world abandoned them.

In conclusion, the advantages of cassettes are that they are easy to record, convenient to handle, cheap, readily available, and easy to skip from cue to cue if each cue is recorded on a separate tape. The disadvantages: difficult to cue up precisely, lower fidelity, and you can't edit by "cutting and pasting."

Compact Discs, or CDs, have become the medium of choice for distributing commercially produced music. If you purchase music for your show, chances are it will come on a compact disc. You can use a CD player to play back sound for your show, as long as the sound on the CD is exactly the sound that you want. You cannot record onto a CD, so you must take whatever is there.

There are machines that allow you to record on CDs and this may be the best choice for archiving material for long periods or for creating CDs for touring shows. The recorders are still fairly expensive to own and are really not cost-effective for most theaters, especially since many service bureaus will make a CD from your tape for under $50.

CDs produce high-quality, distortion-free sound. A CD is a digital medium (see the "digital versus analog" sidebar) and is therefore free of most kinds of noise. CDs suffer the same cueing problem as cassettes, however. Lower quality CD players have also been known to skip, just like a record player.

In conclusion: The biggest advantage of CDs is high-fidelity sound; most commercially available sound is in this format. The disadvantages: cannot be recorded (except on units specifically designed to do so), difficult to cue up precisely, and lower-quality units can skip.

There is a new CD technology known as the **MiniDisc**™ that is beginning to appear in theaters in increasing numbers. The MiniDisc is smaller than a CD and requires a different kind of player. Made by Sony, the MiniDisc is a recordable compact disc that offers the same fidelity of regular CDs, but allows you to record (and rerecord) your own. You can insert marker points to run cues more precisely and even change the order of cues on the disk. While they have been prohibitively expensive until recently, the prices are dropping to reasonable levels: as of this writing, a good player/recorder can be had for around $300 and a reuseable, seventy-four minute blank disk for around $6. (The manufacturer claims that they can be rerecorded up to one million times.) They also have a write-protect tab like a computer disk to prevent accidental erasures. If you use MiniDiscs and your show is traveling, you will have to carry the player with you, since most theaters won't have them. If you can handle owning the player, though, MiniDisks are a high-fidelity option.

One note about MiniDisks: they are only made by Sony, so the long-term availability of equipment, disks, and service depends on Sony's commitment to the format. If you want to archive material for your biographer, you may want to pick a format that is widely supported.

Reel-to-reel tape decks used to be the most common decks used at the semi-pro and professional levels, but they are quickly being replaced by digital audio tape (**DAT**) and by **samplers**. Reel-to-reels are still useful, though, and even though they require a little more skill to use, they are still a great option for sound playback.

Reel-to-reels solve (or at least improve on) most of the problems you encounter with cassettes. Tapes are larger and move faster so they have higher fidelity. The playback head is visible so the tape can be cued up accurately. The tape itself can be pulled off the reels to be edited. So why are they giving way to the new media? Answer: availability, operator skill, and noise.

Simply put, nobody makes affordable reel-to-reel tape machines any more. There is a bright spot, however. Right now, many recording studios are upgrading to digital equipment, so lots of older analog stuff (like reel-to-reel machines) is being tossed, creating a wave of useful equipment for theaters.

The lack of common usage means that reel-to-reel users often have trouble finding recording tape and other supplies. As of this writing, only professional audio stores and Radio Shack still carried these items.

Reel-to-reel requires a certain amount of expertise to operate. It is not rocket science. Anyone can do it, but it is still harder than pushing "record" or "play" on a cassette. Because all the cues are strung together on one tape, you cannot switch quickly from one cue to another if, for example, the director decides to back up or skip to another part of the show during rehearsal. Reel-to-reel decks do have counters, but they can become useless if you have been doing a lot of cutting and pasting, or if cues have been rearranged. Sometimes you get stuck doing a "hunt and peck" routine. With cassettes, you just pull out whatever tape you need and drop it in the machine. You may have to rewind a lengthy cue, but it is a lot easier than hunting through a long reel-to-reel tape for a particular cue.

During one of my college summers, I worked at a summer theater that was doing *Ten Little Indians,* the Agatha Christie murder mystery in which ten people are each accused of a terrible crime and then assassinated, one by one, by a maniacal killer. The key to the whole show is a recording of a mysterious voice that the butler plays for all the assembled guests. This recording (played by the butler in response to written instructions by a mysteriously absent "host") reads off the entire litany of crimes to the assembled guests.

"Doctor Edward Armstrong," booms the recording, "You killed Louisa Mary Clees! Miss Jane Hampshire, you caused the death of Jonathan Smith . . ." and so on, until everybody has been accused. Then, after a moment of stunned silence, the recording ostensibly starts over and plays for a moment until the horrified butler runs over and shuts it off.

Of course, the record player on stage was a fake and the actual recordings were on a reel-to-reel tape machine in the control booth. In order to create the cues, we made two recordings: one full-length rendition with all the accusations, and one rendition with only the first one, which we would play when the recording was supposed to "start over." We figured that we didn't need two full-length ones since the butler would "shut off" the second one right away.

The problem began when I finished playing the previous cue. It was a long wind and storm cue that was much too long for the scene. When the storm scene was over, I always fast-forwarded the tape up to where the "accusation" was. Somehow, I glanced away from the machine just as the beginning of the cue went past. When the next cue came by, I stopped the tape and set it up to play the cue. The *second* accusation cue. The one with only one accusation. And nothing else.

"Doctor Edward Armstrong," boomed the recording, "You killed Louisa Mary Clees . . ." and *stopped*. Silence on the stage. Nobody moved. I look down at the tape and saw a totally different cue coming up. I realize. Wrong cue.

I did what every young theater technician would do: I panicked. I hastily rewound the tape and hit the first leader I saw. Same cue again.

"Doctor Edward Armstrong," boomed the recording, "You killed Louisa Mary Clees . . ." Silence. The actors were beginning to panic. The play is *based* on this cue.

Now I'm frantic. I desperately rewound the tape again as the actors begin to shuffle around on stage, glancing around and trying to imagine how to get out of this one. Finally, the unlucky actor playing Dr. Armstrong looks up at the booth.

"But really . . ." he said with plaintive British accent, "I can't be the *only* guilty one."

At which point, I finally played the proper cue and the show went on. I had learned my lesson: Always mark the leader of a cue and always *check it* before you play it.

Another problem with reel-to-reel tape is breakage. The tapes do occasionally break, especially at the points where they have been edited. To prevent this, buy the shortest possible tape. The way tape companies make longer-playing tapes without making the reels bigger is by making the tape itself thinner. Thus, tape from a two-hour reel is more prone to break than tape from a thirty-minute reel.

Finally, there's the noise, and I don't mean over the sound system. When you push "play" on a reel-to-reel machine, you can hear a big "*ka-chunk*" as the recording heads click into place over the tape. This noise prevents the use of reel-to-reels outside of an enclosed booth. This can be a pain in the rear because the best place to put a sound person is out in the audience where he can hear the show. If you are using a reel-to-reel tape deck, you have to put the sound person in a booth where he cannot hear, or have two people—one to set the sound levels out in the house and one to run the tape deck in the booth.

So, in conclusion: The advantages of reel-to-reel are "cut and paste" editing, precise cueing, and higher fidelity than cassettes. The disadvantages: tape stock is not readily available, it's harder to skip around, tapes can break, and the loud noise of heads engaging.

Vinyl LPs, what we use to call "records," have all but disappeared from the live stage, except for those low-fidelity holdouts—nightclub disk jockeys. You might use records if you need something that was recorded commercially before the early eighties, but I do not recommend using them in live situations. If the records see any amount of usage, they will develop surface damage and attract dust that will add noise to the sound. They can skip and jump and they are hard to cue up precisely. If you do have an older recording, rerecord it onto one of the tape formats for use in your show. Of course, you cannot record onto an LP.

DJs still like vinyl records because they can mess with the tempo of the music. Spin the turntable more slowly and the music slows down. Spin it faster, and the music speeds up. A DJ will have two turntables so one can be playing while he is setting up the other one. You will see him in the DJ booth with headphones on, adjusting the speed of the turntable so that the next song will come on at the same tempo as the one that is currently playing. By adjusting the speeds of the turntables, the DJ can keep the crowd dancing at the same boogie tempo throughout the night. If the DJ is skilled, the crowd may not even notice when one record ends and another begins.

In conclusion: the advantages of LPs are that older commercial material may only be available in this format and the speed of playback can be adjusted. The disadvantages: noisy, impossible to record on, and they tend to skip.

Digital audiotape, more commonly known by its acronym **DAT**, is swiftly supplanting reel-to-reel in most professional and semi-pro applications. DAT tape looks like a smaller version of a cassette tape and, in fact, it operates the same way, except that it stores sound in a digital format. Digital tape produces higher fidelity than any kind of analog tape. If there is a hiss in your system, it isn't coming from the DAT. They produce so little noise in the sound system that they can be considered silent. Furthermore, they don't make a loud noise when you start them up, so they can be set up outside an enclosed booth.

DAT is as easy to use as a cassette. Simply load the tape, push "play" and you're on. Tape is available at stereo stores and pro audio dealers for about twice the price of an analog cassette. Precise start points can be marked electronically on the tape so exact cueing is possible. The DAT also accesses cues much faster than any other kind of tape, so you can keep an entire show on one tape and still skip around during rehearsal. It also starts up faster then a reel-to-reel when you hit the "play" button so it's easier to start the cue at exactly the right moment. The tape is still enclosed so you can't cut and paste it like a reel-to-reel, but all in all, DAT offers the easiest use of any tape medium.

The primary disadvantage of DAT players is cost. Currently, decent DAT players are hovering around a $1,000, versus about $300 for a good cassette player. Expect costs to drop, however, and even if they don't, most theaters with a commitment to good sound quality should give them a look.

In conclusion: the advantages of DAT are the highest fidelity, it's easy to locate cues, the fastest-engaging tape, and silent operation. The disadvantages: machines are more expensive and it's impossible to "cut and paste."

Samplers are the newest addition to the playback arsenal and perhaps the most difficult to talk about because, in a sampler, there is no "tape" where the sound is recorded. A sampler takes the incoming signal and, like a DAT, changes it into a set of numbers. Unlike a DAT, however, it does not record those numbers on tape—it sends them into a computer memory. This process of listening to a sound and converting it into a digital form is called "sampling." The computer "samples" the sound every fraction of a second and assigns a number to what it hears, storing a numerical record of the rising and falling pitches of sound.

Lest you think that this method of recording sound is imprecise, you should know that the sampling process is happening extremely quickly. A good sampler can do it over forty thousand times per second. This value is known as the **sampling rate** and it determines the fidelity of the recording. The higher the sampling rate, the more values that are being stored per second, and the better the sound quality of the recording. The fact that cues are held in an electronic memory (instead of on tape) is a sampler's best and worst feature. The cues can be accessed instantly, in any order, but you can only have as many cues as you have memory in the computer.

Sound tends to eat up memory fairly quickly. As an example, a sound approximately twelve seconds long, when sampled at a fairly high rate could use up to a megabyte (one million bytes) of memory space. This entire book that you are reading takes up about a megabyte on my computer. Think about that for a moment. You are holding the same amount of information as twelve seconds of high-quality sampled sound. Gives you new respect for your ears, doesn't it? Of course, we can sample at a slower rate so it takes up less memory space, but then we start to lose sound quality, just as when we ran the analog tape at a slower speed.

High-quality samplers will have lots of memory (up to sixty-four megabytes as of this writing), but we're still not talking about a machine where you want to record two minutes of scene-change music. Samplers are best used for moments when you need a short sound to happen in exactly the right place.

Samplers are generally attached to a piano-like keyboard. This is because they were first created to play back samples of musical notes, and they still do that impeccably. It is possible to get, for example, samples of saxophone notes. By plugging these samples into the keyboard, a keyboardist can imitate a saxophone player. Samples exist for strings, guitars, woodwinds, sitars, you name it, so a keyboardist with a sampler has an incredible range of instruments at her command. What matters to us, however, is that the sampler can assign any sound to any note. Imagine the sound of a dog barking coming out when you hit a note on the keyboard. Assign the same sound to different keys and hit them all at once. Presto! a pack of dogs outside the door. Assign a wind sound to another note and a crack of thunder to a third and you are ready for a Sherlock Holmes mystery. Samplers can also create loops so that the sound of the wind starts over every time it gets to the end. Sometimes, a sound designer will just tape down that key and the sound of wind will continue as long as necessary.

With all of these sounds assigned to different keys on the keyboard, it is easy to understand the flexibility of a sampler. Want a sound? Hit a key. Want the same sound again? Hit the key again. No waiting to access the cue. No pause before the sound happens. No clanking heads engaging. Just sound. Right where you want it. Samplers are best when timing is critical. I did a show once where an actor mimed opening a large barn door. Since the cue had to start precisely when he reached out his hand, we put the cue on a sampler. When his hand grasped the air where the handle would be, the operator hit the key and that was that.

Samplers are also extremely useful when you are putting cues together, whether or not you decide to use the sampler to play them back during the show. You could, for example, take all of those "Hound of the Baskervilles" sounds I mentioned above, put them all on a sampler, and then mix and match, trying different combinations until you get one you like. Then, record those sounds onto the tape and use it for the show. The possibilities are huge. If you ever get to use a sampler, be careful. The addiction factor is high.

So, to conclude: the advantages of samplers are the instant access to cues, better control over timing and duration of cue, tremendous flexibility and possibilities for "tricks," and an excellent tool for building cues. The disadvantages: limited sampler memory can only record short cues and costs are high.

Mixers: Telling the Sound Where to Go

Mixers are among the most visually daunting objects in technical theater. Their considerable width, carpeted with buttons and knobs, gives them a menacingly complicated appearance. I think technicians get into the fact

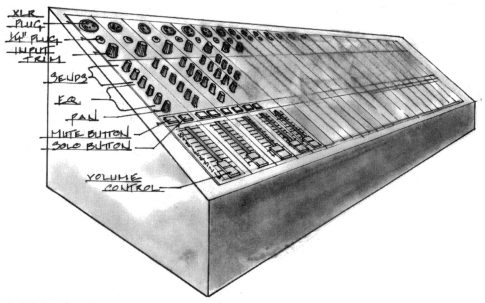

XLR
PLUG
1/4" PLUG
INPUT
TRIM

SENDS

EQ.

PAN

MUTE BUTTON
SOLO BUTTON

VOLUME
CONTROL

Fig. 32. A typical mixer

that the mixer looks so, well, "technical." But let's face it: A mixer is just a big freeway interchange where sound enters from all different directions, gets shunted around, and gets spit out in new directions. Whatever else you forget about mixers, remember this, a mixer just takes in sound, reorganizes it, and sends it out somewhere else. That's all.

Most mixers are made up of four parts: **input modules**, **equalization**, **auxiliary sends** and **returns**, and **output channels**. Big words for simple things. Actually, equalization and auxiliary sends are contained within the input module, so let's do that first. Then we'll do the returns and the outputs. This section is best enjoyed if you are sitting in front of a mixer, so go sit in the sound booth, if you have one.

Input Modules

Any source of sound that we have mentioned so far can be fed into a mixer. A mixer has a number of places to plug things in—inputs. In fact, the first way in which we usually describe a mixer is by saying how many inputs it has. A "sixteen-channel" mixer has sixteen places to plug things in. A microphone would take up one of those places. A tape deck or CD player would take up two places, since these items put out a stereo signal. Stereo signals need two inputs, a left and a right.

Looking at a mixer, we see that the input modules are laid out in columns, each column containing a set of identical controls. One of the reasons that mixers have so many knobs is that each of its functions is duplicated for each input module. Each input module may only have six knobs (for example), but multiply that by sixteen inputs (for example) and suddenly you have a forest of ninety-six knobs.

The controls for each module are laid out in a vertical column. You can think about the sound entering the module at the top and flowing downward. There are exceptions to this idea, but let's not muddy the pool.

An input module begins with an input where you plug in the incoming signal. This input may be on the top, front, or back of the mixer. This input may be a quarter-inch plug or an RCA plug (for unbalanced input) or, for a microphone input, it may be an XLR plug (balanced input).

After the sound enters the module, the first thing it meets is an input level control, also known as the **input trim**. Remember when I said that there were different levels of signal—mic level and line level? The input trim (sometimes called "input gain") allows you to boost a mic signal up to where the mixer can use it. This control may just be a switch between "line" or "mic," or it may be a rotating level control that you adjust. If you are feeding the mixer a mic-level signal, you turn the input level up. Turn it down for a line-level signal.

After going through the input control, the signal hits the **equalization**, or **EQ** controls, if there are any. EQ is just like the treble and bass controls on your stereo. Mixers may have two controls, one for the high end (treble) and one for the low end (bass), or they may have three or four, all to shape the color of a sound, boosting it or cutting it wherever necessary.

After EQ, it's time for the **sends**. Remember how I said that a mixer is a traffic interchange? Well, these are the first exits. A sound engineer will often want to send some sound somewhere else, like into an effects processor, to mess with it, or a monitor system, so people backstage can hear the sound. For these purposes (and many more), the engineer opens up an "exit" (a **send**). It's important to understand that turning on a send does not mean that all the sound goes out that way and none of it continues down the input module. In that sense, it isn't like traffic at all. Making some of the sound turn off the freeway doesn't reduce the amount that continues onward. Then again, traffic seems like that sometimes, too.

The next thing that the signal usually encounters is some sort of routing that tells it which **output** it is destined for, that is, which way it is going to exit the mixer. Depending on how many outputs you have, there may be several switches and knobs here, or only one. There might be buttons for various Master or Submaster outputs, but no matter what it says, it's basically just telling the sound which way is out. One control that is common in this area is a **pan** control. A mixer is usually sending out a stereo signal, and a pan control tells the sound which side of that stereo signal the sound is going to. The pan knob might be turned all the way to the right (known as "hard right"), which means that the sound is only going out the right channel, or it might be set all the way the other way ("hard left") which means that it is going entirely to the left. Or, it may be set anywhere in between, including right in the center. In this last case ("panned center"), the sound would go equally to the left and right sides.

Two other controls that may be found in this area are **mute** and **solo**. Mute simply turns this channel off. Solo turns every channel off *except* this one. Solo is often used during setup to hear a channel by itself in order to set volume, EQ, or search out a problem. In most cases, the solo switch doesn't affect the main output, only a monitor signal that the engineer is listening to.

Way down at the bottom of the module is the volume control. This is usually a long slider.

Auxiliary Returns

Let's go back to that signal that took the exit marked "send." As I said, one use of a send is to feed sound to an **effects processor** (see "Effects Processing" below).

By plugging a cable into the opening marked "send" on the back of the mixer, we can connect that signal to the sound processor. Then, we take another cable out of the processor and back to the mixer where we plug it into the socket marked "return." We have now created an **effects loop**. The sound travels from the input module, out the send, through the processor, and back to the mixer through the return.

When the signal gets back, however, it does not go back to the input module. Rather, it goes into the main outputs along with the other sounds that are coming directly from the input modules. A signal coming from a send does not necessarily have to go to an effects processor, or return to the mixer. It may go to a tape player or a monitor, for instance, and never return at all. Every sound setup is unique, and mixers are designed to be flexible. Remember, the mixer is just a big audio cloverleaf.

Effects Processing: Sound Sculpting

Besides simply amplifying sound, or recording it, sound equipment is capable of performing a dizzying variety of tricks on the sound itself before it spits it out.

Ever record yourself talking, singing, or playing an instrument and then wonder why it doesn't sound as good as a recording on the radio or an album? Of course, the pros record on higher-quality microphones and tape decks, but another big reason is that professionally recorded sounds are being *processed*. If you want to experience a quick example of processing, try listening to your local public radio station for a while, preferably an NPR newscast or something like that. Once you have gotten used to the quality of the voices, switch the dial over to your local rock-and-roll station and listen to the DJ. Sound different? It should. The rock-and-roll DJ's voice is being processed to make it more dynamic, richer, and more in line with the voices on the records he is playing. NPR processes announcers' voices as well, but in more subtle ways.

Processing comes in various forms, discussed below.

Reverb

If you've sat in a large church or a well-designed concert hall recently, than you've experienced reverb in its natural state. **Reverb** is just sound bouncing around in a space—caroming off hard surfaces and coming at your ears from all directions. The more places it has to go, and the fewer absorbent places that exist in the room, the longer the sound bounces around. We refer to the span of time that the sound bounces around as the **reverberation time**. The reverb time is the time that it takes a sound to completely die out in a particular space. A good theater, where the clarity of the spoken word is all-important, will have a relatively short reverb time—from one to two seconds. A concert hall, where we are more concerned about the richness of the sound than the intelligibility of speech, should have a longer reverb time, two and a half seconds or more. Large churches will have reverberation times of four, five, even ten seconds.

In the early days of recording, it was common to have a "reverb room" in the studio. This was a room with a speaker at one end and a microphone at the other. Sound was played into the room through the speaker and rerecorded through the other microphone. In this way, sound engineers added the natural reverberations of a space to the voices. These days, this effect can be recreated electronically by an **effects processor**. The sound is fed into the processor from the mixer and the circuitry inside the box processes it, adding reverb to it. When the sound comes out, it sounds as though the original sound were created in another kind of space. Most processors let you choose what kind of space you would like to imitate, both in size and quality. It might have options like "small room," "ensemble hall," or "concert stage," as well as "warm," "dark," or "rich." By adjusting the processor, you can choose what kind of reverb you want. Want more reverb time? Dial up a larger room. Want to make a voice sound cold and distant? Try the "dark" setting. Some boxes provide literally hundreds of options like "Wood Concert Hall," and "Empty Gymnasium." It can get pretty fun. By altering the balance between the "dry," unprocessed sound and the "wet," processed sound, the engineer can decide how heavy to make the effect. Too dry, and the effect may go unnoticed. Too wet, and the performer will be singing in Carlsbad Caverns.

An effects processor is something every medium-size-and-up theater should own. It will help you produce better sound effects tapes as well as make offstage voices sound more interesting. Other organizations may also choose to own them in order to make their sound systems more flexible. Rock-and-roll bands can't live without them.

Of course, no processor can approach the acoustics of a large concert hall or, best of all, an old-style cathedral. Many classical artists take advantage of these spaces and record their albums there. Please attend these concerts so that you can bask in the best thing the Laws of Physics ever did for music—rich, natural reverb. For some reason, modern church designers always put in carpets. From a musical perspective, that's a sin.

Equalization

Anyone who has ever made a tape at home and then played it back in the theater will understand the need for **EQ**. The tape sounds different in different spaces. Acoustically speaking, every room in the world is different, depending on the textures it has (carpets, furniture, paneling, and so on) as well as the shape of the room itself. Every room will kill certain frequencies and accentuate others.

But wasn't there EQ in the mixer? Yes, there was, but only a few controls. A true equalizer is a separate unit that lives outside the mixer. It has a long row of sliders or knobs that increase or decrease the amount of sound at each frequency. It takes time and experience to set up, not to mention a certain amount of trial-and-error. It also takes a sharp-eared technician. Once the sound is optimized for a space, you should put a lock on that EQ and leave it forever, or at least until you get different carpets.

Besides this kind of colorization, EQ also provides an important function in getting rid of feedback. The shape of the room will cause some frequencies to feed back more than others. Because EQ allows you to decrease those specific frequencies, it can allow you to push the overall volume up higher. Live music depends heavily on EQ for this reason.

Compression and Limiting

Ever go to an amateur night and listen to a bunch of people who don't really know how to use a microphone? As they sing or speak, their voices may get louder or softer. They may pull the mic away from their mouth, or get it too close, causing the sound to die away or boom out like Moses. An overexcited performer might yell into the mic, causing the sound system to overload and distort. Compression and limiting help audio people to deal with these problems.

A **compressor** and a **limiter** are two different versions of the same thing. Both devices follow the sound level and, when it climbs above a certain volume, pull it down. Compressors use a ratio to determine how much to reduce the sound. If they are set at 4:1, then they drop the volume one decibel for every four decibels it is over the limit. A limiter is less subtle: You give it a volume level and it prevents the sound from ever getting louder than that level—an audio "line in the sand." Because they reduce the really high sound levels, compressors and limiters help guard against overloads. This means you can bring the overall volume up without worrying about distortion ruining your speakers. The softer voices will be more audible and the louder voices won't be so annoying.

Because they are so similar in function, compressors and limiters are often built into the same unit.

Amplification: We're Going to Pump You Up

Having been pre-amplified, routed, and processed, our heroic sound wave now exits the mixer and heads for the gym to build some real muscle.

Remember, up to this point, the sound has only existed at mic or **line level**. While these levels are good enough for the electronics in your system, they are not strong enough to really create audible sound. Therefore, the sound has to go through some kind of **amplifier** before the audience can hear it.

Amplifiers come in lots of different sizes but only two common types: **mono** and **stereo**. A mono amp has one input and one output. A stereo amp has two separate inputs and two separate outputs. In fact, it's really like having two separate amplifiers. The manufacturers just package them in one box for convenience.

When you play an album on your home stereo, the sound going to the left and right speakers is slightly different because studio engineers go to great lengths to make it that way. After all, you have two ears, and by giving those ears slightly different sound, the engineers can give the illusion that all the instruments you are hearing are located at different places in space. Therefore, every home stereo is . . . um, stereo.

In the theater, however, this does not work and here's why:

In order for stereo imaging (the two-dollar name for this effect) to work, the output from the two speakers has to reach your ears at approximately the same time and volume. This is not too hard in your living room: Your speakers are about the same distance from you most of the time. In the theater, however, the vast majority of the audience is not sitting dead center in the middle of the auditorium where both speakers would be the same distance away. Most of them will hear one speaker much more strongly than the other, and the stereo imaging will be lost. For this reason, *most sound in the theater is mono, not stereo.* This means that you will not have to have two separate audio signals, even if you have speakers on both sides of the stage.

You might still need a stereo amp, however. Since theater speakers are quite large, each speaker needs its own amplifier. You can use one side of a stereo amp for one speaker and the other side for the other speaker. Just make sure that they are both getting the same signal.

A stereo setup is also useful for sound effects. Directors often want an effect to appear to be coming from one side of the stage or the other. Having a stereo setup allows you to send part of the audio signal (a car starting, a barking dog, gunshots, whatever) to one speaker and not the other.

One final note about keeping your system happy:

When turning your system on, always turn the amp on *last.* When turning your system off, always turn the amp off *first.* Other kinds of electronic equipment, such as mixers, decks, and processors, can send dangerous "pops" through the system when they turn on or off. Making sure the amp is off when this happens will prevent damage to your speakers. So, remember:

Amplifiers are last on, first off.

You can remember this by thinking of your amp as the most dangerous element in the system. Because it is the most dangerous (at least to the other equipment), it should be on the least amount of time.

Speakers: The Bottom Line

If you are buying a new sound system, my advice is to be economical everywhere *except* the speakers. The quality of your sound system is more dependent on your speakers than anything else.

Here's how speakers work: In your speakers there is a curved piece of cardboard-like material, called the **speaker cone**. This cone has a magnet attached to it. Remember the magnet in the microphone—the one that moved and created an electrical signal? This one works the same way, only backwards. Instead of the magnet moving the electricity, here the electricity moves the magnet. This magnet has to be a lot bigger than the one in the microphone since it has to move the cone enough to create large waves of pressure in the air: sound waves.

Speakers have one statistic that you should be aware of: **resistance**. Resistance describes what kind of opposition the signal is going to run into when it gets to the speaker, and it is measured in **ohms**. There are two common kinds of speaker: 8 ohms and 4 ohms (occasionally you might find a 2-ohm speaker). All you need to know is that the resistance of the speaker should match the amp. Your amp will probably say on the back which kind of speaker it is calibrated for. Look for something that says: "100 watts into 8 ohms" or something like that. If the resistance is mismatched, it can cause a variety of problems, some of them potentially damaging.

If you are plugging in speakers, make sure they are "in phase." The positive terminal on the amp must be attached to the positive terminal on the speaker. Same with the negative terminal. Plus sign to plus sign and minus sign to minus sign. If you are not sure which is which, try it one way or the other. Hooking up speakers out of phase will not damage them—they will just sound bad. The most common symptom is a lack of bass. If your system uses quarter-inch plugs for the speakers, you're in luck. They only go together one way.

One final thing about speakers: Proper speaker placement within the space is critical. Speakers are "directional": they are made to throw sound in a particular direction. High-end signals, like flutes, cymbals, and violins, are more directional than low-end ones. The high-end signals will go in whatever direction the speaker is pointed and they will stop when they hit a wall. The low-end signals will go in all directions, regardless of which way the speakers are pointed, and they tend to seep through walls. That is why, when the guy in the apartment upstairs turns on his stereo, you only hear the bass. Bass notes are less directional. Take a moment to notice the effect before you ask him to turn it down. You might get peace and quiet by just asking him to turn down the bass a little. Worth a try, anyway.

Some lucky theaters have speakers specifically designed for very low-end sounds. These are called **subwoofers** and they are wonderful for creating rich, full sound. Because low-end sounds are nondirectional, you can put a subwoofer anywhere in the theater and every one will hear it. Dance clubs almost always have subwoofers—it sends the beat right into your bloodstream.

Proper speaker placement is also critical to avoid feedback. Try not to put speakers where they will pump sound into microphones. It is not always that simple, however. If you have lots of speakers and/or lots of microphones, you may get stuck with some feedback-prone positions. For another thing, singers in bands want to be able to hear themselves, so it is necessary to install speakers, or **monitors**, pointing directly at them, which means directly at the microphones. Sound engineers use equalization to deal with these problems. If you have consistent feedback, try adjusting your speaker placements.

Since theater sound is generally mono, you do not have to worry about getting a good stereo setup, but you do want the sound to appear to come from the direction of the stage. It usually isn't practical to put the speakers right in front of the performers, however, so there is some trickery involved.

The most common trick is to put the speakers directly over the stage. We determine the location of a sound by hearing it arrive at our two ears at different times. (Our brain is capable of distinguishing differences as little as three-thousandths of a second, which is the time it takes for a sound to travel from one side of our head to the other.) Since our ears are on the sides of our head, not the top or the bottom, we distinguish left and right much better than up and down. If you have ever stood on a balcony over someone's head and tried to get his attention, you know what I mean. You keep shouting his name and he keeps looking around, trying to figure out where you are. "No, you ninny, look *up!*" you shout, and round and round he goes, trying to figure out where you are. It's not his fault. Our ears have evolved to find things that are on the same level as we are. I guess saber-tooth tigers didn't drop down from above very often.

By putting the speakers directly over the stage, then, we fool the audience a little. It's difficult to distinguish between sounds coming from straight in front and those coming from a higher position.

From the microphone to the mixer, through the processors, the returns, the outputs, the amps, and the speakers, all in thousandths of a second. It is a strange and wonderful journey.

Making Tapes for the Show

There are few skills more useful for a theater artist than the ability to make a good show tape. It might be a rehearsal tape for a dance company, a mood-creating tape for a theater rehearsal, a presentation tape for a sales proposal, or just an idea tape passed between two artists. Since sound is so emotionally evocative, the ability to carry a piece of it around is precious indeed. It is also useful to note that the *quality* of that recording will have more of an effect on the listener than you might think, regardless of the content. You need look no further than the shopping channels to prove that people are swayed by clear, consistent presentation.

If you do not know how to make a tape from your home stereo system, it is time to learn. Since they all vary, I cannot get too deep into the details here, but the principles are basically the same for all systems. In fact, the principles are basically the same for all kinds of tapes in all kinds of systems so, by understanding how to do it in your living room, you are well on your way to understanding how they do it in megadollar sound studios.

The Backstage Survival Guide to Making a Show Tape

- *Get your source material and your destination tape.* Your source material is whatever sound you want to be on the tape: CDs, vinyl records, other tapes, a microphone to record someone talking, whatever. The destination tape is the tape that you are recording onto—the one that will be used in the theater.

- *Create a signal path.* Somehow the sound will need to get from where it is now (the source), to where you want it to be (the destination). This may be as simple as flipping the dial on your stereo to PHONO, or it may be more complicated, particularly if there is more than one source involved. If you have more than one source, you will need to plug all of the sources into a mixer in order to create a single source. Then, you plug the output of the mixer into the input of the tape deck. *It is not possible with a standard home stereo to combine two different sources.* It is also not possible to add something to an existing tape without erasing what is already there. If you want to combine two different sources or add something to an existing tape, you need a mixer.

- *Play the source material.* Turn on the record player, start the CD, speak into the microphone, do whatever you are going to do on the tape. While you are doing it, watch the meters on the tape deck so you can . . .

- *Set a level.* Adjust the inputs of the tape deck so that the levels peak at about 3db. The stronger the signal you record, the more it will rise above the inherent noise on the tape. This is called increasing the **signal-noise ratio**. Translation: If you record a strong signal, you don't have to play back the tape as loud, and therefore, you won't hear the hiss of the tape as much.

- *Decide how you want to begin and end the recording.* Remember, you cannot add something later without erasing what you have recorded, which means that, once the tape is recorded, you cannot make the music crossfade into something else. You can start the next recording after the first one is finished, of course, but there will have to be a break between the two programs.

    You also cannot make something fade out on a tape after you have recorded it. If you want the fade to be on the tape, you have to put it there when you are recording. Actually, I almost never record a fade out or a fade in on a theatrical tape. It is usually better to have control of it during the performance. Of course, there are reasons to record fades. Maybe you are making a tape for the car and you just want to have a song fade out. Perhaps you have several songs in a row for your slide presentation and you want the middle one to fade out before the last one starts. The point is, you have to make those decisions at this point.

- *Stop the source material.* Rewind, reset, go back to the top.
- *Set the destination tape at the beginning.* Most cassettes have a non-recordable "leader" at the beginning. Use a pencil or your fingernail to advance the tape to the beginning of the brown recordable part. This is an important step. If you do not do this, you will not record the first five seconds of your program. It is particularly important to start a recording at the exact beginning of a tape for a theater cue. You want the operator to be able to set the tape up at the end of the leader, push "play" and hear the cue *right now*.
- *Push "Record."* And then . . .
- *Play the source material.* Start the tape, play the CD, start talking, whatever.
- *Push "Stop"* when you're done.
- *Check your work.* Rewind and find out if it really happened. Don't ever, ever, ever play a tape for an audience if you have not listened to it ahead of time. I would tell you all the horror stories I know about people who did not follow this advice, but I don't have the space.

CHAPTER 8

Properties: Research, Detail, and Crafts

Unlike most things in the theater, prop work is most often done by individuals. Carpenters, electricians, riggers—all these people tend to work in crews, but props are most often created by people working solo. **Props** are chosen (or invented) by the **scenic designer** or **prop designer**, working alone; realized by a craftsperson or located by a researcher, working alone; placed by a single prop person backstage; and, if they are handled during the show, tend to be handled by a single actor.

Prop work is composed of three distinct types of work, and as such, is populated by three fairly distinct types of people. It's worth it to take the time to recognize which type your prop person is. Of course, many prop people are a combination of more than one type and every now and then, you meet someone who embodies all three (*hire her!*), so take these definitions loosely. They are offered here because of the intimate, one-on-one nature of prop work, as well as the necessity of getting to know the people in this department on a personal basis. The following are not individual job titles, just some general personality types that you will likely encounter.

The Artisan

Some people have a gift for creation and imitation. These people take great joy in mastering long lists of materials and techniques while devising new and previously unheard-of ways to construct anything the designer can invent. This process is not so much mental struggle as mental exercise to them, and they generally have flexible minds: able to see peas as pearls, pop tops as chain mail, and washing machine agitators as royal crowns. They are problem-solvers, more often discouraged by bureaucratic obstacles than overwhelmed by an unsolved design problem. They can make anything of the free junk most folks throw in a dumpster. And the best ones can do it by Thursday. These people are often called "crafts" people and they are best called in to construct particular pieces, such as fantasy props or furniture.

The Detailer

Look in the dictionary under the words "mind-numbing detail" and you will find the reference: "see also: props." There are shows in the world without a lot of props, but don't hold your breath waiting for one to come along. Someone has to coordinate the sheer numbers of props, particularly in shows with complicating factors such as real food, animals, multiple scene changes, or trick props that have to light up, explode, break, or fire on cue. Fortunately, there are people in the world who take joy in making sense of this kind of detail. These people live with lists on legal pads and ballpoint pens hung around their necks. They will not rest until their clipboard has a long list of check marks and completed quests. The telephone is a shrine to them. They know how to combine errands to save time. They can read a map. These people are invaluable in heavy prop shows and low-budget theaters that must do a lot of borrowing and begging.

The Researcher

All propmasters inevitably collect a long list of antiques stores, junk shops, and bargain stores where they find many of the pieces that they need for shows. A true researcher goes even further, mentally (or physically) cataloging thousands of pieces all over town, taking joy in searching out the perfectly odd prop. For her, prop work is a quest—a journey into a wilderness of goofy, unexpected, hidden treasures. She is inventive with her sources, and will call places you and I would never think of. I once watched Jolene Obertin, the prop coordinator at Seattle Rep and a true researcher, find a ten-inch-high scale model of the Statue of Liberty in two minutes flat without leaving her desk. She got it on her second phone call—to the gift shop at (where else?) the Statue of Liberty in New York City. (They ship, for a small fee.)

So, now that we've met the prop staff, let's get down to business.

Making the Prop List: When to Buy, Borrow, or Build

Prop Genesis, v. 1

In the beginning, there was the Script. And the Script listed all the props that were necessary for the action to take place, as well as a few more that were mentioned because they were used in the original New York production.

Prop Genesis, v. 2

And the Director said, "Let there be a Concept," and he saw that many props were needed to realize his Vision, so he turned to the Stage Manager and said: "Can we get a stuffed alligator to hang up there?"

Prop Genesis, v. 3

And the Producer said, "Let there be a Design," and the designer called for many more props, either by sketching them in great detail or by writing little notes in the margins like "fill shelves with books and other stuff."

Prop Genesis, v. 4

And the Producer hired the Actors, who realized as rehearsal progressed that they needed notebooks and pens, funny hats and noses, and cigarettes with long, elegant filters or they, too, would not realize their Vision.

Prop Genesis, v. 5

And the Propmaster saw that order needed to be put upon the land, and so she made the **Prop List**, which contained every prop that she had heard of in her travels. And she was sore afraid—for the list was long and compli-cated. Yet she took heart, for Opening Night was six weeks away and she had no time to Freak Out.

And so was born the Prop List. And it was Long.

Setting Up the Prop List

Everything begins with The List. The prop list should contain every prop that will finally end up on stage, and it should be compiled as early in the production process as possible. Like everybody else, prop people like to know what is expected of them early in the game.

The list should identify a prop as one of three categories: **set props**, **personal props**, and **set dressing**.

Set props are pre-set on the stage and generally left there. They are handled, sat on, picked up, dialed, or passed around by actors, as opposed to set dressings, which are considered purely decorative. Set props include furniture, lamps, appliances, rugs, phones, and so on. They are the most important props since (a) they are large enough to be clearly seen by the audience and (b) they are used by actors.

Personal props, since they are also employed by the actors, are also high

For Our Eyes Only   *Prop List*

TYPE	ITEM	PRE-SET POSITION	USED BY
Set	Seltzer Bottle	Drink table	
Set	Dictionary	Side table	
Set	Table Lamp	Side table	
Set	Candlestick	Hearth	
Set	Coffee Table	Down center	
Set	Sofa	Center	
Set	Rocking chair	Left	
Set	Drink Table	Wall stage left	
Set	Side Table	By sofa	
Personal	Giant Key	SL prop table	Andre
Personal	Cigarettes	SL prop table	Rick
Personal	Matches	SR prop table	Rick
Personal	Walking Stick	SR prop table	Mrs. Doddyworth
Personal	Letter from Paul	SL prop table	Susan
Personal	Dead Chicken	SR prop table	Paulina
Personal	Journal	SL prop table	Kitty
Dressing	Painting of Grandpa	SR wall	
Dressing	Bowling Trophy	UC shelf	
Dressing	Sailing Calendar	Kitchen wall	
Dressing	Bulletin Board	Kitchen wall	
Dressing	Newspaper Clippings	SL wall	
Dressing	Feathered Headdress	SL wall	

Fig. 33. A prop list

on the list of priorities. They rank second only because they are smaller, and, relatively speaking, they require a little less effort since their appearance is less noticeable to the audience. Personal props are preset on the prop table and carried onstage by actors. They include things like pens, cigarettes, documents, money, and anything else handheld that is assigned to a particular actor.

Set dressing is the lowest priority since it doesn't affect the action. Set dressing includes things like pictures on the wall, knick-knacks to fill up shelves, draperies, and anything else that fills up empty space and helps to communicate the nature of the space to the audience. In some situations, set dressing doesn't even appear on the prop list since it consists of whatever the designer and prop master can find in the prop room. Nevertheless, efforts should be made to get these props on the list, since it will make it easier for the prop people to pull things from storage. Furthermore, if those people know what you are looking for, they can keep an eye out during their shopping trips.

Once the list is under way, the next step is to divide the props into four other categories: build, buy, pull, and borrow. This is where the detailers come in. The decision about where to get the prop depends on several factors:

Money is, of course, the basis of all such decisions. A prop master balances the money available in his budget against the money needed to buy a prop. If the budget will support it, buying a prop is the least labor-intensive way to get a prop.

Available labor, which is another way of talking about money, will determine what can be built. This is where the artisans come in. Prop building requires a number of different skills including carpentry, sewing, foam carving, plastic molding, and more. Prop artisans are unusual craftspeople, and prop-building technique is unlike anything else. A household furniture builder, for example, will be surprised at how his creations are treated on stage and will hold his head in dismay as the joints come loose.

Time, the third leg of the logistics stool, determines what you have time to make.

Availability means "Can I find it?" With period shows, this is a major factor. Sixteenth-century furniture doesn't grow on street corners. Nor do specialty props, that is, props that sprang from the mind of a sadistic playwright. The show *Ten Little Indians,* for example, requires a set of ten porcelain Indians, all of which get destroyed every night. No, no, thank *you,* Dame Agatha Christie.

So . . .

Buying a prop saves time and labor, but you are dependent on availability and budget.

Building a prop is usually cheaper then buying and solves the availability problem, but you need the necessary talent.

Borrowing saves time and money, but it is completely dependent on availability (and the good will of the lender).

Pulling a prop from stock is always the best option but, if you don't have it, you can't pull it.

Furniture: Why the Stage Isn't Like Real Life

There is one really unfortunate thing about stage props. Many of them bear a striking resemblance to things we have in our own homes, like tables, chairs, and sofas. It isn't unusual, therefore, particularly in low-budget theater, for people to raid their own homes and the homes of others to find furniture for their shows. On the contrary, go visit the home of any community theater luminary and he will probably have a story for every piece in his living room: "Oh, yes, that's the sofa from *The Boy Friend,* and that chest was used in *Man of La Mancha,* and the desk is from *Harvey . . ."* and so on and on.

Most theaters can't afford to buy furniture for every production and it is simply impossible to have every kind of furniture that you need in stock. Hence, theaters borrow all the time. This is not a bad thing, but you should proceed with caution. Let me illustrate with two stories.

Some years ago, I did a production of *The Music Man,* the musical comedy about everybody's favorite con man, Harold Hill. In the second act, while trying to seduce the town librarian, Hill sings "Marian, the Librarian" to her in the middle of the town library, which is full of chairs and tables. The song becomes a raucous dance number, all the more fun because it is going on in the normally sedate library, with Marian frantically trying to shush everyone back into silence. Fun stuff. At least it was fun until the choreographer decided to introduce a little Donald O'Conner choreography with the chairs. You may be familiar with O'Conner's very physical dance routines, particularly the ones involving furniture. Our choreographer created a very exciting sequence that had all the dancers leaping onto a chair, stepping up onto the back of the chair and then riding it down backwards until the chair landed on its back on the floor. Really fun.

And really dangerous. The chairs and tables had been borrowed from a local high school and they were built entirely of wood. There was no way that they were going to put up with that kind of strain and, sure enough, after a couple of weeks of rehearsal, most of them were broken. We were very fortunate to escape without a broken dancer as well.

Household furniture is made to be sat on, slept on, eaten on, even made love on, but it is *not* made to be jumped on, danced on, stomped on, or marched on. It is also not made to be thrown, dropped, kicked, or used as a weapon in a fight. This doesn't mean that you *can't* do all these things (and more) with household furniture, it just means that it wasn't *designed* for it.

Even if your play is devoid of violence or dancing, you will find that stage furniture goes through more punishment than the furniture in your home. For one thing, it gets moved around all the time. If you're anything like me, your living room furniture hasn't moved since you vacuumed under it the last time your mother came to visit. Theatrical furniture gets moved all the time, sometimes several times a day, if you have scene changes. It gets thrown up onto storage shelves, dropped in the wings, and loaded into pickup trucks. All this moving is very hard on the joints that hold furniture together, and they will weaken and come apart much more rapidly than furniture at home. Furthermore, actors are much more con-cerned with portraying a character on stage than they are with sitting down properly. They will collapse harder into a stage chair than the one at home and, no matter what their stage mother tells them, they will invariably lean back. Bottom line? The stage is not like life and prop furniture feels the pain.

What to do? Well, sometimes you have to build furniture especially for this kind of punishment. Those chairs that Donald O'Conner is flinging around in his dance routines were specially built out of steel to stand up to his needs. Sometimes, rather than building a piece from scratch, you need only fortify regular furniture with extra steel or wire. One common trick is to add an "X" of tightly wound wire between the four legs of a chair.

Step one: Talk to your propmaster. Tell her which pieces of furniture will receive special abuse and how often. Then, *listen*

Fig. 34. A chair strengthened with wire

to the propmaster. If she tells you that a chair is not strong enough for what you have in mind, don't dismiss her input as alarmist. It might save you a broken chair (or a broken arm) later.

Besides keeping your performers healthy, it is also important to keep relationships with lenders healthy. When I did *The Miracle Worker* a few years back, I brought in my own dining room table for the famous breakfast scene. In this scene, the young Helen Keller falls into a rage because her teacher, Annie Sullivan, forces her to eat her breakfast with a spoon instead of with her customary fingers. In response, she hurls her spoon violently down on the table. Annie puts it back, Helen throws it down. They repeat this pattern over and over until Helen finally gives in.

I delivered the table to rehearsal and didn't check back with the stage manager for a week or so. When we went to pick up the table for the first tech rehearsal, I was amazed to find the top of the table deeply gouged from the repeated spoon attacks. One-quarter of the table (the quarter that the actress could reach from where she sat) was completely stripped of its finish. After just a few rehearsals, the action of the scene had laid waste to the table. Because it was my own table, the only person I had to worry about was me, but if the table had come from another source, I would have had a real problem. Instead, I had another one of those "Look, there are the gouges that Helen Keller put on my table" stories that abound at theater people's dinner parties. Had the table been borrowed from a member of the theater's board of directors, it might have been a source of anguish, especially since a felt pad would have prevented the entire thing.

The moral? Be aware that theatrical action takes a higher toll on furniture, and, whenever possible, take steps to prevent the damage.

Weapons: Safety and Proper Handling

As with doors and windows, the first question to ask about a gun is: Does it need to be practical? In other words, does it need to fire? If not, then by all means, don't use a real gun on stage. The only exception to this is in an *extremely* intimate theater where the audience can clearly see that a prop gun is being used. Other than that, there is no compelling reason to use a real gun on stage if the gun isn't fired. Even if it is fired, a starter pistol that can fire only blanks should be used, if possible.

The first problem with guns and, in fact, with any weapon at all, is theft. I tell my students over and over, "*Weapons walk.*" This has been demonstrated over and over. There is a fascination with weapons, both among actors and technicians. Somehow, when you put a weapon in someone's hands, it brings out a primal hunter-killer personality, and he won't want to give that violent talisman back. Lured by television and movie images of weapons, people get a charge out of carrying and using them. Hence, when there are weapons around backstage, if you don't go to absurd lengths to protect them, they will walk away. They will, they will, they will. Trust me.

If you have weapons in a show, whether they are practical or not, there should be one person (usually a prop person or a stage manager) who looks after them personally. If possible, the location of their storage place should not be common knowledge and they should be kept under lock and key. If a gun must fire, have the person responsible load it at the last possible moment and hand it to the actor just before the actor goes on stage. When the actor comes off, the same person should be there to receive and unload the gun. If you are using a real gun, be aware that, in some states, the person handling the gun may need a firearm license.

SAFETY NOTE: *All guns, even blank guns, are dangerous. As I am writing this, we are mourning the death of Jason Lee, a young actor tragically killed on a movie set by a gun that was firing blanks. This accident was highly unusual, but it still reminds us of the extreme care that must be taken with all firearms. Even though blank pistols do not have a bullet in them, they still emit a blast that can be harmful or even deadly. They often throw out wadding or other materials with deadly force.* Never fire a blank gun when it is pressed against a person's head or body. Never fire a gun when it is pointed at a person's face. *Back off. Aim lower, or to the side. The audience will be startled by the gun going off anyway and they will never know the difference.*

_____

One other note about guns: It is not unusual for a blank cartridge to misfire or not fire at all. Therefore, when you load a blank gun, load all the chambers, just in case. Actors, take note. If you pull the trigger and the gun doesn't fire, pull the trigger again, and again. Nine times out of ten, you will get the bang on the second or third try. Also, if you are handling a gun on stage, learn the location and operation of any safety switch. Otherwise, you may unwittingly flip that switch and be left with an inoperative gun, and there aren't many ad-libs that will get you out of that one.

There is one legendary story about an actor whose gun wouldn't fire, even after repeatedly pulling the trigger. After looking around helplessly for a knife, a rope, *anything* lethal he could use to cover the moment, he finally cried out "Aha! I will kill you with my *poison ring!*"

Of course, any blades you use should be blunted. If the blade is being handled so close to the audience that they can see that it is blunt, then you are handling the blade too close to the audience. Any blocking that requires a blade to be thrown or kicked across the stage should be rehearsed fanatically. If you do have a weapon being thrown or kicked, you should block the moment in such a way so that, if the actor misses, the weapon will fall harmlessly against the scenery or backstage. Never stage a fight with weapons out in the audience. All stage fights should be rehearsed before every performance.

During a production of *Henry IV, Part One,* at Brown University, the actor playing Hotspur caught the tip of a sword across his forehead and began to bleed profusely. He finished the fight, died dramatically, and was dragged offstage. As it happened, there was a critic in the audience who gave us this review: "The fights were admirably staged, although the bloody death of Hotspur felt overdone."

Handling Props During the Show: Prop Tables

It is essential to have good prop tables. Find a big table to put by each entrance to the set. Cover the table with a large sheet of white paper (usually called "butcher paper" and available from an art store), and, using the real props, draw their outlines on the table with magic marker. That way, you can tell at a glance whether you have everything. Props should be

Fig. 35. A prop table

preset on the table by whichever entrance they come in, and actors should be trained to pick them up just before they enter the scene and drop them off as they leave. Props should never be taken to the dressing room, with the exception of costume props, like watches and jewelry (they're usually handled by the costume people anyway). Actors get attached to props and they sometimes want to keep those props with them, but this practice inevitably results in the actor suddenly realizing, seconds before his entrance, that the critical walking stick is hanging on the back of his dressing room chair. I have seen enough mad dashes to the dressing room by frantic stage managers to state this without reservation: Leave the props on the prop table. I've said it before, and I'll say it again: Actors aren't stupid, they just have a lot to think about.

CHAPTER 9

Stage Management

Theater is complicated. Theater is stressful. Theater is a lot of hard work by a lot of people all trying to work on the same project at different times and in different places. Sometimes these places are in different cities, states, or countries. All of these people have different ideas, different methods, and different definitions of the word "deadline." What to do? Hire a **stage manager**.

Stage managers are helpful people. They have to be. Their job description includes words like "Eye of the Hurricane" and "Safe Port in a Storm." They are at the center of everything. They are the communication link between everybody and everybody. This puts them in a position of uniquely intense stress. As the joke goes: How many stage managers does it take to change a light bulb? Answer: "One. And it's on my list."

Still, even with all this access and ability, many stage managers are not given the tasks that they should be given. Furthermore, since stage management does not necessarily require a lot of technical skills, it is a job often taken over by nontechnical people. For these reasons, all nontechnical people should know what a stage manager does.

Before beginning this discussion, I should mention that "stage manager" is a term with several variations. One of the primary variations is **production manager**. In a large theater company, there is often one person who oversees the entire production process. This is particularly true when one theater is producing more than one show at a time. This person is responsible for overall scheduling and logistics for the entire operation, while each individual show is run by a stage manager.

Communication: The Central Issue

Throughout the show, from concept to close, the stage manager must be in communication with the cast, the shops, the producers, and the director. One of the SM's primary responsibilities is to relay the director's thoughts to everybody else. If the director suddenly decides that an actor should be reading a book during a particular scene, it is up to the SM to ask him all the questions that the prop people will ask: What kind of a book? Hardcover or soft? What color? Any particular title? How big? How thick? Where does the actor get it from? Does that mean we need a bookshelf? and so on. Some of these questions may be initially dismissed as unnecessary, but it is surprising how much details begin to matter once it is too late to change them. It's up to the stage manager to find out these details ahead of time, *before* the propmaster shows up with a small red paperback and finds out that the director really wanted a thick, black, scholarly text. If the propmaster is making a second (or third) trip to storage, muttering under her breath, then the stage manager hasn't done his job.

An experienced stage manager knows that any change that happens during a rehearsal affects somebody who is not there, and it is up to the SM to let that person know. The most important examples are the times when scenery, props, or costumes will be stressed or abused by some kind of action. These include (but are not limited to) fights breaking out, liquids being spilled or thrown, objects being broken, pies in the face, actors having to crawl, run, climb, grab, hide, fall, collapse, or die. If someone stands up in the house during a final dress rehearsal and says: "What do you mean she's going to bleed on that dress?" then the SM hasn't done his job. *It is the stage manager's job to eliminate surprises.*

Besides personal one-on-one communication, the SM should create and maintain several other avenues of communication:

The Contact Sheet

This is a list of everyone related to the show: cast, designers, crew, and anyone else who may need to be contacted about the show. It should include work and home phone numbers, fax numbers, and any other way to contact that person, including e-mail addresses, if they exist. It should also include pertinent phone numbers at the theater, such as backstage, the production office, or the box office. It does not hurt to list the numbers of pizza take-out places and local drinking establishments, particularly if large contingents of show personnel hang out there. Don't forget cab companies and public transportation information lines. Dance companies will generally include a physical therapist. Musicals may list a music store. The stage manager's number should be in bold. Cast and crew should know that, if they have a crisis, they should call 911, and immediately thereafter, the stage manager.

Everyone involved with the show should get one. Update them as things change.

The Callboard

The second major communication thing that the SM should take care of is the **callboard**. This is a centrally located bulletin board that contains information that the cast and crew should know. This might include (but is not limited to):

- **Contact Sheet:** Of course, you should also give a copy to everyone in the show, but hey, people lose 'em.
- **Sign-in Sheet:** This is a checklist with each person's name on it with a space for each night of technical rehearsal or performance. The cast and crew should be trained to sign in as soon as they get to the theater.
- Rehearsal Schedule: From the prompt book (see later in chapter).
- Today's Calls: This is a list showing what is happening today, where it is happening, and who should be there.
- Next Day's Calls: Same thing, but for tomorrow.
- Reviews: Some people put up all of them, but I only like to see the good ones.
- **Scene Breakdown:** From the prompt book (see later in chapter).
- Directions: To the rehearsal space, to the theater, to the shops (for costume fittings, for example), to company parties, etc. Anywhere that people might have to go. Remember to include information on public transportation.
- Telegrams, Postcards, Congratulatory Notes: Anything that keeps people's spirits up.
- Rules and Regulations: Find out what the appropriate rules and regs are in your theater. Professional shows are required to post union regulations as well so make sure you are in compliance.

Basically, anything that the cast and crew needs to know should be on the callboard. This does not preclude spoken announcements. In fact, it is always best to give people information more than once. Announce it, then post it.

If you are a performer, make a habit of checking the callboard every day. And, of course, sign in as soon as you arrive at rehearsal.

From Coffee Shop to Load-Out: Schedules

The creation of a show can begin anywhere from three weeks (or less) to three years (or more) before opening night. The production cycle breaks down into four major blocks: **preproduction**, **production**, the **run**, and **closing**; and there are different schedule needs for each.

Preproduction

This is the time before the show is cast, before the shop has started building a set, before anybody other than the major players—the director, the designers, and whoever is putting up the money—has started working. This is a time for major decisions to be made: Which play are we doing? What time period are we setting it in? When do we open? How much money will we spend on each area? Because these decisions are so important to the process, they need to be made up front. It's up to the stage manager to see that they get made and that everybody else knows what the answers are. Consequently, the first events the stage manager should schedule are **concept meetings**. Concept meetings are "pie-in-the-sky" brainstorming sessions between the director and the designers. The stage manager need not (and should not) attend. These meetings are for drinking amaretto and philosophizing about Shakespeare's mother. It is here that the general concepts for the show should be decided (or, in the case of a strong-willed director, shared).

Once those concepts are agreed upon, the scenery and costume designers go off to their monk's quarters and come up with renderings and floorplans. After the designers have had some time to create (at least a few weeks), it is time to hold the **design conference**. Here the designers present their work and field questions from the director and other staff members. Lighting and sound designers, without the ability to show renderings, may give vivid descriptions.

Once things are moving along, it's time for the first of several **production meetings**, to which the heads of all departments should be invited. Production meetings are for sharing logistical information and for solving problems involving time, space, and money.

It is essential to recognize the differences between these meetings and not allow one to become another. As soon as a production meeting descends into conversations about whether to put the heroine in a red dress, you have slipped into a design conference. If you begin to debate the artistic integrity of red-coated heroines, you have landed in a concept meeting. In either case, you are wasting the time of the other people at the table, and the stage manager should gently but firmly call a halt to it.

This does not mean that you can't go back and have a design conference once you have started production meetings. On the contrary, if you discover a design problem in a production meeting, you should table the issue and sequester the relevant people at a nearby coffee shop to work it out. Likewise, if the design meetings are not going well because of inconsistencies in the concept, it will be necessary to backtrack there as well.

The stage manager should run the design conferences and production meetings. The head of each area (scenery, costumes, lighting, props, audio) should speak in turn, relaying progress reports and potential problems to the group. The stage manager should facilitate the discussion and move things along swiftly, not allowing lengthy discussions to erupt. These longer discussions must, I repeat, *must* be carried out in smaller one-on-one (-on-one) meetings and not in the larger meetings. If a design conference or production meeting takes longer than an hour, you have a problem.

Production

Once the design is complete and actors have been chosen, the show moves into production. Suddenly, a lot more people are involved, and these people are a lot more spread out. You will probably never get all these people into the same room until you tap the keg on opening night.

Much of the scheduling during the production period is handled by the individual shops. The SM should not worry about scheduling when each piece of scenery gets built or when the propmaster makes her run to the antiques store. Once you are in production, the SM should concentrate on scheduling rehearsals.

Production meetings still continue during this period, of course, and the stage manager should continue to schedule and run them. Most theater staffs find that a weekly one-hour production meeting does the job. The SM must also assume the position of attendance cop. As people get busy, priorities tend to shift, and members of the production staff will begin to find excuses not to attend. The SM must be unrelenting in reminding these people to show up. One way to improve attendance is to make the production meeting a regularly scheduled event, say, every Tuesday at 3 P.M.

The other important schedule that the SM should oversee during the rehearsal period is **costume fittings**. The costume shop should provide a list of which actors they need to see and the stage manager should build a schedule that ensures that these fittings happen.

Tech Week

The final countdown to opening night is hellish for everyone, but especially so for the stage manager. Every theater and staff approaches tech week differently, but it is usually a step-by-step process that slowly grows in complication each night. First the actors get on stage with the scenery, then come the lights, then the costumes, then the makeup and hair. Each night more elements should be thrown into the mix.

The center of this hurricane should be the stage manager. Again, many directors do not use the SM to the fullest extent, choosing to run these rehearsals themselves. Rest assured, this is counterproductive. A director should be concerned with what the audience will see and hear and how they will react. If he takes on the job of making sure that all the details get taken care of, then he will not have the kind of mental space necessary to create the show. Of course, many directors in smaller community or school shows habitually operate without stage managers, but these directors lose a lot of stomach lining as well. If you do not have stage managers available, then it is time to start developing them, for the sake of everybody in the show.

The Run

In many professional theaters, the director leaves the show in the hands of the stage manager after opening night. These SMs make a report to the producer every night about the quality of the show and sometimes schedule "brush-up" rehearsals to maintain the quality of the show.

In smaller theaters, the director maintains contact with the show after opening night, but he should still let the stage manager handle the moment-to-moment management of the show. This management does not include artistic decisions, however, just logistical ones.

Closing

When the show is closing, the stage manager should, with the technical director, compose a plan of attack for **striking** the show.

The mood at strike will differ widely depending on the production, and may even differ among people working on the same show. Younger, less experienced performers are usually sentimental and a little sad. Older performers, who know that the next show is waiting in the wings, may be more philosophical. Staff that has been working on a long-running show may be downright relieved. I myself have always enjoyed strike. To me, it seems like a way of restoring order to the world, of decreasing entropy. In any case, strike can be quick and efficient, or it can be interminably painful. Most of that difference comes from how it is planned.

First, determine what jobs can be done by unskilled labor and which jobs require skilled technicians and special tools. The first category includes cleaning, transporting, and general destruction. The second includes removing machinery, disassembling complicated scenery (especially when it is being saved) and anything involving rigging. Divide your forces into teams, with each team having a crew head. Write out their jobs on a separate sheet of paper and give it to them. Make sure that all the spaces in the theater are covered, especially dressing rooms and storage places.

Most important, have a checkout sheet that people have to sign out on. Give that sheet to one person and have her enforce attendance. It's a funny thing, but no matter what you do, there always seem to be fewer people around at the end of strike than there were at the beginning. Go figure.

In addition to the strike after the final performance, the stage manager should confirm that all borrowed props and costumes are returned to their rightful owners and that the theater itself is left clean.

Lists and Lists and Lists of Lists

A stage manager should be the repository of all information about a show, with the exception of some specific technical information that the shops require for construction. If you are not sure if the SM needs to know something, then she needs to know it. SMs are the enemies of trees. Paper is their life. Of course, computers are important, and much information is kept on them, but no SM worth her stopwatch would forgo having a hard copy on a real piece of paper somewhere.

Here is a list of some of the lists that the Stage Manager should have. This is *not* a complete list.

- *Contact Sheet:* This is a complete list of names, addresses, and phone numbers for everyone working on the show. Be sure to update it as people move around. Unfortunately, the SM needs to be a bit of a gossip (always collecting info, never giving it out), because it may be necessary to contact someone in the evening, which means knowing where his romantic interests lie.
- *Costume Plot:* This is a complete list of every costume that a character wears, and when they wear it. The plot should also show where quick changes happen. A quick change is defined as any costume change where the actor does not have time to get back to the dressing room and has to change clothes in the wings.
- *Prop List:* This is a complete list of all props, showing what they are and where they start on the set. See "Properties" for more info.
- *Scene Breakdown:* This is a list of all the scenes in the show, showing the name of the scene ("Act Two, Scene Four," "Brazilian Samba," or whatever name scheme you are using), who is in each one, and page numbers where they begin and end.
- *Lighting Cue Sheet:* This is a list of all the lighting cues showing when they happen and what they do ("All lights go out except special on Agnes"). See "Lighting" for more info.
- *Sound Cue Sheet:* This is a list of all the sound cues showing when they happen and what they do ("Pounding Surf"). See chapter 7 for more info.

Biblical Scholarship: Keeping the Prompt Book

By now it should be clear that one of the stage manager's primary jobs is to collect information. All that information needs to be kept in one, easily accessible place. That place is the **prompt book**, or **prompt script**. (I prefer the first term since the book holds a lot of things besides the script.)

The prompt book should be a large, three-ring binder with the stage manager's name, address, and phone number on the front and back. In that binder resides every piece of information needed to produce the show. Often, it is the only thing kept when a show ends. If a show is later revived, the staff will depend on it.

In most production situations, the prompt book should never leave the theater. Do not take it home. Do not risk forgetting it, losing it, or leaving it in the trunk when your car gets stolen. Often, companies will keep two identical prompt books, one for the SM and a backup for the ASM. This is particularly necessary if you have several different rehearsal locations and the books get carried all over town.

Besides all the lists and schedules above, the prompt book should contain the authoritative copy of the script, showing all cuts and revisions, as well as all **blocking** (the actors' movements) and sound and lighting cues.

Before you start the rehearsal period, make a photocopy of every page in your script onto 8½-by-11-inch paper. Since most scripts are smaller than that, you will end up with a large border of white space around the text.

When a particular movement is determined in rehearsal, make a small, vertical mark next to the word in the script where the actor starts to move. Then draw a long horizontal line all the way out to the *left* side of the page. Write the movement on the line, out in the white margin.

Abbreviate everything. It's the only way you will fit all the information on the page. Write in all caps to ensure legibility. All characters and objects on the stage should be reduced to as few letters as possible (try for three), and all movements should be referred to as *crossing*, abbreviated as "X." It doesn't matter if they are walking, running, stumbling, skipping, fleeing, or crawling. If they are moving, they are crossing. Use "NTR" and "XIT" for comings and goings.

If Hamlet, rapidly dying from the touch of a poison dagger, staggers to the throne and falls, you write: HAM X THRN, FALL.

If Lenny, caught up in George's vision of a beatific future on the rabbit farm, runs to the top of the platform downstage left, you write: LEN X PLAT DL.

If Mame enters from the central door upstage (doesn't she always?), sweeps to a cafe table downstage right, and sits, you write: MAM NTR UC, X DR, SIT.

For shows with large casts, it will not always be practical to notate blocking in this way. For crowd scenes, get a floorplan on 8½-by-11-inch paper and make a bunch of copies. Insert a floorplan into the script when you need one and draw out the blocking on it with names and arrows. For a show with lots of crowd scenes (like a musical), take your script to a copy shop and have them photocopy the floorplan on the back of every page.

When it comes time to write the lighting and sound cues in the script, use the margin to the *right* of the text. Draw a small vertical line next to the word where the cue happens, then draw the line out to the edge of the paper. Write the cue on this line, once again abbreviating everything. Lighting cues are "LQ." Sound cues are "SQ." Cues should be numbered to help you keep them straight.

In some cases, a cue might be a **visual**. This means that the cue doesn't happen on a line; it happens on something that the actor *does,* like turning on a light switch.

(While we're on the subject, every now and then someone gets the idea that the stage lights should actually be tied to the light switch on the set so that, when the actor hits the switch, the lights come on. I do not recommend it. Sure enough, some night the actor will miss the switch, or forget, or the lead will be sick and the understudy will go on and nobody will have told him about it. As I have been saying throughout this book, actors are not stupid, just preoccupied. I say, protect the actor and let the technician take up the slack. Make the light switch a fake one and bring the lights up when the actor gestures in the general direction of the switch.)

Lastly, each cue should have a **warning** about a minute before it happens, so the operators will be ready when the time comes. All warnings should be notated in the script just like cues. There is no need in the prompt book to write what a lighting or sound cue really does, just that it happens.

So, if the lights come up on Peter's bedroom in the early morning (light cue one) and the alarm clock rings (sound cue one), Peter shuts it off, gets out of bed and turns on the light switch, you write:

LQ 1
SQ 1
SQ 1 END ON VISUAL (PET TRN OFF)
LQ 2 ON VISUAL (PET HIT LIGHT SWCH)

Of course, remember that all things change, so mark all blocking and cues in *pencil.*

The prompt book should be maintained with the goal that the stage manager could be removed at any moment and the assistant would still

ACT 2, SCENE 5

AT LIGHTS UP, CHA, MAU | *Charley and Maude come out of the house and sit in the porch swing.*
NTR UC, X SWING, SIT

CHARLEY
That was a wonderful dinner, my sweet. What ominous looking clouds.
Looks like rain.

MAUDE
Charley, be a dear and turn on that porch light, won't you?

CHARLEY
CHA X SWITCH | Why sure, I'd love to.

Charley goes to the light switch and turns it on. | VISUAL   LQ 43

MAUDE
Thanks ever so much.

CHARLEY
CHA X SWING, SIT | Maude, darling, there's something that I've been wanting to tell you.   SQ 18

A car is heard offstage.

MAUDE
MAU STAND | Is that a car coming up the driveway? Whoever could it be?

CHARLEY
I don't know, but they had better hurry up and get inside. The rain is
starting. | LQ 44, SQ 19

*There is a flash of lightning, followed by a clap of thunder. A torrent of
rain begins to fall.*

CHARLEY
What did I tell you?

ABBY (offstage)
Hello! Anybody home?

MAUDE
Why, it's Abby and Ricky! Come on up out of the rain.

ABBY, RICK, NTR DR | *Abby and Ricky dash in, running from the rain. They have newspapers
X PORCH | over their heads.*

ABBY
Well, then, what a sudden downpour!

Fig. 36. A typical prompt script page

know everything necessary to run the show. Other things that should be in
a prompt book:

- *Program Copy:* This includes a list of every person working on the
  show with their proper title. Circulate a copy of this list around
  rehearsals and shops so that each person can initial their name,
  confirming that it is spelled correctly. Program copy may also include

acknowledgments of individuals or businesses that have provided support to the show, biographies of people in the production, as well as comments or quotes that the director would like to include.

- *Publicity Information:* This varies widely depending on your situation, but it might include press releases, schedules of interviews, reviews, or biographies of people in the production.
- *Any other piece of information that relates to the show in any way.* Remember, if it is a piece of paper, the prompt book should contain a copy.

I witnessed an event at Seattle Rep that proved the validity of this statement. We were doing an absurdly complicated production of *Caucasian Chalk Circle.* There were hundreds of light and sound cues, dozens of costume and set changes, and thirty-six computer-controlled projectors. Running the show was a nightmare job: The stage manager was calling cues continuously for over two hours. As it happened, the SM had become pregnant prior to the start of production, and by the time tech week arrived, she was quite far along. The pregnancy never interfered with her duties until, one night, right in the middle of a performance, she suddenly fainted. As the wardrobe staff (the only free hands at that moment) rushed to the light booth to care for her, the ASM sprinted from backstage, slid breathlessly into her chair and headset, and began to read the cues from the book. The show continued seamlessly and neither the audience nor the actors were aware of the problem. That kind of a save can only happen when the prompt book is accurate and up-to-date. Mother and baby are doing fine, by the way.

Preparing the Rehearsal Space and Running Rehearsals

Another of the stage manager's missions is to run rehearsals and call the show. A stage manager should make sure that the rehearsal starts on time (never delayed by tardy actors) and ends on time (never held over by a suddenly inspired director). Of course, once the rehearsal has started, the director is in charge until the SM gently tells him that time has expired. Diplomatically, of course.

To prepare the space for rehearsal, the first thing to do is **tape the stage**. Get hold of several rolls of **spike tape**, a cloth-backed, colored tape sold by theatrical supply stores. Spike tape will not harm floors, tears easily, and comes in a rainbow of colors. You can get away with colored vinyl tape from the hardware store, but spike tape is a lot easier to work with.

Get a copy of the floorplan from the set designer. Using the spike tape, mark out the shape of the set on the floor of the rehearsal space. Make a complete outline of each platform, showing all doors and windows. For a staircase, outline each step and make an arrow that shows which way is up. Use different colors as necessary. Show the edge of the apron and any other feature of the set that may impede movement.

There are lots of different kinds of rehearsals in the production process and the SM's duties will vary with each one:

First Read-through

This is the first time that the entire cast will be in the same room together and is generally a jolly affair. The material is fresh, the energy is high, and no one has any grudges yet. Make the most of it. Designers will sometimes show up to say hello and meet the cast.

There will be a lot of bookkeeping and logistics at this rehearsal and you should do it all before you start reading. Once the scripts come out, you will have lost everyone's attention to the material. The cast should get a copy of the rehearsal schedule and the contact sheet. Ask them to notify you of conflicts immediately, if not sooner.

A representative of the costume shop (the designer, more often than not) should be at first rehearsal to take measurements. As some people are not comfortable having a measuring tape wrapped around their bodies in public, it is best to set this process up in an adjoining room. The designer can quietly pull people out of the main room while the script is being read. Actors with major roles may have to be measured during a break.

Once the bookkeeping is over, the cast should read the script from beginning to end, stopping only for intermissions. The SM or an assistant should read the stage directions.

One more tip for this rehearsal: You should time the read-through. More often than not, the production will run about as long on opening night as it runs in first read-through. You'll impress the heck out of the box office if you give them an accurate running time two months before the show opens. Especially if you're right.

People Needed for First Read-Through: *Director, Cast, SM and ASM, Representive from costume shop (costume designer), Other designers (optional)*

Table Work

Most directors will want to spend some time tearing the script apart while sitting around a table with the actors. Sometimes, the stage manager can skip these rehearsals, since they are mostly discussion, but you should still make sure they start and stop on time. Go make phone calls or something while they do all that artistic stuff.

People Needed for Table Work: *Director, Cast, Stage manager (only at beginning and end)*

Blocking rehearsals, Scenework, Polishing, Dance rehearsals, Music rehearsal, Act run-throughs, etc.: Every director is different. Every production is different. Every director will construct a rehearsal period his own way. You may have any or all of these rehearsals in your schedule. Make sure that the appropriate performers are called for each one, along with the SM or ASM.

Another important job for the SM in these rehearsals is to be **on book** once the actors are **off book**. In other words, once the actors have put their scripts down and are reciting the lines from memory, someone else in the room should be following the script. If an actor has a memory failure, he should call out "Line" and the SM should immediately read the next sentence that the actor is supposed to say. Don't try to act it, just read it. Read one sentence and stop. If the actor needs more, he will ask for it. One note to actors: There is no need to break character or look at the SM when you need a line. Stay where you are, stay in the moment, and ask for the line. A good SM will provide it quickly and cleanly.

First Run-through

Also known as "stumble-through." This is the first time that the cast attempts to run the show from top to bottom without stopping. Besides its obvious value to the cast and the director, first run-through is also very important to another member of the production: the lighting designer. She cannot design the lighting until she knows where the actors are at each moment of the play. First run-through must be scheduled well before lighting load-in (see below).

People Needed for First Run-through: *Director, Cast, Stage manager and ASM, Lighting designer*

Paper Tech

Tech Week, the time when we add the scenery, lighting, and costumes to the production, is approaching. Before it ever starts, the designers (minus the costume designer) should gather with the director to talk through scene shifts, light cues, sound cues, and special effects. If design meetings have been used wisely and the director and designers have done their homework, then most of the decisions about what these cues will look like will have already been made. The paper tech should consist of communicating this information to the stage manager so it can be written into the prompt book. By the end of this meeting, the stage manager should know where all the lighting, sound, and scene-change cues occur during the show.

People Needed for Paper Tech: *Director, Stage manager, Lighting designer, Scenery designer (if there are scene changes), Sound designer, Any special effects people*

Load-in

If your set is not constructed in the theater itself, then you will need to schedule a time to deliver it and set it up. Talk to the technical director and determine how much time will be needed. Props should also arrive during load-in, but not until the first rush of scenery is over. Costumes should *not* be brought into the theater at this point.

People Needed for Load-in: *Technical director, Stage crew, Propmaster, Prop crew*

Lighting Load-in

Lighting and scenery crews can work side-by-side sometimes, but for the most part, it is best to assign them separate hours onstage. Once these hours are determined, the heads of the two crews can negotiate with each other. Often, the lighting crew can start hanging lights in the "front-of-house" positions (out over the audience) while the scenery crew works on stage. Once the lighting crew begins working on the lighting over the stage, the scenery crew will have to curtail its operations. Focusing sessions, with their need for quiet and darkness, should be done with only the lighting crew present.

People Needed for Lighting Load-in: *Lighting designer, Lighting crew, Dimmerboard operator*

Lighting Rehearsal

Once the lights are hung and focused, the director and the lighting designer should sit in the dark theater and set all the light cues. Someone (an ASM, for example) should be recruited to walk around on stage so that the designer and director can see what the lights will look like on a person. If light cues are designed with only the scenery onstage, the actors' faces will almost always look too dark during the show. The stage manager (or her assistant) should be present to make sure that all the cues in the prompt book are accounted for. All necessary operators should attend as well, although, if follow spots are being used, you can usually get by with just one person to operate them. The cast should *not* attend.

> People Needed for Lighting Rehearsal*: Director, Stage manager (or ASM), Lighting designer, Dimmerboard operator, Follow spot operators (if appropriate), Stage walker*

Sound Rehearsal

Basically the same thing as the lighting rehearsal above, except with sound cues. The director should set volumes for all the cues, remembering that the cues will sound softer when the theater is full of people. If microphones are being used, someone should be onstage to talk into them. If "live" sound effects are being used (offstage noises, thunder claps, etc.), they should be tested during this rehearsal.

> People Needed for Sound Rehearsal: *Director, Stage manager (or ASM), Sound designer, Sound board operator, Anyone needed to produce "live" effects., Microphone talker*

Special Rehearsals

Occasionally, a show will have a complicated or potentially dangerous effect that will require a special rehearsal. This includes magic tricks, animal tricks, firearms, explosions, trick doors, traps, stage violence, and any other effect that requires some extra tweaking that could best be done when everyone else is not standing around watching. This rehearsal should happen before first tech and may take anywhere from five minutes to several hours. You should consider having one any time a particular effect is beginning to look complicated. They are obligatory for shows where people are flown or engaging in stage combat.

_____

People Needed for Special Rehearsals: *Director, Stage manager, Any crew or cast that perform the effect*

_____

Dry Tech

The dry tech is a chance to run through all the cues on stage without the actors. Having actors onstage while the tech crew is going through their cues for the first time is wasteful for everybody. It is hard for the actors to remain patient and involved during the long silences while the crew is tweaking their equipment around, and the crew does not need all those bodies in the way. So, have the first tech rehearsal "dry," that is, without the performers.

_____

People Needed for Dry Tech Rehearsal: *Director, Stage manager and ASM, Lighting designer, Scenery designer, Sound designer, All running crews (except costume and makeup)*

_____

Cue to Cue (frequently abbreviated "Q2Q")

Now, and only now, should the actors take the stage again. They will not go through the entire show, however. A Q2Q rehearsal jumps through the show, only performing the lines right before and after a technical cue. The process works like this: Start at the beginning of the show. Run the opening sequence of cues, including house lights going out, curtain (if you have one) going up, and so on. Then, the stage manager should find a line in the script that is thirty seconds or so before the next cue and tell the actors to skip to there and wait. Actors should hold until the SM says "Go ahead, please." When the SM gives the word, the actors begin speaking and, at the appropriate moment in the script, the cue is run. The SM calls out "Hold, please," and checks with the director to see if the cue was satisfactory. If not, then corrections are made and the cue is run again. Once the director is happy, the stage manager calls out a new starting place for the actors and the process begins again with the next cue. This kind of work is hard on actors, to be sure, but it is necessary to get through the show in one pass, and it helps ensure that the run-throughs coming later will go more smoothly, at least from the technical standpoint. If the show is fairly simple technically, the staff may forgo this rehearsal and go straight to the first tech run-through, stopping only for disasters.

People needed for Cue-to-Cue rehearsal: *Everyone from the dry tech plus:*
The Cast

Since this is the first time that the crew and the actors are really working
together, it is a good time to present:

The Actors' Backstage Survival Guide to Tech Rehearsal

- *Prepare to be bored.* Tech rehearsal takes longer than you think it will
  and *a lot* longer than you think it should. Keep in mind that while
  you—the actors—have been rehearsing for weeks, this is the first time
  the crew has been able to run the show. Remember *your* first run-
  through? Bring a book, a deck of cards, your cell phone, whatever you
  need to occupy yourself when you are not needed on stage. When
  you *are* needed, be prepared to stand on stage doing nothing for
  substantial periods. There is actually a great deal of activity going on
  around you. Lists are being altered, computers are being programmed,
  a thousand details are being attended to. It just *feels* like nothing is
  happening.
- *Find your light.* See that stressed-out person sitting in the audience,
  hunched over a desk full of mind-numbing drawings, squinting at
  the stage and mumbling cabalistic strings of numbers into a headset?
  That's the lighting designer; and she is trying to make you look good.
  Help her out by paying attention to the pools of light you are standing in. Become sensitive to what it feels like to have strong light on
  you and what it feels like to stand in shadow. When you are standing
  in a pool of light, be aware of where the edge of it is so that you don't
  deliver your most impassioned monologue with half your face in
  shadow. Sometimes moving six inches will make the difference
  between good and bad light. Mark your spots during tech rehearsal
  and you will never have to think about it during performance. This
  doesn't mean that you have to tell the lighting designer that you are
  poorly lit. Believe me, she knows when something isn't working. Just
  be aware of where the light is so that you can use it to best effect.
- *Be consistent in your timing and your blocking.* The lighting designer is
  also using this time to program light cues. A good lighting designer
  will track your movements around the stage so that the right amount
  of light is in the right place at the right time. If you have already read
  the lighting chapter, you know that lighting works like the camera in
  film—it focuses attention in the proper place and lets the director

"zoom in" on the action. The more consistent you are in your movements, the more attention can be focused on you. If your movements change from night to night, the designer will be forced to light the stage more generally, robbing you of the visual focus that you so richly deserve. I encourage actors to use a tech rehearsal as an opportunity to train themselves. Learn to use your tools—your body and your voice—consistently and the tech people will be able to help you.

- *Do not wear white.* Creating a balance of light onstage is a delicate operation. An actor in white will upset the balance of light, making one side of the stage appear brighter than the other. When the actor comes on in the real costume during dress rehearsal, one side of the stage will be too dark. Of course, if your real costume is white, then you should wear white to tech rehearsal.

- *Maintain quiet in the theater.* Tech rehearsal requires a number of people to communicate with each other in a clear manner. This becomes insanely difficult if there is extraneous noise in the theater, even just a little. Help the process move quickly by being silent.

- *Do not disappear.* If the tech staff can build up a good rhythm, they can fly through the rehearsal on eagle's wings. The fastest way to break that rhythm is to have to stop and send somebody to find an actor. If you are the actor that had to be hunted down, do not be surprised at the cold wind of resentment that hits you when you finally make it to the stage. Stay aware of what is happening onstage and when you will be needed.

First Tech

If you have already done a Q2Q, then this rehearsal should be a run-through with no stops. Any work left to do should be fairly minor and definitely should not interfere with the action. If there are major pieces of scenery, lighting effects, or sound cues that are missing at this point, you should seriously consider cutting them and doing without.

People Needed for First Tech Rehearsal: *Same as cue-to-cue*

Second Tech

A repeat of first tech, but with slightly higher stakes. If a technical effect that has any bearing on the actors is still not done, cut it. Then do not dwell on it. These things happen, and part of the experience of live theater is the opening night deadline. If this were film, we could just shoot it later and it would only cost us money. This is not film, however, and the box office is not about to postpone the show because the tree swing effect had too many problems to make it onstage. Let it go. Use what you have.

Actors should not wear costumes for this rehearsal unless they are difficult to move in (period clothing, masks, soap bubble costumes), must be changed or altered as part of the action (like an actor who gets dressed or undressed onstage), or require insanely fast changes. The only other reason to wear a real costume at tech rehearsal is if it does tricks, like the exploding hat in *Annie Get Your Gun*.

People Needed for Second Tech Rehearsal: *Same as First Tech*

First Dress

Time for the costumes! By this point, the show should only stop if someone's dress is falling off. Actors should keep going, no matter what, unless they hear "hold" from the stage manager. First Dress is sometimes preceded by a **costume parade**, where the director and costume designer sit in the audience while each of the actors is brought onstage to show how their costumes, hair, and makeup look under the lighting. Costume parades can be a time-consuming pill to swallow, but they are almost always beneficial, giving the director and designer valuable time to focus on the costumes without distractions.

People Needed for First Dress Rehearsal (and Costume Parade)*: Same as tech rehearsals plus: Costume designer, Makeup designer (if there is one), Wig designer (if there is one), Costume and makeup running crews*

Second Dress

The costume shop will still be working at this point, so no one should freak out if a few chorus members are still in their blue jeans. If a costume *effect* (breakaways, magic tricks, etc.) or a fast change is not working, alter it or cut it. The decision to cut a costume is often harder than cutting a prop or scenery because almost every change in costume, makeup, or hair will affect an actor. Remember, though: the audience is not going to walk out saying, "I would have loved the show, but that wig spoiled everything!"

People Needed for Second Dress Rehearsal: *Same as First Dress*

Final Dress

If there is any aspect of the final dress that differs from the real performance (other than the lack of an audience), you have a problem. Final dress should be a performance. If possible, it should start at the same time as a real performance and should follow performance protocol. The actors should not stroll through the house in their costumes and the show should never stop for any reason other than an unsafe situation (when a real performance should stop as well). If anything is missing, do not even think about whether to cut it. It's gone, by definition.

People Needed for Final Dress Rehearsal: *Everyone who will be in the theater for a performance (except ushers and front-of-house staff)*

And so ends Tech Week.
Still breathing? Good! Time for the fun part.

Opening Night and the Run

Because you had a successful dress rehearsal (you did, didn't you?), you have already experienced a real performance, right? So you don't have anything to worry about, right? Because everything is going to happen just like it did in rehearsal, right?

Well . . . maybe.

There is a kind of electrical force that flows through the backstage area when the audience—a real audience, not just the house staff and invited friends who slip in at dress rehearsal—starts flowing in the auditorium doors. The force is exciting. It is the reason we do this insanity, after all. It is also dangerous. The best rehearsed, most reliable parts of a sure-fire production will suddenly turn difficult and unpredictable in front of a paying audience, so it is up to the stage manager to maintain consistency and calm throughout the production.

Because of this phenomenon, many theaters perform "previews." These are real performances for real audiences (usually paying cut-rate ticket prices), but everybody in the house knows that the show is still considered imperfect and changes are still being made. In this case, critics agree not to review the show until it "opens."

Once opening night is over, things calm down for the SM. The nightly schedule should be the same as final dress, with the possible additions of post-show parties, brush-up and understudy rehearsals, photo calls, and strike. Parties are up to you, but let's talk about the other three.

Photo Calls

We all love photos of our shows. We all hate photo calls. There. I've said it. Now we can get past it.

There is no good time to take photos of the show. If you do it during a rehearsal, that insane clicking of the shutter can drive actors mad. Plus, the photo quality is lower since people are moving and there never seems to be enough light.

If you get people together before a performance to pose, then everyone is thinking about the show and feeling pressured, knowing that every minute they are out here on the stage is a minute when they could be backstage getting ready. The time pressure can be crippling and the end result can suffer from people's nervousness. On the other hand, getting people together after the show is sometimes impossible, what with post-show euphoria setting in and friends trying to pull them out the door to a party. Schedule a photo call after a show and you are likely to suffer a constant whine of "Can we go yet?"

Still, there is less tension after a show than before, so in most cases the best time is after, but try to find time after a dress rehearsal rather than a performance. At least you are not competing with the party.

Before the photo call begins, the SM should ask the director and designers which moments in the show they would like to photograph. Each moment should be identified with a scene number, a page number, and a light cue. Then, type this list up in reverse—from the latest moment in the show to the earliest. That's because, after a rehearsal, the costumes and set are setup for the end of the show. As you progress through the shoot, the costumes and sets get changed in reverse. When you are done, the stage should be preset for the next night's show (a little selling point you can use to convince unwilling technicians to participate). Give the list to the set, lighting, and costume designers (the sound people get to go home early, for once) so they know what you need and when. Keep things moving and you can get a very complete set of pictures in a minimal amount of time.

People Needed at Photo Call: *Director, Stage manager and ASM, Cast, Lighting staff, Stage crew, Costume crew*

Brush-up and Understudy Rehearsals

If your show runs for more than one weekend, it is normal to schedule a brush-up rehearsal before the second weekend, particularly with a nonprofessional cast. Brush-ups are notorious for getting giggly and out-of-hand, so it is up to the SM to maintain discipline, supported by the director. One smirk from either one of you, and that will be the end of it. It is important that neither of these people put themselves in the position of "I would be joking around with you guys, but old Mr. Serious there wouldn't like it." The director and SM must present a united front at brush-up, otherwise discipline will fly out the window.

If possible, brush-up should happen on the set, but generally a full tech rehearsal is not necessary. Technicians have the luxury of being able to consult lists and notes during the show, and brush-up exists mostly to jog the actors' memories.

People Needed at Brush-up: *Director, Stage manager and ASM, Cast*

If your show has **understudies** (actors who have agreed to take over another actor's role in case of illness), then the stage manager should schedule rehearsals after opening night to allow these actors to be trained. In the professional theater, the director leaves after opening night, so understudy rehearsals are run by the stage manager who is responsible for maintaining the director's intentions.

People Needed at Understudy Rehearsals: *Director (if possible), Stage manager, Cast members who appear in the scenes with the understudies.*

The Payoff: Calling the Show

Once again, the stage manager is not responsible for deciding if the lightning flash goes before or after the thunder roll, she just tells everyone when to do it. Every person backstage should have a nerve wired up to the stage manager's voice, and that nerve should fire when the SM says the magic word: "Go."

Go

Go means "Do it *now*." It should always be said at the end of a sentence, as in: "Lighting cue 49. Go," and it should never be ignored unless there is a question of safety. This means that, even if you think the stage manager is calling the cue in the wrong place, you should run it when the SM says so. (Likewise, the SM should never say the "G-word" unless he means it.) If it is in the wrong place, the SM will be so informed by the designer or director and will adjust the timing. If operators start taking cues on their own initiative, it will be much harder to track down who got it wrong.

Half-Hour

In some companies, the stage manager will announce that one hour remains until the show, but in most cases, the first call comes thirty minutes before the show, at a time traditionally referred to as **half-hour**. At half-hour, the SM should confirm that everybody is in the theater for that evening's rehearsal or performance. If someone has not arrived by half-hour, it is time to make alternative plans: Prepare the understudy, find someone else to run the lightboard, etc. If you are not in the theater by half-hour, you have created a problem for somebody.

Personally, I have always found the call of half-hour to be reassuring and exciting. It means: "Heads up, everybody. We're doing a show."

Pre-show Calls

The proper form for all pre-show calls is: "Half-hour, ladies and gentlemen. The call is half-hour. Half-hour, please" or something very similar. A trifle formal perhaps, but why not? Theater is an honorable profession with deep traditions and half-hour calls are a well-worn comfort to us all.

All pre-show calls should be answered (unless the SM is announcing over an intercom and cannot hear you). The proper answer to a pre-show call is a cheerful "thank you." This tells the SM that you appreciate her dearly and, more importantly, that you heard her.

Pre-show calls should also be made at fifteen minutes, ten minutes (usually accompanied by the "crew to places" call), and five minutes, using the same format and getting the same response.

If the show is not going up at the proper time, then the SM should announce backstage: "Ladies and Gentlemen, we are holding for <how many> minutes due to <whatever the reason>." Usually, holds are because the audience is late getting in, but occasionally, some other kind of problem will crop up.

About two minutes before the show, after being told by the front-of-house staff that the audience is almost seated, the stage manager should make the stomach-tightening announcement of "Places, ladies and gentlemen. The call is places. Places, please." The ASM should confirm that those actors who are on at the top of the show are in place.

Once places has been called, the show may start at any time, so heads up!

Once the show has started, it is up to the individual actors to be in the right place at the right time. They must not depend on the stage manager for calls once the curtain has gone up.

Headset Etiquette

Generally, the stage manager, her assistants, and the operators will be connected by a headset system during the show.

Nonessential conversation must be kept to an absolute minimum on the headset. It produces distraction that *will* cause mistakes.

This is an extremely hard policy for a stage manager to enforce, but it is essential. The stage manager is concentrating on a great many things, and chatter on the headset is one more thing that must be filtered out in order to keep a clear head. Make it easy. Keep it down.

It is a *huge* temptation to indulge in gossip and meanness on the headset. If you allow this kind of thing to go on unchecked, rest assured that sooner or later, these comments will find their way to their subject and feelings will be hurt. On several occasions, I have heard comments made over a headset about someone who was actually listening in at the time. Not good. The moral is: Be professional over the headset. In fact, there is no reason for people to have their microphones turned on, unless they are responding to something the SM says.

One other piece of headset etiquette: If you are going to take your headset off, make sure that the mic switch is turned off. Having an open, untended microphone backstage makes it hard to hear on the line. Besides, the "CLUNK" of a mic being laid down on a table is painful to hear. Get in the habit of checking the mic before you take your headset off.

Calling Cues

The stage manager's prompt book should be marked before the show with all the cues, so calling the show is basically a process of reading from the book. About a minute before each cue, the SM should warn the operators over the headset, like this: "Warning, Lights 49." If there are cues happening close together (or simultaneously), the format is: "Warning, Lights 49 and Sound 7." If you warn too early, people will relax between the warn and the cue. Too late, and they will not be ready in time.

When the cue comes, your goal is to say "Go" at the exact moment that you want the cue to happen. The format is: "Lights 49 . . . Go" so you have to anticipate a little bit and start talking before the actual moment happens. It takes practice to get Warns and Gos in the right place, but that is why we have rehearsal.

If more than one cue is happening simultaneously, then the format is: "Lights 49 and Sound 7 *together* . . . Go."

When the SM gives a warning, operators should respond so the SM knows they are ready, saying, for example: "Lights warned." Responding to a Go is usually not necessary since the SM can see whether or not a cue happened.

Note that, when calling a warning, you say "warning" and then the cue number. When calling a cue, it is the other way around: the cue number and then the "Go." Just one more way of avoiding confusion.

After the Show

After the last cue, when the stage lights are down, the house lights are up, and the show is really over, the stage manager should thank everybody on the headset and then get off it. If corrections, or notes need to be given, they are best done in person.

CHAPTER 10

How to Do a Show in a Hotel: Corporate Theater

Shareholder meetings, conferences, corporate parties, product rollouts, news conferences, kickoff meetings. You might not think of these as "theater," but think again. What is theater? Someone stands on a stage and speaks, emotes, demonstrates, sings, pleads, presents, listens, and, in some way, performs for an audience of people who may or may not be interested. I call it theater. Even with all the theaters in the world, from community to Broadway, there is probably more theater done in hotels than anywhere else.

Doing a show in a hotel, however, has an entirely different set of problems to attend to. While you have the same general areas to worry about—lighting, scenery, sound, and so forth—hotels present a different set of solutions.

Lighting: Trees, Trusses, and the Demon Track Light

The first question you will need to ask about lighting is "How many lighting instruments do I need?" Like so many things in lighting, the answer may come down to "How many can you afford?" but I'll try to give you a rough guide to use.

If you are hiring a lighting company, here are the questions that they will be asking:

- *How big is the stage?* Obviously, the bigger the stage, the more lights you will need.
- *Are you shooting video or image mag?* **Image mag** means that the image

of the speaker is, quite literally, "magnified" by pointing a video camera at him/her and projecting the picture on a large screen so that people sitting far away can see. You will need bright light, or the face on the screen will look shadowy and dark.

- *Are the performers staying in one place, or moving around?* You can save money if you are principally lighting a podium. If you have dancers, though, or a big awards ceremony, then you will need bright light all over the stage.

- *Do you need follow spots?* Do you have runway models? Lounge singers? A roving emcee who likes to go into the audience? Consider (strongly) a follow spot. If you have talking heads at a podium, forget it. If you have a band, it's a nice touch.

- *How "professional" do you want it to look?* Brighter lighting with more colors and more "looks" will help your show look more professional and slick. There is no point in spending a lot of money on a flashy set and then lighting it poorly. For that matter, there's no point in renting an expensive ballroom and then making the whole thing look cheap by underlighting the stage that everyone is looking at.

- *How "theatrical" do you want it to look?* "Theatrical" means lots of colors. Remember, you can't change the color in each individual instrument during the show. If you want the stage to be blue for one number and red for the next one, then you need a set of blue lights and a set of red ones.

- *How "flashy" do you want it to look?* "Flashy" means theatrical but more so. This is where you spend the big money on moving spot-lights, mirror balls, and lots and lots of colored back light.

If you are doing it yourself, however, you will still want to have the answers to these questions when you meet with representatives of the rental company. They can help you come up with the lighting package that you need. Read through the following section to get a general idea, then talk to them about what you want to do.

Think about how big your stage is. Mentally divide the stage into eight-by-eight-foot squares. For each square, you will need two lights from the front. This is a good rule of thumb since hotel stages are generally made from four-foot-wide platforms, so the stage size is almost always a multiple of four. So, for example, a sixteen-by-twenty-four-foot stage divides nicely into six eight-foot squares so you will need twelve lights. If you are having a band or some other kind of entertainment, you may wish to add trees upstage as well, to provide colored lights and back light. For back light, figure on one instrument for every six-by-six-foot square. Our sixteen-by-twenty-four-foot stage, then, has eight areas, so figure another eight lights for back light.

If all you have is speakers at a podium, you can get away without the back light, *unless* (are you tired of hearing this exception yet?) you want good videotape of the event. Video loves back light.

Track Lights

Any event in a hotel begins with a meeting with hotel personnel. During the course of the meeting, the subject of lighting will invariably come up and, two times out of three, they will try to tell you that they have lighting already installed in the room and don't worry about it.

What they are talking about is **track lights** and they are almost always inadequate for what you are trying to do. Track lights are wonderful for chic living rooms, restaurants, and art galleries, but lousy, lousy, lousy for theater. Generally, they do not put out enough light to illuminate a stage, plus it is very difficult to aim them in the right direction. They are generally at least twenty feet in the air and I have never been successful at getting the maintenance guy to show up before the performance and turn them the right direction.

The only time that track lighting really works is for a small meeting where you don't particularly care about shifting the focus up to a stage or a podium. If you could do your meeting in an ordinary office conference room, then you can do your meeting in a hotel without adding any lighting.

In most cases, however, you will want to bring in your own lighting equipment, especially if you want to videotape the event. If you have any kind of artistic performance—like a band, dancers, a magician, a guy in a bunny suit, or anything else—you will want to bring in lighting.

Besides making it possible for the audience to see the performers clearly, additional lighting adds an air of pizzazz to the occasion. People will listen more closely to a speaker who is well lit. Focusing attention on the stage and turning the lights down in the audience turns the event into a "show," making whatever is happening on stage more special. It also adds variety to what might otherwise be a long day of meetings.

So, now that you've decided that you need real theatrical lighting for your event, how do you get what you need?

There are two levels of lighting for hotel shows: trees (or booms) and trusses.

Trees

A **lighting tree** is a pretty simple thing: a vertical pole with a horizontal crossbar, held up by a flat or folding, triangular base. There are variations, of course. Some of them come in three separate pieces: pole, crossbar, and base. Some of them come as a folding unit that unfolds like a camera tripod. They vary in height from six to twelve feet.

Lighting instruments attach to trees the same way they attach to any other pipe in a regular theater. Put the C-clamp on the lighting instrument over the pipe and tighten the bolt. If you are going to set it up yourself, make sure you have a ladder at least as tall as the crossbar on the tree and that ubiquitous lighting tool, the eight-inch Crescent wrench.

When using trees, you do want to get the lights as far up as you can, since you are still trying to get that same forty-five degree angle that you used in the regular theater. You don't often get it with trees, but you should try. Many trees use a telescoping action to push the crossbar higher, but beware. Don't push the crossbar up too high, or the tree will become top-heavy and might fall over. Most trees have a mark showing the upper limit. Find it and pay attention to it. If you are renting the trees, ask the rental company where the mark is.

Each tree can usually hold four lighting instruments—six if they are small. Larger instruments include PAR 64s (the automobile headlight instrument) and all ellipsoidals. Smaller instruments include six-inch fresnels and any PAR smaller than a 64. I do *not* recommend overloading them. Again, they will be top-heavy and unstable.

Here are three sample arrangements of trees for three sizes of show:

- *Small show* (a speaker or small musical group): Two lighting trees, each tree contains four six-inch fresnels
- *Medium show* (five-piece dance band or awards ceremony): Four lighting trees, two trees in front of the stage with four PAR 64s each; two trees in back of the stage with four six-inch fresnels each
- *Large show* (large chorus, "big band," or beauty pageant): six lighting trees, two trees at downstage corners of stage with four PAR 64s each; two trees directly in front of the stage have four six-by-nine ellipsoidals; two trees in back of the stage have four six-inch fresnels each; portable follow spot in the back of the audience

Trusses

If you are doing a larger-scale show, you will want a **truss** or two. A truss is a horizontal gridwork of pipes that hangs across the front of a stage. Because it runs the full width of the stage and is higher in the air, it provides a far better lighting angle than trees do. Because it is much longer and stronger than a tree, it can hold many more lighting instruments. The downside? A truss requires professional riggers and much more time and money to install. Two lighting trees can be set up by two people in an hour or two. A full-size truss might take a professional crew of four riggers twelve hours to rig, including the time necessary to hang and focus the lights.

Hanging a truss is not something to do yourself, but for medium- and high-budget shows, it is a far better option for lighting a stage. To really look good, a large stage should have at least two trusses, one in front of the stage and one in back to provide back light.

Trees versus Trusses

Trying to decide between them? Here's the rule of thumb. If you can afford a truss, get one. If your stage is thirty feet across or less and you don't have a lot of money, use trees; either two, four, or six of them, depending on your budget and the size of the show. If your stage is wider than thirty feet, you need a truss. If you are really determined to make the show look great, get two trusses, one in front and one in back.

Power

Now that you have made your decision about trees and trusses, let's talk about where you are going to get enough power for all these lights.

If you haven't already, this would be a good time to go read the "The Birds and the Bees: Where Does Power Come From?" section in chapter 6.

There are three levels of power available to you:

- If you are working with a small lighting setup, you may be able to plug into the wall and be done with it. A normal wall circuit is 15 amps, so you must make sure that you are not trying to use more than 1,500 watts of lighting instruments (100 volts $\times$ 15 amps = 1,500 watts). For example, PAR lamps often come in 350-watt sizes, so you could hang four of them (1,400 watts) and still plug the whole mess into a 15-amp wall circuit. If you have two separate circuits (ask the hotel which outlets to use), you could plug one set of four into one outlet, one set into another outlet, and have eight 350-watt PARs to light your stage—perfectly adequate for a small platform with a podium and a chalkboard.
- If you need more than two circuits, but you don't need more than fifteen amps at a time, the hotel can provide a group of circuits all in one place. In this scheme, the hotel electrician opens up a special circuit in the wall and plugs in a suitcase-sized **breakout box**. A breakout box is simply a box that plugs into a high amperage (usually thirty- or fifty-amp) outlet and has a whole mess of plugs on it. You can plug lots of different things into this box, including your slide projector and laptop charger, but make sure that you ask the electrician what the *total capacity* of the box is. It may have four outlets, for example, each of which can take fifteen amps individually, but the total capacity of the box may be only fifty amps, instead of sixty. Ask, and ye shall not blow the circuit breaker.

- If your lighting setup is too big for wall circuits, then you must ask the hotel to provide more power. A large lighting setup may require hundreds of amps, far more than a wall circuit can provide. In this case, the hotel can provide a **power drop**, which is a fancy name for hooking your dimmer pack directly into their hotel's power system, bypassing the regular plugs and circuit breakers. I am not going to bother you with a lot of detail here because this job must be handled by qualified personnel. What you should know is, if you need more power than normal wall circuits, you must ask the hotel management for it. Some hotels are easier to work with than others. Smaller, older hotels with antiquated power systems (not to mention antiquated staffs) will be more likely to give you a hassle. Large, modern hotels do this kind of thing all the time and shouldn't give you any trouble. In any case, you will want a trained crew person to be handling the setup because it involves sticking bare wires into a big metal box full of power. No place for an amateur.

Portable Dimmers and Control Boards

Your rental company should provide you with a list of available dimmer packs and control boards, depending on how many lighting instruments you are hanging. The rental house will probably have pre-assembled lighting packages with instruments and dimmers already picked out. Once you know what is available, call the hotel staff to see what kind of power they can give you. If your system can be plugged into wall circuits, you should be able to handle it yourself. If you need a power drop, then you will need to hire someone who can do it for you.

Don't know where to start? First of all, decide whether you are using trees or trusses. If trusses, then sit back and let the experts make the decisions. If trees, then determine what size show you have. Call the rental company and find out what your options are for dimmers and control boards. Then call the hotel to make arrangements to get enough power.

House Lights

This is one area (the only one, really) where hotels have made it easy to do theater. Most conference and ballrooms have a variety of different house lights that can be mixed and matched for different looks. Turn the chandelier off and leave the wall washers at a glow for the slide show. Put the chandelier at half strength for the ballroom dancing. Point the track lights at the decorations and turn everything else off for a dramatic moment.

As soon as you get into the space, get someone from the hotel staff to show you all the different "looks" that the house lights can create. Sometimes the hotel management will insist on having their own person run it, but many places will show you how the lights are programmed and then let you handle it. In any case, try very hard to get them to leave that little door that hides the switches *unlocked*. Nothing is worse than waiting around to set up a slide projector while someone is paging a maintenance guy with a key.

Sound: Plug and Play, or Truck It In

Sound in hotels is almost always provided by the hotel itself, unless you have a band or a very large event. Many hotel ballrooms and conference rooms, particularly modern ones, are set up to "plug and play." In other words, you take a microphone, stick it in the wall, turn up a volume knob, and you are ready to go. No further setup is required because the amplifier is built into the walls and the speakers are already in the ceiling. Note that plug-and-play systems are rarely set up to accept cables from a CD player or tape player so, if you want to play relaxing music before your presentation, you'd better bring your daughter's boom box (a thoroughly acceptable low-tech solution, in my book).

Here are the questions that the hotel audio-visual staff will want answered when you are requesting a sound system:

- *How many microphones do you need?* If you have a panel discussion, do you want a microphone for each person or will they be amenable to passing one microphone among them? Don't forget to have a microphone placed in the audience if you want audience members to ask questions.
- *What kind of stands do you want?* Here are the options: **podium stand** (also known as a *gooseneck*), for a speaker who is addressing the audience in a formal way, from a podium; **straight stand**, for a speaker who is standing up, but does not require a podium; **boom stand**, for a speaker (or singer) who is playing a musical instrument or sitting in a wheelchair; **table stand**, for a person seated at a table, such as a panel discussion; or none, for speakers who are walking around with the microphone or have it mounted on their bodies, like a lavaliere microphone. Speaking of which . . .
- *Do you need a lavaliere microphone?* **Lavaliere**, or lav mikes, are small, pencil eraser–sized microphones that attach to a lapel or a collar and allow the speaker to operate "hands-free." Very useful when the speaker likes to use a pointer *and* carry notes.
- *Do you need wireless microphones?* Do you want your speakers to be able to walk around unencumbered by a cable dragging along behind them? It's generally more expensive, but it's often worth it, particularly for more animated speakers. Absolutely essential for speakers who want to walk around the audience, Donahue-style.

- *What else do you need?* Do you need to play tapes or CDs? How about videotapes? Does your slide show have a soundtrack? Make sure that the hotel knows about any other kind of sound that you might want to put through their system.

Scenery: Four Feet by Whatever

Scenery in the hotel ballroom is generally limited to what you bring in yourself, with two exceptions. Bare, no-nonsense platforming, and drapery to dress it up.

Platforms

Hotel platforms are usually folding platform sections in multiples of four feet. Common sizes include four by four, four by six, and four by eight. Basically, you can have any size and shape of stage that you want, as long as it can be built out of four-foot squares. The sections have little levers underneath them that allow them to lock together in various configurations. Because they don't require nailing or bolting, they are also quick and easy to change, even at the last minute. When you discover that the four-piece band you hired is actually a ten-piece ensemble, call in the hotel staff and have them throw on a few more platforms. Assuming that the *room* is big enough, of course.

As for heights, portable platforms usually come in a variety of heights at eight-inch increments (eight, sixteen , twenty-four, etc.), but many hotels have made a somewhat arbitrary decision to buy platforms of one specific height. Find out what is available, but be ready to compromise on this one. Some hotels have simply decided that twenty-four inches (or thirty-six, or thirty . . .) is the right height for everybody. Whatever height you order, make sure that you specify steps. I always order a set for every side, on principle.

Drapery

The drapes will come in two varieties: borders, and pipe-and-drape.
- *Borders.* Borders are all those pre-fab little curtains that hotels slap (generally with Velcro) on all sides of the portable platforms to make them look like they really aren't so portable. I have seen some hotel impresarios hire scenery shops to make borders to match the rest of the show but, trust me, it usually isn't worth it. Only the first row can really see them, and if everyone is looking down there, your show has a problem and it isn't the scenery. Concentrate your time and money on making scenery for the stage itself. You are going to need it to hide the . . .

- *Pipe-and-drape.* Pipe-and-drape is the hotel world's answer to the question: "How can we hide these peach-colored walls for the least amount of money?" Pipe-and-drape is a very common system where drapes with pockets sewn into the top are slid over pipes that are then hung atop slender stands. The drapes are very lightweight, which means that they are easy to put up, but completely transparent to sound. Any sound that is made backstage will be heard out front. Since the drapes aren't very thick, they also will not hide all the light from backstage. Turn off all lights backstage or they will be seen through the drapes.

Projectors and Projection Systems

Almost all hotel shows (other than weddings) seem to require some sort of projection. In choosing a projector and a projection system, here are the questions to consider:

- *How big is the room?*

For a small conference room, a standard slide projector will suffice. The standard slide projector is the Kodak Ektagraphic carousel projector. That's the one you see everywhere that has the round tray on the top. The regular trays hold 80 slides. You can buy trays that hold 120, but I wouldn't recommend using them unless you *absolutely* have to, since the slots are smaller and the slides have a tendency to stick. While we're on the subject, if you are having slides made for a presentation, have them mounted in plastic frames (instead of cardboard). They are less likely to jam.

Try to use rear projection if you can. It looks a lot cleaner and your audience won't have to listen to the fan in the projector. You can only do it, though, if you have enough space behind the screen.

For a large ballroom, you will need either a rear-projection screen with specially "brightened" projectors (the Ektagraphic version is called a "Brightlight") or a xenon slide projector from the rear of the audience. The xenon will be considerably more expensive, but it will be worth it. It is seriously bright.

- *Do you need a dissolve unit?*

For really slick presentations, you can use a dissolve unit. This little gem hooks up two or more projectors to a single controller, allowing you to fade from a slide in the first projector to a slide in the second one and back again. Instead of the slides snapping on and off, they fade gently from one to the next, offering a more professional look. Remember, you have to load the first slide in tray #1, the second one in tray #2, the third in tray #1 again, then #2 and so on. If you have a visiting speaker, she has probably loaded up the slides in a single tray and you should forget about the

Fig. 39. The "keystone effect"

dissolve. If you are making your own presentation, though, the extra time and expense are often worth it.

• *Are you projecting video?*

If you are, you will need to rent a large-screen video projector. Be prepared to pay $500–$1,000 or more for a high-quality one. If you need to display a computer screen, make sure that the projector is compatible with your computer.

• *Can you turn the rest of the lights off?*

And the answer is *yes,* because that is the only way that you are going to get a good image on the screen. If you have a speaker onstage, try to tie him down to the podium and put a little bit of light on him. Try not to give him a wireless mic in this situation. You'll never be able to keep him in the light.

• *What kind of screen do you need?*

Get the biggest one you can for the room. Will you be using front or rear projection? Rear projection screens can be used for front projection, but not vice versa. The sharpest rear projection screens are the black ones, followed by grey, then white. The black screens, however, are less visible if you are not directly in front, so if your seating area is wider than it is deep, get a white or grey screen.

• *What kind of lens do you need on the projector?*

Let the staff at the rental place help you figure this one out. They will want to know how big the screen will be and how far away the projector will be.

Playing Twenty (or More) Questions: Things to Ask and to Know

In order to smoothly stage a hotel show, you will want to know the answers to a lot of questions. Hotel staffs seem to come in two varieties, very helpful and very not. I have a lot of compassion for them, however. A convention staff in a busy hotel helps stage dozens of shows every month. Every one of those shows are the "only show we do all year" to some group of people. To a convention staffer, though, your show is number twenty-four out of fifty-one shows that they are doing this month alone. My advice: Be prepared with a list of questions and get them all answered at your initial meeting with the hotel staff. This is when the staff will be at their most helpful and least stressed.

• *Is there an in-house convention services office?*

Since you might be having your meeting *in* the convention services office, this may be an irrelevant question. Even at a small out-of-the-way hotel, however, there is someone who can help you. These are the people who can answer your questions about almost anything, from lighting to platforming to dressing rooms.

• *Where is the loading dock? What is the access like to the room?*

Everyone who is bringing in equipment will want to know how far the loading dock is from the space, the number of steps (hopefully none) that must be descended or climbed, the width of the doors into the space, and where the freight elevator is. Audio-visual companies or bands will often need bellman's carts to carry equipment.

• *Is there a floorplan available for the room?*

Very useful for lighting and scenery companies, not to mention your own strategic planning.

• *Is there an in-house audio-visual company?*

If there is, then these folks will probably handle most of your AV equipment needs. Even if you are bringing in equipment from the outside, you will want to make friends with the in-house guys. They may be your only hope when your last slide projector bulb goes out.

• *Which lighting and sound company do they recommend?*

This does not always give you the name of who you should use. Some hotels will advertise in-house lighting and sound companies and then simply run down to the local rental house and rent equipment for the show, charging you an extra fifty percent for their trouble. Do some research: Find out who they recommend and then call the local rental shops and compare prices. For that matter, ask the rental houses if they have ever worked in this hotel before.

• *What kind of lighting is built into the room?*

What do the house lights look like? Is there track lighting? Where are the controls? Do you need to have hotel staff to operate them?

• *What kind of power is available in the room?*

As I said above in the lighting section, you may have several different options when it comes to power. Find out how many outlets are in the room and how many amps each of them can take. Some hotels have breakout boxes that can give you more outlets. If you are planning a larger lighting load-in, schedule a time when your lighting person can meet the hotel's electrician to complete the power drop (some people call it the "tie-in"). One final word about power: *Make sure you get the sound and lighting systems on different circuits.* Otherwise the sound system will buzz when the lights turn on. If you have a video system, make sure that it gets its own power as well.

• *How high is the ceiling in the room?*

This will affect the height of the scenery and the lighting trees.

• *What kind of platforming is available in the room?*

How high? What sizes? Stairs? Borders? Handrails? What kind of surface is on the stage? Unless you have dancers, carpet is the way to go. If you do have dancers, they will need a slick surface, so you should arrange to have dance floor or a masonite surface put down.

• *Are there ladders available?*

With modern insurance regulations, the hotel may be loath to lend out their equipment, but you can ask.

• *Do they have a map with directions already printed?*

Very helpful for getting all the right people to all the right places.

• *Where are the bathrooms?*

Do you need separate dressing rooms for entertainers?

• *Where is security?*

Who are you going to call if there is an accident, an intruder, a theft, a lost child, a lost wallet?

Of course, the hotel management will have some questions of their own, so you will want to have answers ready to the following questions:

• *How many people are coming?*

The single most critical number. It determines the size of the room, the staff required, the number of meals to be served, and more.

• *Do you need platforming?*

Trust me, the answer is yes. Now, how much platforming is another matter. I've given you a quick and easy guide for estimating below. Find the type of event you are staging, then decide if you are doing a tight show (you are on a budget and you need to squeeze), an average show (you want people to be comfortable, but you aren't here to show off), or a spacious show (you've got a generous budget, and it's the event of the year). All sizes are specified width by depth. Remember, these are only rough guesses, and you may need more or less space for any number of reasons. Just remember, platforming is cheap, and you can always take away what you don't need.

	TIGHT	AVERAGE	SPACIOUS
Speaker			
alone on stage	8 × 8	16 × 8	30 × 12
with six chairs	16 × 8	24 × 12	40 × 16
Bands			
grand piano	12 × 8	24 × 12	40 × 24
string quartet	8 × 8	12 × 12	30 × 16
five-piece dance band	24 × 12	36 × 20	44 × 40
twelve-piece band	30 × 20	40 × 20	48 × 24
"Big Band"	30 × 20	40 × 20	48 × 24
Awards Ceremony	12 × 12	20 × 12	44 × 16

• *What other kinds of space will you need at the hotel?*

You may need additional space besides the main room. Here is a short list of possibilities to consider:

– Office space
– Storage space (essential if you have a band coming)
– Backstage space (room to store scenery or props)
– Dressing-room space
– Green-room space (where performers await their entrances)
– Parking space
– Space to feed cast and workers
– Space to sell tickets or souvenirs

• *Do you need phones in the space?*

In this era of cell phones, you may be reachable without a phone in your space, but remember, this is usually an easy one for the hotel, and you never know who's going to have a flat tire and need a last-minute lift. While we're on the subject, how about a fax? A photocopier?

• *Do you need security?*

Will you need to restrict access to backstage or to sensitive materials (such as unreleased products or trade secrets)? Is there expensive equipment that will need to be stored in a safe place? Where can performers leave valuables during a performance? Do you need "backstage passes" to monitor access?

• *Are you providing food for cast and/or crew?*

After years of working conventions, meetings, and parties as a crew member, musician and speaker, I have one piece of advice for a successful event—feed your people. Hungry people are angry people. People who have to run across the street to a fast food restaurant for dinner between the load-in and the show are stressed people. People who sit down and have dinner together are friends. Feeding your crew and your performers is one of the best investments you can make in your event. And the better you feed them, the better your investment. It is demoralizing as a performer to watch your audience eating prime rib while you are choking down your dry ham sandwich. At least get the good mustard.

CHAPTER 11

The Essentials: Things You Should Know and Things You Should Own

Every theater in the world is different, but some things never change. Here is a short list of essentials that every person backstage should know or own.

Things Every Theater Person Should Know

- *Stage directions:* On stage, directions are always from the actor's perspective, not the audience's. That is, if you, the actor, are facing the audience, **stage left** is to your left and **stage right** is to your right. If you really want to talk about things from the audience's perspective (when you are talking about seating arrangements, for example), you say **house left** and **house right**. As far as the other dimension goes, **upstage** is away from the audience, **downstage** is toward the audience. (In the early days of Elizabethan theater, the audience sat on a flat surface and the stage was pitched to allow the actors to be seen. Hence, when you moved away from the audience, you really were moving "up." Nowadays, the audience is generally on a sloping surface and the stage is flat, but the term persists.)
- *"Heads!":* No doubt about it, backstage can be a dangerous place. This is particularly true when one person is working over another person's head. Fingers get sweaty, people get careless, things get dropped. If you do drop something, don't swear, don't berate yourself for being a clumsy oaf, don't do anything except yell "HEADS!" Heads is the all-purpose, look-out-or-you'll-get-socked-in-the-head shout and if you

are going to be hanging out backstage, you should begin to train yourself to yell it whenever you see danger coming from above. Any other word might not do the trick. Of course, if you hear someone above you yell "heads," get away quickly. Do not look up. Do not ask questions. Run. If you are onstage, and the call comes from above, head for the wings. You are almost always safest against a wall.

Besides using "heads" in emergencies, technicians will sometimes use it in calmer situations to alert people on stage that something is about to be lowered. In this case, they will follow it with the name of what is coming down, as in "Heads up! Ballroom drop coming in!" Pay attention to these calls. They are made for your safety.

- *Where the callboard is:* In theater, communication is everything. The primary way that technical people tell nontechnical people things (and vice versa) is by posting them on the callboard. Find it. Read it.
- *How big ten feet is:* I have been involved with a lot of conversations about how big something should be, and most people have trouble visualizing a dimension. Once, when doing a show with an extremely polite director of Kabuki theater, we translated his beautiful water-color renderings into shop drawings by asking him repeatedly, "How tall is this one? How about this one?" and studiously writing down the heights he called out. Once the entire set was built, he came to the shop to see it all set up. He smiled graciously, looking carefully at each piece we had built. "Very nice." he said, smiling politely, "It's very nice, but it should be *much* bigger . . ." He gestured up towards the shop ceiling, three times as high as the scenery. After he left, we built him a new set that reached the roof. We grumbled, of course, but we did get a good catch phrase: "Very nice, but *much* bigger . . ."

Ten feet is a good baseline dimension to begin visualizing size. If you have a feel for ten feet, then you can judge larger distances by multiplying it and smaller distances by dividing it. Find something in your life that is ten feet long, like your dining room, a hallway, your car, anything you are familiar with. Then, when someone says, "Hey, will five feet be enough?" you can think, okay, that's half the length of my dining room, and you will have a handle on it. It's also useful to find a couple of measurements on your own body. I know, for instance, that if I stand and reach up, it is exactly eight feet to the last knuckle on my middle finger. It may sound trivial, but you have no idea how many times that distance has come in handy when I needed a rough measurement and I didn't have a tape measure. Another good one is a dollar bill, which is just a shade over six inches long.

- *The difference between an ellipsoidal and a fresnel:* These two lighting instruments are the basis of almost every light plot in the theater, and you should be able to tell them apart. The ellipsoidal (often called a "Leko" after one popular brand) is the one that puts out a sharp-edged light that can be shuttered and shaped. The fresnel puts out a soft-edged light that cannot be shuttered, but blends more easily. The fresnel can be spotted by the circular ridges on the lens. Ellipsoidals have smooth lenses.

- *The difference between a flat and a platform:* Flats are walls, platforms are floors. Mixing up these two is the quickest way to show your amateur stripes.

Things Every Show Person Should Own

- *This book:* Hey, if I don't think you need it, why should you?
- *A Mini-Maglite:* The toughest, brightest, small flashlight made. Forget about all the little colored lenses—they're a pain to put in and you'll lose them anyway.
- *A Swiss Army knife:* A regular folding knife is OK, but you'd be surprised what you can do with that screw driver. The corkscrew comes in handy at a cast party, too.
- *A tape measure:* At least sixteen feet long, longer if you don't mind carrying the weight around.
- *An eight-inch Crescent™ adjustable wrench:* The one essential tool for doing lighting.
- *A clipboard with a pen attached:* Put your name on it, or kiss it good-bye.
- *A set of black clothes including black tennis shoes:* Essential for fading into the background backstage.

Things Every Show Place Should Own

- *A roll of black, two-inch-wide gaffer's tape:* A cloth-based tape that has held more sets together than I can count. Don't let them sell you "duct tape." It has a gooey adhesive that stays behind when you take the tape off. Black masking tape is also insufficient—it's just not strong enough. Go to your theatrical supplier and pay the extra couple of bucks for the good stuff.
- *A Mikita cordless screwdriver:* There is a time for brand loyalty and this is it. The Mikita is the ultimate stage tool—strong, light, and adaptable. The Jeep of the modern theater.
- *Phillips-head drywall screws:* Drywall screws go in and out of wood quickly, and they are quite strong. Keep several sizes around, like 1¼ inches, 1⅝ inches, and 2 inches for use with the Mikita cordless.

- *A fifty-foot tape measure:* Or longer. You should be able to measure all the way across your stage diagonally.
- *A roll of one-inch-wide white gaffer's tape:* The best way to make things visible in the backstage area. Phosphorescent or "glow" tape will work on the stage itself, but behind the scenes it will not get enough light on it to "charge up." Use white tape backstage to mark pathways, obstacles, and stairs.
- *Aluminum utility lights covered with blue color filters:* For "running lights." Sprinkle them around the stage to light prop tables, walkways, and exits. Make sure you take a look from the audience during a blackout to see if the light is spilling on stage.
- *A callboard:* a bulletin board where the performers and technicians can look to see schedules, announcements, phone numbers, and maps to the opening night party. Everyone should get trained to look here for info.
- *Tie line:* A black, cotton/polyester line about the thickness of a shoelace, but stronger. Use it to tie up cables, draperies, rope, and everything else.
- *A hot glue gun:* The props coordinator at Seattle Rep once told me, "If I can't fix it with hot glue, tie line, and gaffer's tape, it wasn't built right to begin with."

In Closing

There are a lot of folks who keep repeating this phrase: "There are no stupid questions."

This is wrong.

I know, because I have asked most of those questions. A stupid question is any question that you wouldn't need to ask if you knew something that someone in your position should know.

Ignorance is like your appendix, though: You only have to get rid of it once. Sometimes the process of learning is about asking stupid, uninformed questions. Sometimes it's about asking intelligent, informed, sophisticated questions that open up new and exciting realms of discussion, but I think it's safe to say that you will need to do the first part before you get to the second.

Sure, the technicians that you ask are going to look at you funny, laugh into their shirts, and roll their eyes. It would be nice if they didn't, but technicians are people, and it is a true fact that people with a particular kind of expertise have a tendency to look down on those who don't have it. However, with luck and tenacity, you will find many enlightened, compassionate technicians who are not afraid to be good teachers for you. Trust me, there are more of them than you think, particularly if they know you are trying to make their lives easier by becoming better informed.

So go ahead and ask your question, no matter how stupid. Sure the person you're talking to might think less of you, but the *next* one won't. Nor will the one after that, or after that. Once you know something, it's yours. And every bit of knowledge will rest on the one before, building higher and higher, until you have a pile of knowledge that will let you reach that last brilliant chocolate chip cookie on the top shelf of wisdom.

Thanks for reading my book. Let me know how you do.

Glossary

a vista: in view of the audience, as in an *a vista* scene change.

ACL (aircraft landing light): a very narrow-beamed instrument, used on airplanes and rock-and-roll lighting plots.

acoustical shells: a large, half-dome–shaped shell used behind choruses and musicians to amplify the sound.

acting areas: a small area of the stage that has its own set of lights. Lighting designers often divide the stage into acting areas in order to create balanced lighting.

actor trap: a slang term assigned to any technical situation that will trip up an inattentive actor, e.g., an uneven step on a staircase.

aircraft cable: thin, steel cable used to hang scenery.

amperage: a measure of power flowing through cables, plugs, and circuit breakers.

amplifier: a electronic device that makes an audio signal strong enough to create sound.

analog: any electronic device that uses constantly changing electrical current to represent constantly changing sound; the opposite of digital.

arbor: in a flying system, the cage where the operators put the counterweight to balance the weight of the scenery.

ASM: see **assistant stage manager**.

assistant stage manager (ASM): the all-purpose technical assistant; the backstage entry-level position.

auxiliary returns (return): an input on a mixer that accepts a signal from an effects processor; part of an "effects loop."

auxiliary sends (send): an output from a mixer used to feed an audio signal to a processor or a monitor.

back light: light coming from upstage of an actor.

balanced (and **unbalanced**) **lines:** two different varieties of cable. Balanced lines require three wires and resist noise. Unbalanced lines require two wires and collect noise.

balcony rail: a lighting position on the front edge of the balcony; originally installed in most Broadway theaters.

ballast: an electronic device used by fluorescent and HMI lights. Necessary to start up these kinds of lights.

barn doors: a color frame with two or four flaps that cut off excess light.

base station: the main station in a headset system; the part that provides the power and connective ability for all the other headsets.

battens: metal pipes that hang over a stage; used for flying scenery and lighting instruments.

beadboard: a flexible, lightweight, synthetic material, commercially marketed as Styrofoam™, among other brands. Sold in sheets.

beam: a horizontal lighting position over the audience.

belt pack: part of a headset system that connects the headset to the rest of the system.

blackout: what happens when you turn all the stage lights off.

blackout drop: a black drop that lives behind a scrim drop, making it fully opaque.

blackout switch: a switch on a lighting control board that turns off all the lights. A very bad idea.

blocking: the movement of the actors onstage.

blueboard: a synthetic material, similar to beadboard but more dense. Sold in sheets.

body mic: a small, almost invisible microphone that mounts on an actor's head or body.

boom: a vertical lighting position, either backstage or in the auditorium.

boom stand: a microphone stand with a horizontal attachment that can reach over a keyboard or other musical instrument.

border: a horizontal drape that runs across the top of the stage, hiding the lighting instruments.

border light: see **strip light**.

bounce: stray light beams that bounce off shiny surfaces and go where they don't belong.

box booms: a lighting position in the auditorium, commonly on either side of the proscenium arch.

box sets: an interior set with three complete walls; the fourth wall is open to the audience.

breakaway: any scenery or prop that is designed to break on cue.

breakaway glass: a fake glass made of a material that can be safely broken without producing dangerously sharp pieces.

breakout box: a group of electrical plugs installed in a single box; used by hotels to provide extra outlets.

bricks: see **counterweights.**

bump buttons: buttons on a lighting control board that "bump" the lights up to full when pressed.

bump cue: a lighting cue (usually at the end of a musical number) that quickly pushes the level of light to a brighter level.

cable: any long, rubbery cord with plugs on each end that carries electricity. The larger ones carry power to lighting instruments; the smaller ones carry data or audio signals.

callboard: the backstage bulletin board where announcements, schedules, and other information is posted.

calling a show: the process of calling out the lighting, sound, and scene-change cues during a performance; usually done by the stage manager over a headset.

calls: the announcements made backstage (usually by the stage manager) telling cast and crew how many minutes remain before curtain time. Also means the specific time that the cast and crew must arrive at the theater.

carbon-arc spot: an older type of follow spot used in large venues that makes light by "arcing" electricity between two carbon electrodes.

castors: the wheels on a platform.

C-clamp: the metal clamp that holds a lighting instrument to the bar it's hanging on. So named because of its C-like shape.

center line: an imaginary line down the center of the stage, from upstage to downstage.

chain pocket: a fabric pouch running the length of a drape along the bottom. It is designed to hold a chain that weighs down the bottom of the drape.

changing booth: a small temporary booth in the wings where an actor can make a costume change without going to the dressing room.

channel (audio): an input on a mixer.

channel (lighting): in computer lighting control boards, a way of controlling a group of dimmers.

charge artist: a scenic painter.

chase effects: special effects, produced by a lighting control board, that cause a series of lights to turn on and off in sequence. Used for marquis lights and fire effects, among other things.

circuit breaker panel: a box containing all the circuit breakers for a building or room.

circuit breakers: electronic devices designed to shut off power if it goes above a certain level. Used to protect electrical systems and prevent fires.

circuit plot: a list of all available circuits in a particular theater.

closing: the last night of a show.

coffin locks: metal brackets embedded in platforms that help lock separate platforms together. So named because they were developed to hold down coffin lids.

color balance: the overall color of the light onstage.

color filter: a piece of colored plastic used to change the color of light.

color frame: the metal frame that holds a color filter.

color scrollers: color frames that hold a roll of color. Used to change color filters in the middle of a performance.

color temperature: a scale used to describe what color a video camera will recognize as white.

company manager: the person who arranges food, lodging, and other details for the cast and crew.

compressor (audio): the electronic device that reduces loud signal levels, making the overall sound level more consistent.

compressor (scenery): an air pump that powers a special type of shop tool (pneumatic tools).

concept meeting: one of the first meetings of the production period, where general concepts are hammered out.

condenser mics: microphones that pick up sound using a small electrical field. Disturbances in the field are detected by the circuitry and converted to an audio signal.

contact sheet: the list of addresses and phone numbers used to keep track of everybody's whereabouts during the production period.

control board (dimmer board): the panel that controls the lighting instruments.

costume fitting: the meeting where costume personnel measure actors and test-fit their costumes.

costume shop manager: the person who decides how to construct the costumes and gives individual workers their assignments.

costume designer: the person who researches the costumes, decides which styles and fabrics to use, and then draws or paints the costumes in renderings.

costume parade: an event held in the theater where each actor walks onstage wearing his or her costumes, one at a time. Designed to show the costumes to the director.

counterweight flying system: a system of moving scenery up into the air using cables and counterweights.

counterweights (bricks): the slabs of iron that are loaded into a counterweight system to offset the weight of the scenery.

cove: a lighting position out in the auditorium where lighting instruments are concealed from view.

craftspeople: people working in properties shops who are proficient in carving, fabrics, and/or any number of other construction skills.

crossfader: the lever on a lighting control board that simultaneously fades all of the channels from one cue to the next.

crossing (a cross): moving from one part of the stage to another, as an actor.

crossover: a passageway that leads from one side of the stage to the other, out of view of the audience.

crotch light: a position on a lighting tree, usually two to three feet off the floor. Generally used in dance.

cue (**cueing**): something that happens at a particular point in the show, such as a change of lighting, scenery, or other technical event. Also used to describe the verbal command to do that thing.

cutters: costume shop workers who cut the fabric for the costumes, using patterns and/or intuition.

cyclorama (cyc): a large backdrop meant to resemble the sky.

DAT: see **digital audio tape.**

dead-hung: scenery or lighting that is hanging in the air and not designed to be moved during the performance, as opposed to "flying" scenery or lighting that is designed to be moved up and down.

deck: the stage floor, or a temporary floor that has been built on top of the permanent floor.

design conference: a meeting that happens early in the production process where designers present their work to the production staff.

designer fabrics (e.g., Rosco): specialty fabrics for the stage, such as slit drape, shimmer cloth, and so on.

deus ex machina: originally, a theatrical device in the ancient Greek theater where a god would appear above the scenery at the end of the play and resolve all the conflicts. Now, any event happening late in the show that, somewhat miraculously, resolves everybody's problems.

diaphragm: the tiny membrane in a microphone that vibrates when sound hits it, allowing the microphone to "hear."

diffusion filters: a specialized form of filter that spreads out the light coming from a lighting instrument. Used to get rid of hard shadows.

digital: any electronic device that represents sound as a string of numbers; the opposite of analog.

digital audio tape (DAT): a high-fidelity tape format for recording any kind of sound.

dimmer: an electronic device that reduces the amount of power that a lighting instrument receives, thereby reducing the light that it is putting out.

dimmer per circuit: a wiring scheme where every circuit in the theater has its own dimmer, thereby eliminating the patch panel.

dimmerboard operator: the person who operates the lighting control board during rehearsals and performances.

director: the person who makes the final judgments on all artistic decisions in the production, subject to the financial approval of the producer.

douser: the control on a follow spot that fades out the light by slowly closing a set of doors.

down light: see **God light.**

downstage: the part of the stage closest to the audience.

draper: a costume shop worker who makes clothes by draping them over a dress form.

dresser: the person who assists actors with their costumes before, during, and after a performance.

dressing room: a space for performers to hang costumes, put on makeup, and otherwise prepare for their show.

drop: a flat piece of fabric, generally painted, that forms part of the scenery.

dry ice: extremely cold ice, formed by freezing carbon dioxide. Used in fog machines. Can burn you if it touches your skin.

dynamic mics: microphones that pick up sound with a tiny, moveable strip of metal. The vibrations of the strip are converted to an electrical signal with a tiny magnet.

Edison plugs: the standard household plug in the United States. Two parallel metal tabs.

effects loop: a loop formed by taking a cable out of a mixer, through an effects processor, then back to the mixer. Used to add effects to sound.

effects processor: an electronic device that adds effects, such as reverb and distortion, to audio signals.

electric: a batten specifically used for lighting instruments.

electrician: the crew member who hangs, adjusts, and operates lighting instruments.

electrics crew: the crew members who hang, adjust, and operate lighting instruments.

ellipsoidal: a type of lighting instrument that produces a sharp-edged beam using an ellipsoidal reflector and one or more lenses.

equalization (EQ): "coloring" a sound by increasing or reducing specific frequencies.

erosion cloth: a very loosely woven cloth used to cover freshly seeded ground. Used in the theater for texture and backgrounds.

escape stair: any staircase out of the audience's view that is used to help actors get off the set.

extreme sightline: the seat in the auditorium that, by the nature of its location, has the best view of backstage. Used to determine masking requirements.

false perspective: a scenic effect that, by exaggerating the effects of perspective, makes a set look bigger than it really is.

false proscenium: a portal that sits in front of or inside the real proscenium, giving the set its own "picture frame."

fast change: a costume change that must be done very quickly, and is therefore done in the wings instead of in the dressing room.

feedback: an annoying noise caused by a sound leaving a speaker and immediately reentering the sound system through the microphone. This round trip is repeated at the speed of light and the resulting blare can be painful and dangerous to equipment.

fidelity: the "trueness" of a sound; how closely it resembles the original source.

fire curtain: the heavy, fire-resistant curtain that seals off the stage from the audience in the event of a fire.

first electric: the most downstage electric; generally contains the greatest number of lighting instruments of any electric.

first hand: the second-in-command in the costume shop, assistant to the costume shop manager.

flats: vertical walls of scenery.

flooding (a Fresnel): the process of moving a Fresnel lamp back in the instrument, thereby making the beam of lighting wider. The opposite of "spotting."

floorplan: the diagram showing the placement of the scenery as viewed from above.

flying: being raised up in the air. To "fly" a piece of scenery is to raise it up using ropes or cables. People may also be flown, but only by trained professionals using special equipment.

flyman: the person who operates the flying system.

focal length: in an ellipsoidal, the distance from the lamp to the point where all the light beams converge. The longer the focal length, the narrower the beam of light that the instrument produces.

focusing: the process of pointing the lighting instruments where the director wants them.

fog machine: a simple machine that produces a ground-hugging fog by melting dry ice.

follow spot: any spotlight that can be moved to follow the movements of an actor.

follow spot operator: the person who operates a moveable spotlight during a performance.

footing: bracing a flat with your foot while it is being raised from a horizontal position to a vertical one.

front-of-house (FOH): anything in the audience. Commonly used to describe staff (such as ushers) and lighting positions.

front light: any light that is coming from downstage of an actor.

front-projection screens: screens that are designed to be projected on from the front, i.e. with the projector behind the audience.

fullness: the number and depth of the folds in a drape. The greater the fullness, the more folds in the drape.

fuse box: a metal panel that contains the fuses.

fuses: small devices that "blow" when the power rises to dangerous levels, shutting off the flow of electricity and preventing fires.

gate (audio): an electronic device that shuts off an audio signal once the level of the signal has dropped to a certain point.

gel: an antique name for lighting color filters, left over from the days when filters were made from animal gelatin.

gel frame: the metal frame that holds the color filter.

glare: the reflection of light from the floor of the stage; caused by lighting instruments pointed downstage over a floor that has been painted a shiny color.

go: the magic word. The universal way to tell someone to do their thing.

gobo: see **template.**

gooseneck (audio): a microphone holder that can be twisted and bent; designed to fit on a podium.

grand drape: the main curtain; a.k.a., the main rag.

green room: a common area where performers wait until it is time to go onstage.

grid: the network of steel beams or pipes over the stage that holds up the rigging.

gripping: moving scenery by picking it up manually.

grommets: small metal rings driven into a drop; designed to hold tie lines.

ground row: a low, horizontal piece of scenery designed to hide lighting instruments on the floor.

half-hour: thirty minutes before the beginning of the performance, when all actors and crew must be in the theater.

hand-held mic: as opposed to a mic on a stand or attached to a performer's body.

hard-wired electric: a hanging pipe that is permanently wired with circuits for lighting instruments.

heads, or tops: the lighting instruments at head height or above on a lighting tree. Generally used in dance.

headsets (headset system): phone-like systems used to keep in touch during a performance.

hemp flying system: a system to fly scenery using hemp ropes and sandbags.

HMI: a type of follow spot that uses a special lamp to create very bright light.

hookup chart: a list showing which circuit and channel is being used for which lighting instruments.

hot spot: the center of a beam of light; the brightest part of the beam.

house left: the left side of the auditorium, from the audience's point of view.

house right: the right side of the auditorium, from the audience's point of view.

image mag: the process of pointing a video camera at a speaker so that his/her image can be projected on a larger screen on the same stage.

impedance: the amount of resistance that an electronic device puts up to an incoming signal. Two varieties: high and low.

industrial felt: a specialty fabric used to make hats, props, and, sometimes, scenery. Looks like felt, but much heavier.

in-ones: the first set of legs behind the proscenium arch. Also used to describe scenes that are played in front of a drop placed just behind the first set of legs.

input module: the part of a mixer that accepts a single input and then adjusts and redirects the signal from that input.

input trim: a control that sets the level of a signal coming into a mixer. Turn down for a line-level signal, up for a microphone.

iris: the control on a follow spot that makes the circle of light bigger or smaller.

irising in/irising out: on a follow spot, making the circle of light smaller (in) or larger (out).

jackknife platform: a platform that pivots on one corner.

juliets: see **box booms**.

knife: a slender piece of metal attached to a platform and sticking down into a groove in the floor. Helps to keep the platform moving straight.

lamp: the thing inside a lighting instrument that makes the light. Often erroneously called a bulb.

lasers: very narrow beams of light produced by specially designed lighting instruments. Can be harmful to your eyes if you look straight into them.

lavaliere (lav) microphones: pencil eraser–sized microphones that are mounted on a collar or lapel.

legs: drapes that hang to the side of the stage, hiding the backstage area.

Leko: a particular brand of ellipsoidal spotlight. This term is often (and erroneously) used to describe any brand of ellipsoidal spot.

light trees: freestanding metal poles with wide bases. Designed to hold lighting instruments.

lighting cues: the instructions that tell the lighting operators what to do and when to do it.

lighting designer: in the theater, the person who decides where the lighting instruments should go, how they should be colored, and which ones should be on at any particular time.

lighting director: on a television set, the person who decides where the lighting instruments should go, how they should be colored, and which ones should be on at any particular time.

lighting inventory: the list of lighting instruments in a theater, showing their size and type.

lighting positions: the various places in a theater where lighting instruments are hung.

lightning box: a special effects device that produces bright, lightning-like flashes of light.

limiter: an electronic device that prevents an audio signal from rising above a certain point.

line level: a particular strength of audio signal in electronic devices, such as tape decks and mixers.

line set: a set of cables that hold one batten in a system for lifting scenery and lighting.

load: something that uses power, like a lighting instrument or an appliance.

loading dock: a place where you can unload scenery, costumes, and other items that you are bringing to the theater.

loading rail: where you go to put weight on the arbor in a flying system.

lock rail: the place where you stand to operate a counterweight flying system. So named because it has a set of locks that prevent the scenery from moving. The locks are mounted on a metal railing.

masking: the draperies or flats that hide backstage from the audience's view.

master carpenter: the person in charge of all the carpenters.

master electrician: the person in charge of all the electricians.

master fader: on a lighting control board, the slider that causes all the lights to fade out.

mic level: a very soft level of audio signal. Generated by a microphone.

mic stand: a metal stand used to hold a microphone.

mid-range: in a sound-system speaker, the part that puts out sound in the middle frequencies.

mids: on a dance lighting tree, the lighting instruments between the crotch lights and the highs. Usually five to eight feet from the floor.

MiniDisc™: a Sony product that allows you to record on a special kind of compact disc.

mixer: an audio device that takes in multiple audio signals, adjusts them, and sends them out to amplifiers and other devices.

monitor mixer: the person who controls which sounds are heard in the monitor speakers (the speakers that the performers listen to) onstage.

monitor speakers: speakers that are designed to help performers hear themselves.

monitor system: a system that allows people backstage (or onstage) to hear what is happening on the stage.

monitors (in the world of sound): wedge-shaped speakers that sit on the edge of the stage and allow singers to hear their own voices. In the world of computers or video: a screen resembling a television screen that shows information (computers) or pictures (video) to an operator.

mono: sound that only requires a single speaker to be played back correctly. As opposed to stereo.

motivational light: where the light in a scene is "supposed" to be coming from, i.e., the sun, an overhead light, etc.

motivational side: the side of the stage where the motivational light is coming from.

movable spotlight: a mechanically operated spotlight that can turn and pan to send light in any direction. Often called a Vari-light after the first company that made them popular.

multi-set shows: a show that requires several distinct sets, such as a large Broadway musical.

muslin: a reasonably priced, commonly used fabric for drops and flats.

mute: a switch that turns off one channel on a mixer.

nap: the "fluffy" part of the fabric.

ohms: in the audio world, a measure of resistance. Used to match speakers to amplifiers.

on (or **off**) **book:** unable (or able) to perform a scene without looking at a script. The stage manager following along in the script during rehearsal is also said to be "on book."

output channels: the places where an audio signal comes out of a mixer.

paint shop: where scenery is painted and otherwise decorated.

pan: move side to side, as a lighting instrument or a camera.

PAR can: a very simple lighting instrument, basically an automobile headlight in a metal housing. Used for rock-and-roll and display.

patch panel: where electrical circuits are assigned to dimmers.

pattern: see **template**.

personal props: props that are carried during a performance, such as guns, cigarettes, and letters.

perspective: the artist's trick that makes a two dimensional space look three-dimensional. The old "train tracks converging in the distance" thing.

phantom power: power that comes to a microphone over an audio wire from the mixer. Necessary for compressor mics.

phone (quarter-inch) **plug:** a long, slender plug used for headphones and many other audio devices.

pickup lines: the cables that attach to a batten and raise it up (fly it out).

pin rail: in a hemp flying system, the place where the ropes are tied off. Occasionally used as a misnomer for the lock rail.

pipe-and-drape: a system of curtains often used in hotels for temporary stage setups.

pipe-ends: lighting instruments hanging at the ends of electrics. Usually focused across the stage and used for side light.

platform: any horizontal playing surface, or a piece thereof.

playing space: the amount of room available onstage for the performance. Does not include wing space, storage, or any part of the stage that is not visible to the audience.

podium stand: see **gooseneck**.

port: the opening on a speaker that lets air in and out.

portal: the archway formed by two legs and a border.

power conditioners: electronic devices that regulate power, removing fluctuations in voltage.

power drop: in a nontheatrical space, the device that allows you to tap into the power system and use higher amperages than single outlets would allow.

practical: able to be operated, like a window or a faucet; also used to describe a "real" lamp or other lighting fixture on a set.

pre-amp: the part of a mixer that amplifies mic-level signals to line level.

preproduction: the time period before actors have begun rehearsal and before the shops have begun to build the show.

preset: on a manual lighting control board, a row of sliders that controls all of the dimmers. Also used to describe the position of a prop at the beginning of a performance.

production: the time period during which the actors are rehearsing and the shops are building the show.

production manager: the person in charge of the technical side of the production. Generally, the technical director and the stage manager report to this person (a.k.a. production stage manager or **PSM**).

production meeting: a meeting of production staff to discuss items of mutual interest.

projection screens: specially designed sheets of plastic fabric used to project slides, video, or film.

projection designer: the person who creates the slides, selects the projectors, and places them backstage.

prompt book (prompt script): the "Bible" compiled by the stage manager, containing all the pertinent information about the show.

prop carpenters: the shop carpenters who build furniture and other props.

prop coordinator : see **propmaster**.

prop designer: the person who selects, designs, and finds the props.

prop list: the master list of all items that could be considered props.

propmaster (prop coordinator): the person in charge of collecting and distributing properties.

props: any item that could be carried by an actor in the course of a show.

props crew: the people backstage who get the props in the right hands at the right times during the performance.

prop table: the table backstage where handheld props are put when they are not being used onstage.

proscenium (pron: pro-SCENE-ee-um) **arch:** the architectural wall that separates the backstage area from the audience.

PSM: see **production manager**.

purchase line: in a flying system, the rope that the operator uses to move the scenery or lighting unit up and down during the performance.

PZM microphone: a microphone that sits on the floor and uses the reflected sounds off the floor to pick up better sound.

rails: the top and bottom boards in a flat.

raked stage (rake): a stage that is slanted, either to increase visibility or to produce false perspective.

rear projection screens: the process of projecting on a screen from the upstage side. Requires a specially designed screen.

reel-to-reel tape deck: a style of tape machine where the tape is passed from one open reel to another across a playback head.

rendering: a drawing or painting that shows what the set or costumes will look like.

resistance: the amount of force that must be overcome to move a speaker and make sound. Measured in ohms.

resistance dimmer: an older style of dimmer that depended on "wasting" energy to dim a lighting instrument.

restore: bringing the lights up or down to where they were before some event (like a musical number) occurred.

reverb: the "echo" effect produced by a large room with hard surfaces; often produced artificially by an effects processor.

reverberation time: the amount of time it takes for a sound to die out in a particular space.

revolve: a stage, or a portion of one, that rotates.

rolling: using wheels to move scenery.

rim light: light that comes from the back or side of a performer. Used to define the edge of the performer and make him distinct from the background.

rise and run: the ratio of stair height (the rise) to stair width (the run).

run: the depth of a stair step, usually used in conjunction with the "rise," the height of the stair. Also the number of performances for a particular show.

sampler: a device that electronically records a sound by changing that sound into millions of numbers.

sampling: the process of recording a sound by turning the analog sound wave into a string of numbers. Sampling happens in samplers and CDs.

sampling rate: the rate at which a sampler makes samples of incoming sound. For example, 44.1 khz means that the sampler makes 44,100 samples per second.

saturation: the amount of color in a pigment or lighting filter. High saturation means deep color.

scene breakdown: a list of scenes showing which characters are in which scenes.

scene-change light: a dim light cue designed to allow a scene change crew to work without the audience feeling that a real scene is going on.

scene shop: where scenery is constructed.

scene-shop manager: the person who maintains the scene shop and, with the TD, decides how the scenery will be built.

scenic artist: a person who applies paint and other forms of decoration to scenery.

scenic designer: the person who designs the look of the scenery and then paints renderings and drafts floorplans.

scoop: a simple lighting instrument composed of a standard bulb and a large reflector.

SCR dimmers: the standard form of electronic dimmer.

scrim: a drop that can be opaque or transparent, depending on how it is lit.

send: on a mixer, the control that allows you to send the audio signal to an external device.

set dressing: decorations that have no function on a set, but are merely placed there to look good.

set props: props that are used only as set dressing and are not handled by actors.

sewn-in fullness: a technique for draperies where the fabric is gathered into folds and permanently sewn that way.

shinbuster: a low instrument on a lighting boom, generally lower than two feet. Used primarily for dance.

short circuit: an electrical fault where the wire leading to a load accidentally touches a wire going away from the load. Can cause fires. A major reason why circuit breakers and fuses are used.

shotgun mic: a microphone designed to pick up sound only directly in front of it.

show drop: a front curtain designed especially for a particular production.

shutter lines: the hard shadows caused by pushing in a shutter on an ellipsoidal.

shutters: the metal tabs on ellipsoidals used to cut off part of the light.

side coves: see **box booms.**

side light: light that comes from stage right or left of the performer.

signal: what sound is called while it is traveling through a sound system. An electrical force.

signal chain: the chain of electronic devices through which an audio signal travels in a sound system.

signal level: the strength of an audio signal as it travels through a sound system. Usually mic level, line level, or speaker level.

signal-noise ratio: the ratio of the loudest part of a signal to the level of noise that exists in the sound system when the signal stops.

sign-in sheet: a list of performers and crew that lives on the callboard. Cast and crew should check off their name when they arrive.

silhouette: a lighting effect when you light the performer only from upstage, or when you light a drop behind her.

skin: the top of a platform, where the actor stands.

smoke machine: a machine that produces billowing smoke that hangs in the air.

snap out (snap to black): an instantaneous blackout.

snow bag (snow cradle): a long bag strung between two battens and filled with artificial snow. Shake it gently and it will "snow" on stage.

solo: on a mixer, a button that turns off every other input.

sound designer: the person who chooses sounds, makes tapes, and designs the sound system.

sound engineer: the person who operates the sound system during a performance.

source: in a sound system, where the signal comes from, e.g., a microphone, a tape deck, etc.

speaker cone: the part of the speaker that makes sound by pushing the air and creating sound waves.

speaker elements: the assemblies that contain the speaker cone and the magnet that makes it move.

speaker level: the level of the audio signal after it leaves the amplifier.

special: a lighting instrument that is used to light a single, isolated person or thing.

spike protector: a device that protects electronic devices from electric "spikes" caused by lighting, electrical faults, or other dangers.

spike tape: colored tape that is used to mark (or "spike") scenery positions onstage.

split fade: a lighting effect where one cue fades down at a different rate than the one that is fading up.

spotting (a Fresnel): the process of moving a Fresnel lamp forward in the instrument, thereby making the beam of lighting narrower. The opposite of "flooding."

stage crew: the crew that works backstage during the show, shifting the scenery.

stage crew chief: the person who decides how the shift will be done and assigns the crew their individual jobs.

stage left: the left side of the stage, from the actor's perspective.

stage manager: the person who runs rehearsals, calls the cues during the show and, in general, organizes things backstage.

stage plug (stage pin, three pin): one of two common types of plugs on stage lighting instruments, it has three round pins and a square, black plug.

stage right: the right side of the stage, from the actor's perspective.

stereo: an audio signal that comes in two parts and must be played through two speakers. Generally designed to give the illusion that the instruments are arranged in space.

stitcher: the costume shop worker who assembles pieces into finished costumes.

stock scenery: scenery that is stored and used for many different productions, e.g., flats and platforms.

straight stand: a microphone stand that does not flex or bend.

straight-run: a rolling platform that only rolls forward and back, as opposed to a swivel platform, which can go any direction you want. Also describes the castor that makes this possible.

straight-run wagon: a rolling platform that only moves forward and back, not side to side.

strike: to take apart a show after the last performance; also, to remove any item from the stage.

strip light: a lighting instrument composed of a string of lamps in a long, metal housing; AKA border light.

subwoofer: a speaker designed to play very low, almost inaudible frequencies. Always used in conjunction with normal speakers.

surge protector: a device used to protect electronic equipment from variations in the power supply.

sweating out a mic: what happens when a drop of sweat covers a small body mic, making it unusable.

swivel: a castor that is able to roll in any direction.

tab: a vertical drape just inside the proscenium that masks performers in the wings. Also a term meaning to pull a drape aside.

table stand: a small microphone stand designed to sit on a table.

tape the stage: the process of depicting the outlines of the set on the rehearsal room floor, using colored tape. Generally done by the stage manager before the first rehearsal.

TD: see **technical director**.

teaser: a horizontal drape across the stage, designed to hide the first electric.

technical director (TD): the person who figures out how the set will be built and then oversees construction; sometimes in charge of lighting as well.

template (pattern, gobo): a metal pattern that, when placed inside an ellipsoidal spotlight, throws a shadow pattern on the stage.

three pin: see **stage pin plug**.

throw distance: the distance from the lighting instrument to the person or thing it is lighting.

tie lines: small cotton lines used to attach drapes and drops to battens.

top hats: round metal objects that are placed in the color frame holder of lighting instruments to cut down on stray light.

tormentor: masking drapes just inside the proscenium that mask the backstage area.

track lighting: permanently installed lighting instruments on tracks in the ceiling. Rarely useful for the stage.

tracking a platform: building a track into the stage that helps to guide a platform to its proper place.

transceiver: the part of a wireless mic that sends out the signal. In a hand-held mic, it is inside the mic; in a body mic, it is a separate unit.

trees: see **lighting trees**.

trims: the heights of flying scenery and masking.

tripping: folding a piece of flying scenery as it goes out. Generally done to save space.

trombone: the lever on a follow spot that allows the operator to make the beam larger or smaller.

truss: a horizontal gridwork structure that is suspended from the ceiling or held up by towers on either end. Designed to hold lighting instruments. Standard equipment for larger industrial shows or rock-and-roll concerts.

tweeter: the speaker element that reproduces the high-end frequencies.

twist-lock: one of two common types of plugs on stage lighting instruments, it has three curved blades that lock when inserted and twisted.

unbalanced line: an audio cable containing only two wires. Generally recognized by the quarter-inch phone plug on the end. Vulnerable to noise, making it a poor choice for microphone cable.

understudies: actors who are trained to replace actors in lead roles if the leads are unable to perform.

unit set: a set that changes very little during a performance, but still creates many locations through changes in props and lighting.

uplight: light that comes from underneath a performer, either from footlights or through a grated or Plexiglas® stage floor.

upstage: the part of the stage furthest from the audience.

valence: a small drapery that runs across the top of the grand drape, hiding the hardware that suspends it.

vinyl LP (a record): a dying medium.

visual cue: a cue that the operator runs when she sees something happen on stage. Warned, but not called by the stage manager.

voltage: a measurement of the strength of electrical power.

wagon: a rolling platform.

walking up a flat: a method of getting a flat from a horizontal position to a vertical one.

warning: what the stage manager gives you about a minute before your cue.

wash light: unfocused, soft light that erases shadows and gives color to a scene.

wattage: a measure of how much power is required to operate a load.

watts per channel: a measure of how much power an amplifier can put out.

webbing: the thick woven fabric at the top of a drape that holds the grommets.

weight rail (loading floor): the walkway where you load counterweights into the arbor in a counterweight flying system.

white balance: what video people do before they shoot to ensure that the colors they are shooting look accurate.

wing space: the amount of space on the stage that is not visible to the audience.

wireless mic: a microphone that does not have to be plugged in to a cord. The mic transmits the sound via radio waves.

woofer: the speaker element that reproduces the low-end frequencies.

xenon arc spot: a type of follow spot that uses a special type of arc lamp. Very powerful, but must be installed permanently.

XLR plugs: a plug with either three prongs or three holes set into a round casing. Used for microphone cables. Called "XLR" because the three pins carry the audio signals for ground ("X"), left ("L"), and right ("R").

yoke: the U-shaped piece of metal that attaches a lighting instrument to a clamp.

zoom ellipsoidal: an ellipsoidal with an adjustable focal length.

Bibliography

Here is a short and incomplete list of some very helpful books that are available if you would like to study technical theater further:

Scenery and Painting

Gillette, J. Michael. *Theatrical Design and Production*. Mountain View, Calif.: Mayfield Publishing, 1997.

Parker, W. Oren and R. Craig Wolf. *Scene Design and Stage Lighting*. New York: Harcourt Brace, 1996.

Pecktal, Lynn. *Designing and Painting for the Theater*. New York: Harcourt Brace, 1975.

Lighting and Projections

Gillette, J. Michael. *Designing with Light*. Mountain View, Calif.: Mayfield Publishing, 1989.

Pilbrow, Richard. *Stage Lighting*. New York: Drama Book Publishers, 1991.

Reid, Francis. *The Stage Lighting Handbook*. London: A&C Black, 1996; New York: Theatre Arts, 1996.

Walne, Graham. *Projection for the Performing Arts*. Oxford: Focal Press, 1995.

Sound

Kaye, Deena and James Lebrecht. *Sound and Music for the Theater*. New York: Backstage Books, 1992.

Props

James, Thurston. *The Theatre Props Handbook.* Cincinnati, Ohio: Betterway Books, 1990.

Stage Management

Bond, Daniel. *Stage Management, A Gentle Art.* London: A&C Black, 1997; New York: Theatre Arts, 1997.

Ionazzi, Daniel. *The Stage Management Handbook.* Cincinnati, Ohio: Betterway Books, 1992.

Kelly, Thomas A. *The Backstage Guide to Stage Management.* New York: Backstage Books, 1991.

General Stagecraft and Rigging

Carter, Paul. *Backstage Forms.* Louisville, Ky.: Broadway Press, 1990.

Carter, Paul. *Backstage Handbook.* Louisville, Ky.: Broadway Press, 1994.

Glerum, Jay O. *Stage Rigging Handbook.* Carbondale, Ill.: Southern Illinois University Press, 1997.

Ionazzi, Daniel. *The Stagecraft Handbook.* Cincinatti, Ohio: Betterway Books, 1996.

Safety

Rossol, Monona. *Stage Fright: Health and Safety in the Theater.* New York: Allworth Press, 1991.

General Conceptualizing and Design

Ingham, Rosemary. *From Page to Stage.* Wordsmith, N.H.: Heinemann, 1998.

Directors Who Must Do It All

Rodgers, James W. and Wanda C. Rodgers. *Play Director's Survival Kit.* New York: Simon and Schuster, 1995.

Index

Books from Allworth Press

Promoting Your Acting Career
by Glen Alterman (softcover, 6 × 9, 224 pages, $18.95)

Creating Your Own Monologue
by Glen Alterman (softcover, 6 × 9, 192 pages, $14.95)

The Screenwriter's Legal Guide, Second Edition
by Stephen F. Breimer (softcover, 6 × 9, 320 pages, $19.95)

Stage Fright: Health and Safety in the Theater
by Monona Rossol (softcover, 6 × 9, 144 pages, $16.95)

Selling Scripts to Hollywood
by Katherine Atwell Herbert (softcover, 6 × 9, 176 pages, $12.95)

Writing Scripts Hollywood Will Love
by Katherine Atwell Herbert (softcover, 6 × 9, 160 pages, $12.95)

Booking and Tour Management for the Performing Arts
by Rena Shagan (softcover, 6 × 9, 272 pages, $19.95)

An Actor's Guide—Your First Year in Hollywood
by Michael Saint Nicholas (softcover, 6 × 9, 256 pages, $16.95)

Making and Marketing Music
by Jodi Summers (softcover, 6 × 9, 240 pages, $18.95)

The Internet Research Guide, Revised Edition
by Timothy K. Maloy (softcover, 6 × 9, 208 pages, $18.95)

The Copyright Guide: A Friendly Guide for Protecting and Profiting from Copyrights *by Lee Wilson* (softcover, 6 × 9, 192 pages, $18.95)

Arts and the Internet: A Guide to the Revolution
by V. A. Shiva (softcover, 6 × 9, 208 pages, $18.95)

Please write to request our free catalog. To order by credit card, call 1-800-491-2808 or send a check or money order to Allworth Press, 10 East 23rd Street, Suite 210, New York, NY 10010. Include $5 for shipping and handling for the first book ordered and $1 for each additional book. Ten dollars plus $1 for each additional book if ordering from Canada. New York State residents must add sales tax.

To see our complete catalog on the World Wide Web, or to order online, you can find us at *www.allworth.com.*